EXTRAORDINARY PRAISE

THREE NIGHTS IN AUGUST

● ● ●

"*Three Nights in August* will be devoured by hard-core strategists who enjoy nothing more than arguing for hours over why a hit-and-run was not called. Yet it is immediately accessible to any fan curious about the more complicated elements of the game. This is because Bissinger does much more than simply dissect 27 innings of baseball. He has the wonderful ability to stop the action in mid-pitch to talk about the people involved."

— **JOHN GRISHAM,** *New York Times Book Review*

"A masterpiece of reporting and writing, and flat-out one of the best books on the subject ever."

— **MARK BOWDEN,** author of *Black Hawk Down*

"Explains baseball to its core . . . the best baseball book I've read in a decade . . . pure joy for fans."

— *DENVER ROCKY MOUNTAIN NEWS*

"Bissinger depicts both the timeless appeal of a game that is rooted in the past and the unsatisfying changes wrought by big-money contracts."

— *WALL STREET JOURNAL*

"A terrific read."

— SPORTSILLUSTRATED.COM

"The Cubs against the Cardinals in the heat of August and of a pennant race — this is baseball at its best."

— **GEORGE F. WILL,** author of *Men at Work: The Craft of Baseball*

"The biggest buzz in sports books [in 2005] was generated by Buzz Bissinger's *Three Nights in August*."

"More than a splendid baseball book, it's a revealing, inspiring portrait of leadership under pressure."

"This book lets you breathe the game."

"Engaging . . . more than enough to please any fan of the national pastime."

"What differentiates *Three Nights* from run-of-the-mill sports books is Bissinger's rapport with La Russa. The Cardinals' manager bares his soul for Bissinger."

"Bissinger does a masterful job of encompassing the entire season —and, indeed, La Russa's entire life—in those three games."

"La Russa is remarkably candid."

"A rare and often exhilarating vantage."

"An opportunity to explore the quirks of the contemporary game."

"Mixing classic baseball stories with little-known details and an exclusive perspective, this work should appeal to any baseball fan."

— *PUBLISHERS WEEKLY,* starred review

"[A] first-rate account of a battle of titans . . . A real treat for scholarly baseball fans, and a better management book than most on the business shelves."

— *KIRKUS REVIEWS,* starred review

"Enthralling."

— *BOOKLIST,* starred review

"La Russa is one of baseball's most intriguing figures. Bissinger is one of our most respected writers. Together, they provide a unique and compelling view inside the game that for so long has fascinated, rewarded, and tortured the Cardinals manager."

— **BOB COSTAS,** HBO and NBC sports commentator

"A great writer. A great manager. A great book filled with surprises. In *Three Nights in August,* Buzz Bissinger has brought to baseball the same magic he brought to football in *Friday Night Lights.*"

— **BILL BELICHICK,** head coach, New England Patriots

"What a great book this is. It takes you closer to the game than you could ever get otherwise."

— **BILL PARCELLS,** head coach, Dallas Cowboys

Handwritten: 1 - 6/15   5 - 2/7   2 - 2/13   6 - 5/23'   3 - 12/42²   7 - 0/11   4 - 18/51ⁿ   8 - 3/1ₚ

DUGOUT AND PHOTOGRAPHERS AREAS

- Ball entering dugout or photographers area: **Out of Play (Award by Book Rule).** *G-4 - 7/5   G.dm - 5/9   K.r - 2/10   m.h - 0/6   B.L. - 2/6   W.ak - 8/27*
- Ball striking top step (lip) of dugout: **In Play.**

BACKSTOP AREA

- Ball going through or lodging in wire screen in back of home plate: **Out of Play (Award by Book Rule).**

OUTFIELD AREA

- Batted ball in flight going over yellow line on top of outfield fence: **Home Run.**
- Fair ball strikes yellow line: **In Play.**
- Fair ball bouncing into field boxes or enclosed area in left or right field corners or going through or under fences: **Two Bases.**

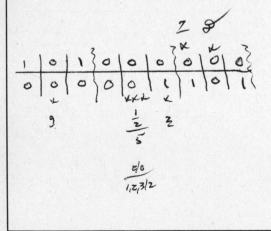

OFFICIAL BATTING ORDER

ST. LOUIS

DATE _____ 8/28/3

	ORIGINAL				CHANGE	ALSO ELIGIBLE
1				B	3-2 F	Cairi
				C	HP	Benz
2				B		Taguchi
				C		Widger
3				B		
				C		
4				B		Palmeiro
				C		
5				B		
				C		
6				B	Harper /8	
				C		
7				B		
				C		
8				B		Fsaro
				C		
9				B	Klein /8	Klein
				C	Taguchi /8	
				D		Harper
				E		Eldred

MANAGER'S SIGNATURE _____

240-51-KR- $\frac{V-F}{VF}$
$0-0$

#1- Stupid v Size

- Careless - Banco

B. Jackson

3-2

OFFICIAL BATTING ORDER

CHICAGO CUBS   8-2   DATE _____ 8/28/03

#	ORIGINAL		CHANGE	ALSO ELIGIBLE
1	LOFTON - 8		B	GLANVILLE A/8
			C	KARROS
2	MARTINEZ - 4		B	MILLER
			C	WOMACK
3	SOSA - 9		B	O'LEARY
			C	GOODWIN
4	ALOU - 7		B	
			C	CLEMENT
5	SIMON - 3		B	ESTES
			C	PRIOR
6	RAMIREZ - 5		B	WOOD
			C	
7	GONZALEZ - 6		B	
			C	
8	BAKO - 2		B	LEICESTER
			C	BOROWSKI
9	ZAMBRANO - 1		B	ALFONSECA
			C	FARNSWORTH
			D	REMLINGER
			E	GUTHRIE

MANAGER'S SIGNATURE _____

THREE NIGHTS IN AUGUST

BOOKS BY BUZZ BISSINGER

Friday Night Lights • *A Prayer for the City* • *Three Nights in August*

The Best American Sports Writing 2003 (editor)

THREE NIGHTS
IN AUGUST

Strategy, Heartbreak, and Joy

Inside the Mind of a Manager

Buzz Bissinger

A MARINER BOOK

HOUGHTON MIFFLIN COMPANY

Boston • New York

First Mariner Books edition 2006

Copyright © 2005 by Tony La Russa and H. G. Bissinger

Afterword copyright © 2006 by H. G. Bissinger

Visit our Web site: www.houghtonmifflinbooks.com.

Library of Congress Cataloging-in-Publication Data
Bissinger, H. G.
    Three nights in August / Buzz Bissinger.
        p.   cm.
    ISBN-13: 978-0-618-71053-9 (pbk.)
    ISBN-10: 0-618-71053-1 (pbk.)
        1. St. Louis Cardinals (Baseball team) 2. Chicago Cubs
    (Baseball team) 3. La Russa, Tony.   I. Title.
    GV875.S74B57   2005
    796.357'09778'66—dc22   2004065134

Book design by Melissa Lotfy

PRINTED IN THE UNITED STATES OF AMERICA

MP 10 9 8 7 6 5 4 3 2 1

To Lisa, Caleb, and Maddy.
A beautiful woman. A beautiful son. A beautiful friend.

—HGB

● ● ●

To Elaine, Bianca, and Devon, and the four-legged companions who have been part of our family. They mean more to me than they did yesterday and less than they will tomorrow.

And to the baseball family—those I have competed with and those I have competed against.

—TLR

I'm as nauseous as I've ever been. I have a terrible headache. My head is pounding. I feel like throwing up and I'm having trouble swallowing. And the beauty of it is, you want to feel like this every day.

—TONY LA RUSSA

CONTENTS

GAME THREE

PREFACE

● ● ● THE FACE made me do it. It left an indelible image with its eternal glower from the dark corner that it occupied. I had always admired intensity in others, but the face of Tony La Russa entered a new dimension, nothing quite like it in all of sports.

I first saw the face in the early 1980s, when La Russa came out of nowhere at the age of thirty-four to manage the Chicago White Sox and took them to a division championship in his third full year of managing. The face simply smoldered; it could have been used as a welding tool or rented out to a tanning salon. A few years later, when he managed the Oakland A's to the World Series three times in a row, the face was a regular fixture on network television and raised even more questions in my mind. Did it *ever* crack a smile? Did it *ever* relax? Did it *ever* loosen up and let down the guard a little bit, even in the orgy of victory? As far I could tell, the answer was no.

I was hooked on the face. I continued to observe it as he stayed with the Oakland A's through 1995. I followed it when he became the manager of the St. Louis Cardinals the following season. Along the way, I became aware of his reputation as a manager, with a polarity of opinion over him such that when *Sports Illustrated* polled players on the game's best five managers and its worst five managers, La Russa appeared on both lists. But I liked seeing that because it meant to me that this was a manager who didn't hold back, who ran his club with a distinct style regardless of the critics' chorus. Had he been any different, surely the face would have broken into a smile at least *once*.

After La Russa came to the Cardinals, I did see moments when the face changed. I saw fatherly pride and self-effacement spread over it when Mark McGwire hit his record-breaking sixty-second home run in 1998. I also saw the face overcome with grief when he and his coaches and his players mourned the passing of the soul of the St. Louis Cardinals, broadcast announcer Jack Buck, followed four days later by the death of beloved pitcher Darryl Kile in his hotel room during a road trip in Chicago. Later that season of 2002, I saw the intensity return, all the features on a collision course to the same hard line across the lips during the National League Championship series that the Cardinals painfully lost to the Giants four games to one.

As a lifelong baseball fan, I found myself more curious about La Russa than about anybody else in the game. Which is why, when out of nowhere, I received a call from La Russa's agent at the end of November 2002 asking whether I might be interested in collaborating on a book with La Russa, my answer was an immediate yes. I jumped at the opportunity, although I also knew that collaborations can be a tricky business. I had been offered them before by the likes of Rudy Giuliani and legendary television producer Roone Arledge, and I had turned them down. But this was different, or at least I told myself it was different, because—at the risk of sounding like some field-of-dreams idiot—my love of baseball has been perhaps the greatest single constant of my life. I knew the game as a fan, which is a wonderful way to know it. But the opportunity to know it through the mind of La Russa—to excavate deep into the game and try to capture the odd and lonely corner of the dugout that he and all managers occupy by virtue of the natural isolation of their craft—was simply too good to pass up.

In the beginning, this was a typical collaboration. I brought along my little mini–cassette recorder to where La Russa lived in northern California. I turned it on and interviewed him at length, thinking that I would listen to the tapes and transcribe them and try to fashion what he said into his own voice. As is common in collaborations, we also have a business arrangement, a split of the proceeds, although the entirety of La Russa's share is going to the Animal Rescue Foundation, known as Tony La Russa's ARF, that he cofounded with his wife, Elaine, in northern California.

The more we talked about the book, the more agreement there was about trying to do something different from the typical as-told-to. La Russa's interest in me as a writer had been on the basis of *Friday Night Lights,* a book I had written about high school football in Texas. He was struck by the voice and observational qualities of the book, and we wondered whether there was a way to fashion that here. We also wondered whether there was a way to write the book with a narrative structure different from the usual season-in-the-life trajectory, a book that would have lasting and universal application no matter what season it took place in.

It was during those conversations that we came up with the idea of crafting the book around the timeless unit of baseball, the three-game series. The one we settled on, against the eternal rival Chicago Cubs, took place in the 2003 season. Had the goal of the book been different — to write about a particular season — it would have made sense to switch gears and write about the Cardinals' magnificent ride of 2004. But that wasn't the goal.

It was also during those conversations that La Russa agreed to give me virtually unlimited access to the Cardinals' clubhouse and the coaches and players and personnel who populate it — not simply for the three-game series that forms the spine of the book but also for the virtual entirety of the 2003 season — to soak up the subculture as much as possible. La Russa understood that in granting such access, he was ceding much of the control of the book to me as its writer. In doing so, he was untying the usual constraints of a collaboration, allowing me wide latitude to report and observe and draw my own conclusions. He also knew that approaching the book in this manner required him to be revealing of not only the strategies he has come to use but also the wrenching personal compromises he has made in order to be the kind of manager he has chosen to be.

La Russa did not waver from the latitude that he promised. I was made privy to dozens of private meetings between the Cardinals coaches and their players. I was able to roam the clubhouse freely. Because of my access, I was also able to probe not only La Russa's mind but also the minds of so many others who populate a clubhouse. La Russa has read what I have written—the place where collaborations can get odious. He has clarified, but in no place has he asked that anything be removed, no matter how candid.

I came into this book as an admirer of La Russa. I leave with even more admiration not simply because of the intellectual complexity with which he reaches his decisions but also because of the place that I believe he occupies in the changing world of baseball.

He seems like a vanishing breed to me, in the same way that Joe Torre of the New York Yankees and Bobby Cox of Atlanta and Lou Piniella of Tampa Bay also seem like the last of their kind. They so clearly love the game. They revel in the history of it. They have values as fine as they are old-fashioned, and they have combined them with the belief that a manager's role is to be shrewd and aggressive and intuitive, that the job is more about unlocking the hearts of players than the mere deciphering of their statistics.

In the fallout of Michael Lewis's provocative book *Moneyball,* baseball front offices are increasingly being populated by thirtysomethings whose most salient qualifications are MBA degrees and who come equipped with a clinical ruthlessness: The skills of players don't even have to be observed but instead can be diagnosed by adept statistical analysis through a computer. These thirtysomethings view players as pieces of an assembly line; the goal is to quantify the inefficiencies that are slowing down production and then to improve on it with cost-effective player parts.

In this new wave of baseball, managers are less *managers* than *middle managers,* functionaries whose strategic options during a game require muzzlement, there only to effect the marching orders coldly calculated and passed down by upper management. It is wrong to say that the new breed doesn't care about baseball. But it's not wrong to say that there is no way they could possibly *love* it, and so much of baseball is about love. They don't have the sense of history, which to the thirtysomethings is largely bunk. They don't have the bus trips or the plane trips. They don't carry along the tradition, because they couldn't care less about the tradition. They have no use for the lore of the game—the poetry of its stories—because it can't be broken down and crunched into a computer. Just as they have no interest in the human ingredients that make a player a player and make a game a game: heart, desire, passion, reactions to pressure. After all, these are emotions, and what point are emotions if they can't be quantified?

La Russa is a baseball man, and he loves the appellation "baseball man." He loves the sound of it, although the term has become increasingly pejorative today because of the very stodginess that it suggests. But La Russa is not some hidebound manager stuck in the Dark Ages. He honors statistics and respects the studies that have been written about them. He pays meticulous attention to matchups. He thinks about slugging percentage and on-base percentage, as they have become the trendy statistics in today's game. They have a place in baseball, but he refuses to be held captive to them, because so much else has a place in baseball. Like Torre and Cox and Piniella, his history in the game makes him powerfully influenced by the very persuasions the thirtysomethings find so pointless: heart, desire, passion, reactions to pressure. After all, these are emotions, and what point is there playing baseball, or any game, if you don't celebrate them?

This book was not conceived as a response to *Moneyball.* Work began months before either La Russa or I had ever heard of Lewis's work. Nor is this book exclusively about La Russa. Because he is the manager, he is at the hub of the wheel of *Three Nights in August.* But the more time I spent in the clubhouse, the more aware I became of all the various spokes that emanate from that hub and make a team that thing called a team.

La Russa represents, to my mind, the best that baseball offers, but this book doesn't sidestep the less noble elements that have associated themselves with the game in the past few decades: the palpable decline in team spirit, the ever-escalating salaries, the burgeoning use of steroids—all are a part of what baseball has become. The sport has a tendency to cannibalize itself, to raise the bar of self-interest just when you thought it couldn't go any higher. The recent scandal of steroid abuse is shocking enough—with its lurid images of players lathering weird creams all over themselves —but what's truly shocking is that this problem has festered for at least a decade. As La Russa pointed out in one of our interviews, everybody in baseball knew for years that steroid use was taking place. But the only two powers that could have done something about it—the owners and the players' union—did nothing until 2002. It's difficult morally to understand that, but not financially, since steroids helped fuel the home-run craze that many who run baseball were convinced was the only way to capture new fans who lacked an interest in the game's subtleties.

It's a cynical notion and it's also wrong. Home runs are electrifying, but so are the dozens of smaller subplots that reveal themselves in every game, strategically and psychologically and emotionally. *Three Nights in August* tries to convey that very resonance, not with nostalgia, but because it is still the essence of this complex and layered game.

FOREWORD

BY TONY LA RUSSA

● ● ● IN THIS BOOK, Buzz Bissinger describes baseball as "complex and layered." I've been involved in professional baseball for over forty years, and the whole time I've been consumed by a drive to understand those complexities and layers. That process began in 1962, when at age seventeen I signed with Charley Finley's Kansas City Athletics. From the beginning of my playing career, "baseball men"—expert managers, coaches, scouts, and executives —tried to explain all the game's layers. They could break down each offensive and defensive play, for instance, showing how my responsibilities as a hitter could be different depending on the inning, score, and number of outs and base runners, if any. Early on, I started learning to "play the scoreboard"—that is, to figure out what play was appropriate at a given moment in the game and how to make it happen.

My education intensified dramatically in 1978, when I started managing the Knoxville Sox in the Double-A Southern League. As a player, your understanding of strategy and other subtleties is limited by the time and energy you must devote to the physical demands of playing. As a manager, however, your efforts to unlock the game's mysteries are no longer limited by physical constraints. You can apply yourself to this learning process during every play, every game—all the time.

By August 1979, I'd had only two partial seasons of minor-league managerial experience and one season in the winter league when Bill Veeck and Roland Hemond gave me an opportunity to manage the Chicago White Sox. At that time, the major leagues were populated largely by legendary managers—veterans so successful that they were recognized by their first names: Sparky, Billy, Earl, Gene, Chuck, Whitey, Tommy, Dick, and Johnny Mac. Against those managers and their teams, the White Sox and their new, thirty-four-year-old skipper were overmatched. To narrow that gap as much as possible, I grabbed at any information I could. Often, the information came from conversations with my legendary opponents, as well as other baseball men who generously shared their wisdom.

Twenty-five years on, I'm still learning. For example, as a former infielder, I'm less skilled at deciding what pitch to call in certain situations than somebody with a background as a pitcher or a catcher. Thousands of times over my two decades of working with pitching coach Dave Duncan, I've asked him what pitch to call. I still don't have Dave's expertise, but I'm getting better.

Aspects of the game that once baffled me—like where to position the defense in various game situations, or where to hit the ball with a runner on first and fewer than two outs (a hit to center or right beats a hit to left; a ground out beats a fly out if the runner is going on the pitch)—have become intelligible after exposure to dozens of expert tutors and postgame analysis of thousands of ballgames. Other mysteries remain. How can a quality team dominate during the regular season, win convincingly in the playoffs, but lose four straight or four of five in the World Series? That has happened to three teams I've managed: the A's in 1988 and 1990 and the 2004 Cardinals. I'm still searching for answers, and I don't like the one I'm left with: that when we suck it's mostly because I suck.

The more I've learned about baseball, the more my affection and respect for this beautiful game have grown. With that realization in mind, I decided several years ago that someday I'd like to be part of a book that described the intricate details of the game that baseball men (and, increasingly, women) have debated and passed along for over a century. Part of my motivation came from the many conversations I've had with fans who wanted to dig deeply into the layers. They would light up when we talked about the complexities of situational at-bats, defensive positioning, and pitching changes, or when we discussed the psychological nuances of the game, from the tactical value of getting a first-pitch strike (or ball, if you're a hitter) to the growing challenges of motivating extremely well-paid guys to put their team's success above their own.

I saw that for fans, too, deeper knowledge could mean greater pleasure. But how do you make inside baseball into a must-read book? I've always been a big reader, and I know that the nonfiction I like best is consistently entertaining, surprising, and honest. But I have enough trouble writing a lineup card, so I knew I had to find an author who could create a book with those qualities. People I respected recommended Buzz Bissinger, whose book *Friday Night Lights* I had enjoyed. Buzz agreed to the project and we had a collaboration going.

I quickly saw how truly gifted a writer Buzz is and how knowledgeable he is about baseball. As we worked together, Buzz's role gradually changed: Our collaboration became Buzz telling the story based on information he got from me and many others—managers, coaches, scouts, front-office people, and players—along with observations he made during a season spent watching the St. Louis Cardinals more closely than any writer has ever watched a ballclub before. All along, I've been aware of the contents of *Three Nights in August,* but it was Buzz who selected which people and events to feature and what stories to tell.

This book is about one three-game series between two teams in 2003. But Buzz and I agreed from the start that *Three Nights* should really be about baseball in general. Much of what you will read here would apply to any team at any time, in any season. My decisions and mistakes are mine alone, but all major-league managers have faced similar situations and have made similar decisions and similar mistakes. In much the same way, the players you'll read about here are particular people, but many of them also represent types of player: the clever veteran, the eager rookie, the spoiled star, the frustrated benchwarmer, the schizophrenic pitcher, the impulsive hitter, among others. Players like these can be found on just about every major-league team, just about every season.

So this book is about the constants of the game. But it is also very much about change. Baseball has changed enormously since I got into it forty years ago. This book describes some of the most notable developments: the growing importance of video, the decline of base stealing, the sharp drop in complete games, the sharp rise in home runs, and so on. The biggest transformation of all has taken place above players' necks.

In the past, the game was simpler. I am not saying it was easier to be a successful major leaguer, just that there were fewer distractions then. A player's survival was tied primarily to playing as good and as hard as he could. He had to focus on mastering the game's fundamentals, because next year's earnings depended on this year's productivity, and there were several replacements waiting in the minor-league talent pool if you failed to produce. If your team made it to the World Series, your bonus check would provide much-needed extra income.

Now a World Series bonus is little incentive for most players, who earn seven or eight figures a year. Now the pool of potential replacements waiting in the minors is much smaller. Now players' contracts give them the opportunity to earn significant money and security regardless of injury or productivity. Now a player's agent, family, friends, and union encourage him to concentrate on his individual numbers, regardless of how much those stats might contribute to the team's effort to win games, because his personal stats dictate how big his salary will be. Now the players' relationship with the media is contentious and the influence of the players' union overpowering.

Now managers and coaches must battle against all that in persuading their teams to play hard enough and selflessly enough to win ballgames. In spring training and throughout the regular season, we establish and explain the fundamental skills players must master to play the game right. But we spend much more time motivating guys to max out their concentration and effort in practice and competition, convincing them to make winning their first priority. So, in that sense, motivation has become more fundamental than the fundamentals. Even the most selfish player can be inspired to put his team first once he realizes he can gain personally from the club's success. If a club becomes a serious contender, every player earns extra credit that can be cashed in at contract time, because the team's impressive performance makes his own performance look more impressive.

Every successful team has fortune on its side. In each organization where I've managed, good fortune has been a constant teammate. I know of no other manager for whom so many pieces have fallen into place as they have for me. Any manager or coach will tell you that the most essential ingredient of success is quality players, and I've had more than my share of them on the Chicago White Sox, Oakland A's, and St. Louis Cardinals.

I've also been fortunate to work for three franchises whose every level has shown the will and the skill to win. In an era when players' attitudes and relationships to their clubs are so fragile, these three teams have had an edge because their players have sensed this coordinated commitment to win throughout the organization. The standards set by Bill Veeck, Jerry Reinsdorf, and the White Sox ownership; Walter Haas and his family with the A's; and Bill DeWitt and the Cardinals ownership were as high as they get. The front offices of Roland Hemond with the White Sox; Sandy Alderson with the A's; Walt Jocketty with the Cardinals; as well as the coaches, trainers, and everyone associated with those three teams—did their utmost to realize those high standards.

My greatest fortune has been the support of my wife, Elaine, and our daughters, Bianca and Devon. Baseball is very hard on families: No other sport requires so much time on the road. Even when your team's playing at home, you spend roughly twelve hours a day, six days a week at the stadium, so your wife unfairly bears the demands and responsibilities of raising your family. Elaine has borne those burdens better than any man could ask for—with strength, with independence—and to a great degree, I owe the resilience of my family and my success as a manager to her.

PROLOGUE

● ● ● TONY LA RUSSA definitely saw things that kept him up at night: changeups without change, sinkers lacking sink, curves refusing curve. Not to mention the time that Fassero, after being told to throw some garbage nowhere near the plate—bowl it, roll it, slice it, dice it, bounce it if he had to—had thrown it so up and so over that Garciaparra couldn't help but lace it past second to tie the game in extra innings. For four months now, that vision had haunted La Russa, not what Fassero had done but what La Russa *hadn't* done: hadn't adequately prepared Fassero for the moment, leaving Fassero exposed.

The explanation for his sleeplessness was simple, maybe. When anybody does the same thing for as long as he had, going on a quarter century, he was bound to see things he couldn't set aside no matter how hard he tried to rationalize. Another explanation was his own personality: intense, smoldering, a glowing object of glower. He barely smiled even when something wonderful happened, as if he were willing himself not to. Some thought he worked too hard, grinded away at it when he would have been better off forgetting it, took the bad things into the night when he should have slept. Even he knew he had gone too far, had made personal compromises he knew were wrong, but it wasn't simply an occupation to him or even a preoccupation.

It was something he loved. And like other managers who have

spent most of their lives around the game, he had an obsessive mind for it: no at-bat unsung, no pitch ever forgotten, no possibility of simply turning it all off at night. He retained more anecdotes —more memories of balls and strikes and beanballs and stolen signs and games won that should have been lost and games lost that should have been won—than any of the half-pound encyclopedias that came out like clockwork. His meticulous personality accounted only partly for his late-night visions. Maybe the very oddity of his chosen profession was also to blame. Maybe it was the fact that he couldn't simply call an employee in when he had performed badly, couldn't simply talk to him privately. With thousands of people watching, he instead had to walk out and fetch the poor soul as if he were a suicide-in-waiting, then take his weapon away from him because clearly he could no longer be trusted with it, might somehow do further harm than he already had. Or maybe it was all those hand gestures he performed six days a week and sometimes seven: the pantomime of wipes and swipes and scratches.

As much as his job tormented him, he knew that managing a baseball team was a wonderful way to spend a life. It could be thrilling when it went right: when you did something that pushed in a run here and there, when you set up a defense and the ball, often so recalcitrant, obediently played right into the hands of that defense. There was exceptional excitement in the fact that for all the preparation you did, and Tony La Russa was always preparing, the game could never be scripted. As much as he knew—and he had spent his life trying to know—things he never could have imagined still routinely happened, an odd fantastic play that even if it went against you still made you secretly smile in wonder. When the game did work right, hummed along with that perfect hum that every fan recognizes, La Russa would think, simply: "Beautiful. Just beautiful baseball."

If the amount of time he had been at it—the very attitude he had about it—made him something of a throwback, it shouldn't imply that he was simply some tired relic waiting for his retirement papers. No one currently managing had won as many games; he was eighth on the all-time list going into this 2003 season and likely to be as high as third by the time he was finished. No one in the modern history of the game had managed for twenty-four *consecutive* years—starting in 1979 with the White Sox, then with the Athletics, and now with the Cardinals for nearly a decade—an amazing feat of security in a job that had no security. No one else had won the Manager of the Year Award *five* times, across four decades, in both leagues, with each of the three teams he had managed: the White Sox in 1983 when he was still in his Wonder Boy thirties, twice with the Oakland A's in 1988 and 1992 in his forties, and then with the Cardinals in 1996 and 2002.

Along the way, in a game generally terrified of innovation, La Russa, now fifty-eight, had come up with innovations. He had refined the concept of the closer into a one-inning pitcher with the exclusive territory of the ninth. He had made a science of situational matchups between hitter and pitcher in the late innings. (Once he used five pitchers in the space of eight pitches.) And, as if to prove that an obsessive mind was hardly perfect, he had even challenged the hallowed concept of the starting rotation. Briefly, instead of having a single starting pitcher for each game, he went with a starting *grouping* of pitchers in which each one was not allowed to pitch longer than three innings. It was in keeping with his reputation for continual tinkering—too much tinkering in the eyes of some—and it was quietly shelved after a handful of games.

After twenty-four years of managing, it was difficult to imagine that he had ever done anything else. He seemed like someone who had bypassed infancy and childhood and adolescence to appear one day in his chosen profession: He seemed that intimate with it. But he still sensed the intrinsic bizarreness of what he did—the idea of spending his life in what looked like a seedy basement nightclub with a long bench instead of chairs and paper cups instead of shot glasses, a club whose denizens had temperaments as stable as a Silicon Valley IPO. Day in and day out, he had to tell them what to do, even though they made millions more than he did and weren't above back-stabbing betrayal and knew that ultimately, he was a lot more expendable than they were. Even so, he controlled their work schedules, kept them in a game or took them out, got them up or sat them down. As a result, he often humiliated them simply by doing his job. They vented their anger through pouty eyes refusing to look at him from the length of that stark bench. They had pride, enormous pride, at least the ones worth worrying about did. They played with a magic to them that he had never had when he'd played, which made the idea of his telling them what to do—deciding the daily flow of their lives—even more dicey.

He made the decisions he made because of a belief that the whole was always more important than the parts. He likened the team to twenty-five puzzle pieces in which everyone threw his piece in. He kept telling them that, and they nodded when he did, having learned early in their entitled lives that the best way to avoid a lecture was to nod. He told them he loved them, cared about them, needed them. And then he did what he had to do: pinch-hit for them, remove them from that rise of dirt, swap them out for someone with a more reliable glove. And then the next day, he had to tell them all over again how much he loved and needed them.

So it was odd, very odd, perhaps the oddest job in America. As odd as an editor editing his upcoming crop of books on a Central Park bench with all his authors gathered around him fuming over every red line and crossout. As odd as a CEO closing a plant by telling each employee that he had found some workers in India who do it smarter and better and cheaper: In other words, you're all being permanently pinch-hit for, but *don't get me wrong, I still think you're all great!*

Day in and day out, he persevered in the face of the fact that when you're a manager, you never have a 100 percent happy day. There was always something taking away from it, inevitably a burnt ego, somebody who felt scorned or didn't get the start he deserved or the at-bat. He still did the things he had to do, and even when he did them right—knew he had done them right—they still went to hell because the game was eternally mischievous, or "cruel," as he liked to put it, simply cruel. Whether Matt Morris would be able to land on his injured ankle when he pitched: That kept him up at night. The seeming indifference of J.D. Drew, his talent only add-ing to his indifference: That kept him up at night. Kerry Robinson's refusal to follow instructions or stick to fundamentals: That kept him up at night. Trying to figure out what to say to Woody Williams after a particularly heartbreaking loss when he had pitched his brains out: That not only kept La Russa up at night but also had him walking the empty streets of Chicago at 2 A.M. in search of the right words.

Sometimes, he stayed awake to work things out: find an answer in the seeming absence of any, pick a situation apart and put it back together and pick it apart and put it back together again. Beneath his taciturn exterior was an optimist, someone convinced that if you thought about something hard enough, grinded through it enough, examined every possible alternative enough, it could be fixed. That is what happened with the elbow.

The elbow was all he saw at night for a while: not simply anybody's elbow but the elbow of the great Pujols, the best hitter in baseball, even if the only people who knew it for sure at the beginning of 2003 lived in St. Louis. In his first two seasons in the majors, Albert Pujols had hit over .300, driven in more than a hundred runs, and hit more than thirty home runs. And although it was early in 2003, only his third season, he was hitting the ball even better than he had the first two: on his way, if he kept it up, to hitting more than thirty home runs once again and driving in more than a hundred runs once again and *leading* the league in average. It was wonderful for Pujols, obviously, another rapid step up the ladder to pre-emi-nence. But it was also wonderful for the Cardinals: more than won-derful, as their pitching was already in the toilet, with both the starters and the relievers combining to run up the highest ERA in the league. The team couldn't succeed without Pujols's hitting.

And then he injured his elbow on a throw from his position in left field and wouldn't be able to throw with any force for three weeks. In the American League, this wouldn't have been a terrible problem. He couldn't field, maybe, but he still could have his regu-lar place in the batting order; he'd simply be the designated hitter.

But in the National League, in which the dimensions of managing afford far less latitude than in its junior counterpart and therefore far more complication, it meant that Pujols could only pinch-hit until his elbow healed.

This could not have happened at a worse moment. The Cardinals had lost two out of three to Arizona in St. Louis, and Arizona was a down club, hitting poorly, waiting to be plucked. Now the Cardinals were going off on a brutal six-game swing to Atlanta and Florida. Yes, it was only April. But La Russa had learned long ago that April is a great time to push, when most other teams are simply trying to settle in, still trying to figure out whether the puzzle pieces actually amount to anything beyond pieces. He had learned that from Sparky Anderson, and the best proof of that had been the Tigers in 1984 under Anderson's skipperdom, when they had started the season 35–5 on their way to winning a World Series.

So much for this year's April push. But La Russa was worried by the road trip in particular because his team rarely played well in Atlanta. Part of it was psychological, maybe: his nemesis Bobby Cox simply a craggy, crafty old fox who regularly beat him. Part of it was also style: The Braves worked the outside of the plate better than any other team in baseball—made a meal out of it as a matter of policy and instructed pitchers who came over, such as Russ Ortiz from San Francisco, to hit that outside corner for a first-pitch strike, the most important pitch in any at-bat—and then get nasty the rest of the at-bat with a mixture on and off the edges of the plate. He was also worried about the Marlins. He knew that they were stoked with pitching, because he had seen them probably half a dozen times in spring training. The Cardinals would be facing their three right-handed stallions still in the brim of their twenties.

The Cards lost the first game in Atlanta. Then they lost the second when Jeff Fassero, on in relief, just lollipopped one up there, put it right on the plate when the one thing, once again, he should have done was put it off the plate. He made the kind of mistake you maybe expected from a rookie but not from a twelve-year veteran, as if he were *bored* by relieving. And it was unfair to simply single out Fassero, as all the relievers had been ineffective, making fatal mistakes.

After the game, as the team bus made its way to the hotel, La Russa suddenly told the driver to stop. To the players, the game was just another game, a tiny forgotten sliver in the longest season in professional sports. They were in the back of the bus, talking, chirping, making plans for what to do with the night ahead. But La Russa was miserable; losing made him miserable, and being in the suffocating bus made him more miserable. So he got off and walked over to Morton's Steak House just off of Peachtree Street in downtown Atlanta. It was an odd choice for a strict vegetarian who refuses to eat anything that, as he puts it, once had a face on it. But Morton's was warm and clubby, and given that La Russa lived in a hotel not only when the team played away but also when it played at home, the restaurant was probably as close as he got to the feel of an intimate dining room during the season.

He requested a table for one; after a loss, he liked eating alone. There was no worse social interaction in the complicated history of social interaction than trying to make conversation with Tony La Russa after a defeat, idle chitchat bouncing off a face that with each innocuous and annoying word spoken, looked more and more like a glacier with a migraine. And he wasn't entirely alone, anyway. He at least had his book with him because he always brought a book, potboiler plot, with him when he ate by himself: in this case, James Paterson's *The Jester,* an appropriate title, given what had happened in the ninth to give the Braves the 4–2 win.

He tried to concentrate on *The Jester* as he ate. He flipped through the pages as he simultaneously poked around his salad and his baked potato, but it was of no use. He had worked his way through the tattered bullpen because he had had no choice but to work his way through the tattered bullpen. But as soon as that disturbing vision left, another took its place. Now he fixated on tomorrow's lineup with the lefty Mike Hampton going for Atlanta. When he thought about the lineup, there loomed the elbow of the great Pujols.

Almost as soon as La Russa started managing in the major

leagues in 1979, he discovered that most hitters, like mules in their ruts, hate to be meddled with. They hate trying a new stance or a new swing, even if it may lead to improvement, believing that they must be doing something right to have gotten to where they have gotten. As a result, when someone starts telling them to do this and do that—someone who may have had trouble hitting .200 in the major leagues—they tend not to have a particularly open mind. They operate on the superstition that if they do anything differently—*anything,* from stepping on a chalk line as they approach the batter's box to the mechanics of the swing itself—the delicate assembly line they have concocted will collapse. It's a mindset opposed to that of pitchers, La Russa has also found over the years. Pitchers will experiment with a new pitch daily—throw with their toes, spray it out their butt, flick it off their tongue—if they think it might gain them something.

Because most hitters don't like any change in their routine, lineups are, from a manager's perspective, as much rooted in Freudian analysis as they are in the traditional elements of wanting someone who makes good contact to hit lead-off and putting your power hitters in the middle, and so on and so forth. A manager has to take into account every hitter's whim, superstition, ego, and reality, difficult enough on a good night but on this particular night in the dark wood Jacuzzi of Morton's, further hampered by the glaring absence of Pujols.

Pujols normally batted third, so that was an immediate hole needing to be filled. But it wasn't that simple: Filling Pujols's slot meant changing other hitters' routines, a situation La Russa describes as the "consequences of consequences." Scott Rolen moved to the third spot from his customary fifth position. But Rolen *liked* hitting fifth. He had been flourishing there, so sweetly sandwiched between Jim Edmonds and Tino Martinez. Fifth is where he wanted to be. Fifth is where he should be. La Russa had already moved him to third in the middle of the Arizona series, and his bat had gone silent. So then he had moved Rolen *back* to fifth and put Edgar Renteria in the third spot. But that led only to another consequence of consequence; deep down, Renteria *liked* hitting seventh because he drove in a bunch of runs in that slot.

The lineup was in tatters without the great Pujols: the karmic gestalt of it completely disrupted, a Freudian analysis cut abruptly short, feng shui in crisis. But life is unfair, and La Russa had no choice but to remove an index card from his breast pocket and scratch out a lineup for tomorrow's game. He knew he would give the first baseman Martinez a rest, as it was a day game, and Martinez was an eleven-year veteran who could use the time off after playing the night before. It gave him another hole to fill, and he picked Eddie Perez off the bench to play first. It wasn't a bad choice at all, as Perez, a free swinger, had some pop in the bat.

Then he started thinking about Perez a little bit: The best way to use Perez—to get the most out of him—was to be judicious. He *could* take it deep, which is why he was such a nice player to use off the bench in the late innings and even to start in small doses. But if, in the baseball vernacular, he got too "exposed"—if he was playing so much that pitchers started routinely exploiting the holes in his swing—his effectiveness could be curtailed. So he had to be careful with how much he used Perez.

On the bottom of the little index card he was using to scrawl out his lineup was Pujols's name, alongside the other bench players who might be called on to pinch-hit. With the injured elbow, that's all that Pujols was now: a bench player, a *possible* pinch hitter good for one at-bat. The more he stared at Pujols's name, the more it looked like a waste there at the bottom of the card, on the bench. And then he started thinking about first base, and it hit him: *What about putting Pujols at first base?*

When La Russa had been a player in the 1960s and 1970s, virtually all his career was spent in the minors. He had learned a lot there, perhaps most of all that it was called the minors for a reason. He knew early on, particularly after he hurt his shoulder, that he was never going to have much of a big-league career. He continued to plug away, trying to compensate for lack of talent with drive and hustle, although he knew that these fine and admirable qualities were a poor substitute for it. He also studied: sat on that bench in the dugout, watching managers make moves, wondering why they had made them, and asking afterward why they had made them and refusing to go away until they had given a sufficiently exhaustive answer. He learned from one of his managers, Loren Babe, that in some situations, you have no choice but to sacrifice defense *altogether* to get the offense you need. Babe gave a player in this category—offensive asset, defensive drawback—three at-bats, getting him out of there by the sixth so as not to risk some defensive late-in-game lapse that could not be overcome. That's what led La Russa to the unlikely notion of Pujols at first base.

But Pujols wasn't simply a defensive liability. Because of his elbow, he *couldn't throw* anything beyond a soft toss. It made the idea of playing him at first seem, like many ideas, nice and intriguing and totally impractical, fractured La Russa logic. But he continued to chew on it. He refused to let go of it, convinced that something was still there, something that could still work. What if La Russa played Pujols at first and ordered him *not to throw,* no matter how great the temptation?

He walked from Morton's to the Ritz-Carlton Hotel with a new spring in his step. He got into bed, lay on a skyscraper of pillows, and, naturally, stayed awake. But instead of seeing lollipops over the plate, he now saw an elbow with angel's wings. After he woke up the next morning, he continued to think about it. He thought about it some more on the way from the hotel to the visitor's clubhouse at Turner Field, and when he got to the clubhouse, he found Barry Weinberg, the trainer, to tell him of his scheme.

Weinberg dutifully processed La Russa's scenario and offered a clear and specific reaction—*You can't do it!*—for the obvious reason that if Pujols in the heat of the moment did make a real throw, it could be a career-threatening injury. La Russa listened to Weinberg's reaction. He always listened to Weinberg's reaction because they had been together for nearly twenty years. He was quite fond of Weinberg and sometimes had dinner with him after the team won. He clearly respected Weinberg. And then he called Pujols into the little office.

Pujols was circumspect when he came in, a body language of politeness at odds not only with his 6'4", 225-pound frame but also with the superstar status that with each day was only further entombing him. He was already a great player—maybe the greatest young player the game had seen since Joe DiMaggio and Ted Williams—but he didn't express it with an equal measure of physical arrogance. When La Russa spoke to him about something, he listened because that's what a player was supposed to do.

La Russa started the conversation by asking Pujols who was the best major-league manager he had ever played for. Pujols dutifully answered, "Tony," which was true as well as tactful, as La Russa was the *only* major-league manager Pujols had ever played for.

"We get along good, don't we?" asked La Russa.

"Yes," replied Pujols.

"Well, you know what, you can get me fired by throwing the ball. If you throw the ball, I'll quit."

Pujols nodded that he understood.

"All we have to do is have you lay out for three weeks and you come out 100 percent. So you have to trust me on this strategy, because it gives us a better chance to win."

So Pujols started at first. And it took all of one inning, actually less than that, for the danger of La Russa's scheme to become apparent. In the bottom of the first, Rafael Furcal got on for Atlanta. It brought up Marcus Giles, who tried to sacrifice Furcal to second with a bunt *toward Pujols*. Furcal made it to second, and he could have easily made it to third had he known that Pujols was under orders not to throw the ball. There were no more major episodes at first base after that, but the Cardinals ended up losing to the Braves 4–3 anyway, when the bullpen imploded again and gave up two runs in the bottom of the ninth.

The team dragged into the Westin Diplomat in Miami at about 3 A.M. after the American Airlines charter flight from Atlanta. The players, exhausted, went to bed. But La Russa couldn't sleep. With the three-game sweep by the Braves, the road trip from hell was half done, and the devil seemed in no mood to relent, not with A.J. Burnett and Josh Beckett and Brad Penny pitching for the Marlins: guys who effortlessly threw 94 mph and 95 mph. In his sleeplessness, he began to further examine the Pujols experiment.

Florida was a different team from Atlanta. The Marlins led the league in stolen bases, with Juan Pierre and Luis Castillo, guys who drove you nuts on the basepaths. And with the word trickling out that Pujols couldn't throw—as a baseball dugout was a greater cauldron of gossip than a Flatbush nail salon—La Russa knew there were even more liabilities. A pitcher, for example, couldn't even make a pick-off move to first, because a runner, aware that Pujols couldn't throw properly, would simply take off to second as if it were a free base. So starting Pujols at first was out, particularly as Martinez was coming back into the lineup anyway to face the Marlin trio of right-handers. But then La Russa considered the out-field dimensions in Florida. Left field there was relatively small, with most of the room in center and right. He conjured and pon-dered—a little bit of this, a little bit of that—until he had another potion.

The next morning, he couldn't wait to try out his newest remedy on somebody. As was his pregame habit, he picked up pitching coach Dave Duncan, bullpen coach Marty Mason, and third-base coach Jose Oquendo in the hotel lobby and they all rode together to the stadium. By now, La Russa was bursting with excitement; on the way there, he told them about his plan to play Pujols in left field and set out the rules he'd devised to make it work:

1. If there's a base hit to left field, Renteria runs out from the shortstop position so Pujols can simply flip the ball to him, which presumably will prevent a runner from trying to stretch a single into a double with the ball in Renteria's glove.
2. If the ball is hit to left center, Pujols fields it and flips it to center fielder Edmonds, who, as Pujols's surrogate, makes the throw back in to prevent an extra base.
3. If a runner on first tries to tag up and go to second on a fly ball to left, Pujols lets him tag up.

Duncan and Oquendo and Mason were receptive. But once in the clubhouse, La Russa had to run the idea past Weinberg because everything involving the players' health had to be run past the trainer. Weinberg's usual answer, based on caution intrinsic to his line of work, was *no,* so La Russa wasn't surprised when Weinberg said that it was an even worse idea than the first-base experiment.

"Tony, he's gonna get hurt. He can't throw."

"I know he can't throw."

La Russa then called the general manager, Walt Jocketty. As it turned out, Jocketty was already aware of his plan. Weinberg, wanting to stop the madness before it became reality, had called him first. But Jocketty became supportive after La Russa convinced him that Pujols, with his intellect for the game, would not give in to any dangerous impulses. It couldn't be said of all players. Maybe it couldn't even be said about most players. But it could be said about Pujols, for whom a nod was more than simply defense against a further lecture.

La Russa knew that it was a risky tactic. He knew that there might be terrible repercussions if it went south, for Pujols and for him. He could be fired if it didn't work: probably *should* be fired because he had jeopardized the exceptional future of an exceptional player. But he also knew that he needed Pujols in the lineup. So he wrote him into left field.

Pujols came up in the top of the first against Burnett. He was hitting third, Rolen fifth, and Renteria seventh. The correct feng shui of the lineup had been restored. Things felt good again. The order of things had been restored. There was a man on first and one out when Pujols settled in at the plate.

He homered on the first pitch. From the corner of his most peculiar office, La Russa whispered the only thing he could possibly whisper: *"Son of a bitch."* Because sometimes it really did work: as it did then, as it must now in the high heat of August—heat born for baseball—with the Cubs coming to town the way every team comes to town this season and all seasons. A three-game series.

GAME
ONE

1

FEAR FACTOR

I

● ● ● WITH THE SERIES against the Cubs set to begin tonight in a matter of hours, Tony La Russa is doing what he has done since he first became a major-league manager at the uncertain age of thirty-four. He is managing out of fear, preparing as if he has never managed before, striving to prove to the world that he possesses the combination of skills essential to the trade: part tactician, part psychologist, and part riverboat gambler.

What few words he utters from his office in the bowels of Busch Stadium are less words than they are contorted mumbles so low off the surface of the floor, you need a fishing net to scoop them up. He is dressed in Cardinals-red undergarments, and, because his office is off to the side of the main locker area, he is oblivious to the players who trickle in one at a time to eventually get dressed. They are easygoing and relaxed, all about the sublimation of pressure. It's pretty much a given in baseball—unlike other sports—that the more hyped you get, the worse off you will be. But La Russa is all about pressure.

Tension emanates from his face like a lighthouse beacon in the fog, visible from miles away. He is already moving into his zone of concentration: the tunnel, as he calls it. By game time, he will be so deep in the tunnel, so riveted on the vagaries of the field in front of him, that the rest of the spectacle—the swells of the crowd, the incessant seagull screech of the vendors, the out-of-town scoreboard with its inning-by-inning warnings—will have no meaning to him. He won't even be aware of them, as if the game exists for him in a pure extract of silence. He isn't quite in that place yet, and from his office, he occasionally does acknowledge a world outside his own. He scowls when somebody turns up the music in the locker room and a blast of "P.I.M.P." by 50 Cent rages into his office without even as much as a courtesy knock, the decibels so high it would blow the door down anyway. He occasionally peeks at the two television sets that hang at opposite corners from the ceiling of his office: one TV running the satellite feed of Cincinnati playing at Pittsburgh and the other showing an old John Wayne movie, *The Fighting Kentuckians*. "Now that's my kind of movie," he says, but he draws no comfort when Wayne starts to sing. "John Wayne singing. That's nice," he says with misery, momentarily lifting his head from the sheaf of the latest statistics on his upcoming opponent. Then he turns back to the columnar murk of the stats in his ceaseless search for slivery edges, possible aberrations that may be of use during the game.

The stapled packet contains the usual baseball breakdown: at-bats and hits and extra-base hits and walks and strikeouts and average for hitters, wins and losses, and innings pitched and runs allowed and hits allowed and home runs allowed by pitchers. La Russa pays special attention to the individual matchups, an essential ingredient of his approach to managing. These sheets detail how each of his hitters has done against Cubs pitchers and how his pitchers have done against Cubs hitters, as well as the flip side: the individual performances of Cubs hitters against Cardinals pitchers and Cubs pitchers against Cardinals hitters.

The term *bench player* doesn't really apply to the Cardinals, because La Russa so frequently plugs utility players into the lineup based on little opportunities he unearths by sifting through the results of their previous experience with players on the opposing team. These individual matchups are so integral to his strategy that he copies them onto 5-by-7-inch preprinted cards that managers normally use to make out the game's lineup. With ritualistic precision, he folds the cards down the middle ten minutes before game time and then slips them into the back pocket of his uniform. During a game, he pulls them out continually, almost like worry beads, peering at them as if in search of evidence that everything is fine, that he is doing exactly *what he needs to be doing.* More practically, he refers to them when deciding who to bring on in relief or who may be the best candidate to pinch-hit.

Matchups aren't foolproof to La Russa, perhaps because nothing is foolproof in baseball. They have their weaknesses, particularly if the statistics are several years old. But they do provide the best indicator of what the competition will be between a pitcher and a hitter. There are some hitters who, never mind their mediocre batting averages, simply tag the living crap out of some pitchers. Conversely, there are pitchers, despite soggy ERAs, who simply do well against particular high-stroke hitters.

But La Russa believes that in virtually all situations, human nature dictates results and that his role as a manager is to recognize the impact of human nature and take the best advantage of it. It sounds simple, maybe, but it isn't simple, because human nature isn't simple, and it's even less simple when applied to the twenty-five pieces of the puzzle. Some need to be left alone, some need a pat on the rump every so often, and some need a swift boot in the rear: fuzzy love or tough love or no love. To a certain degree, matchups are a compact reflection of the human psyche, in this instance the effect of confidence on performance. A hitter who has gained early success against a pitcher may simply continue to build on that. He *believes* he can see the ball better when it's thrown by that pitcher, even though there is no physical truth that he can. It's moot, immaterial; the octane of confidence itself is enough to propel him. It's the same with certain pitchers. Their curve may have less break, less tumble, less of that 12-to-6 plummet than their colleagues' curves, but they begin to succeed with it against a given hitter. They begin to feel, to *know,* that the poor little guy 60 feet and 6 inches down the road from them can't do anything with it. And it actually turns out that way.

But matchups also tell the truth about skill—the numbers, like the needle at the start of a lie detector test, are just the beginning of what will be revealed. So when La Russa looks at the matchup numbers that he has been handed, numbers he is familiar with because the Cardinals have already played the Cubs nine times before, it isn't the numbers he cares about as much as the stories behind them: ways to find a remedy for a hitter who has consistently lousy numbers against a sinkerballer (start hitting the ball the other way instead of always trying to pull it and roll over the ball with weak grounders), or the anomalies of right-handed relievers who, against the grain of baseball, actually do better against lefties and how to make use of that (instead of the conventional wisdom of putting in a lefty pinch-hitter, go with a righty). Of all the hours spent preparing before a game, many of them La Russa spends searching for the explanations of these matchup numbers, a slice of seemingly buried narrative that during the season can single-handedly change the outcome of the four or five games that—in La Russa's estimation—a manager can change.

The more La Russa scrutinizes these matchups, the less he likes them. Usually, they offer hope at some point in a series, but not this time. Over the next three nights, the Cards will confront three dominating pitchers. Adding to La Russa's anxiety, giving it the true crisp of darkness, is an acute animus: *the Cubs*.

The rivalry between the Cubs and the Cardinals is probably the oldest and perhaps the best in baseball, no matter how the Red Sox and Yankees spit and spite at each other. That's a tabloid-fueled soap opera about money and ego and sound bites. That's a pair of bratty high-priced supermodels trying to trip each other in their stilettos on the runway. But the Cards-Cubs epic is about roots and geography and territorial rights. It's entwined in the Midwestern blood and therefore refreshing and honest and even heroic. It isn't simply two teams throwing tantrums at each other but two feudal city-states with eternal fans far beyond their own walls, spread throughout not only the Midwest but also deep into the South and the West. The Cubs started amassing their empire through WGN, its crystal-clear radio waves sweeping out of Chicago into Iowa and

Wisconsin and the Dakotas. Until the Boston Braves moved to Milwaukee in 1953, no other National League team was in the upper Midwest.

As for the Cardinals, they were for a period of time baseball's *westernmost* team, and its *southernmost,* too, until the Dodgers moved to Los Angeles in 1958. The Cardinals' retort to WGN was KMOX, whose fifty thousand watts fed millions starved for big-league baseball. Carried by its powerful signal, Cardinals games rolled south from St. Louis, across Missouri into Arkansas and Mississippi, and west into Oklahoma and Texas and even beyond, if the night sky was right.

In Peoria and Decatur and dozens of smaller Illinois farm towns, factions developed, with half the population tuning in to WGN and half turning on KMOX. But the rivalry goes farther back than radio, deep into baseball's mythic youth.

It might have originated on June 24, 1905, when the Cubs' Ed Reulbach and the Cards' Jack Taylor each pitched eighteen-inning complete games before the Cubbies won 2–1. The mutual contempt was only sharpened by more recent heroics, such as the nine showdowns in the late 1960s and early 1970s between the Cubs' Fergie Jenkins and the Cards' Bob Gibson. In seven of these duels, both men pitched a complete game, four were decided by one run, and two of them produced a final score of 1–0. Once, in 95-degree St. Louis heat, as terrible a heat as this hemisphere can muster, both pitchers went the distance undaunted by the departure of homeplate umpire Shag Crawford, who found the weather so insufferable that even he quit in the middle of the game. St. Louis fans also hearken back to Bruce Sutter's split-fingered fastball, perhaps the greatest contribution to pitching since Mordecai "Three Fingers" Brown refined the curve ball. Cubs fans exult in the memory of Ryne Sandberg's stroking that splitter for two back-to-back homers in 1984, a deliciousness made more delicious because Sutter had once been a Cub himself before going over to the dark side.

The inevitable implosion of the Cubs—the sad fury of their futility—only gave the rivalry an added extra, with nothing more fun for a Cards fan than to watch the Cubs self-destruct with their own special brand of pathos. Their knack for misfortune has proved itself thousands of times but rarely more eloquently than in "Broglio-for-Brock," a term synonymous in some circles with *idiocy, absurdity, ridiculousness,* and *senselessness.* Broglio-for-Brock was born in June 1964; at first, Cubs fans thought that they had gotten the better of the deal. They didn't mind at all when Lou Brock was sent to the Cardinals along with Jack Spring and Paul Toth in return for Ernie Broglio, Bobby Shantz, and Doug Clemens. Brock's statistics at the time were middling at best. He struck out often, got thrown out stealing nearly half the times he tried, and had an aggregate batting average with the Cubs of .255 over four years. Broglio, on the other hand, was a hard-throwing pitcher who had been 18 and 8 in 1963. The fact that he was only 3 and 5 in 1964, an indication of arm trouble, didn't seem to bother the Cubs' hierarchy.

As a Cardinal, Brock became one of the greatest players in the history of the game, leading the National League eight times in stealing, finishing five times in the top-ten voting for most valuable player, and getting inducted into the Baseball Hall of Fame in 1985. After the trade, Broglio subsequently won seven games and lost nineteen before leaving baseball two years later. Whether it's true or not, and it probably isn't, it is still considered to be the worst trade that has ever taken place in baseball. Cubs fans have never forgotten it, partially because Cardinals fans will never let them forget it, and it makes every series they play touched by trauma.

II

THIS SEASON, La Russa feels a special competitive edge against the Cubs because they're for real. He pays particular notice to the two pitchers who embody the team's newfound swagger and success: those punk rockers Mark Prior and Kerry Wood. They're the best 1-2 in the game this year, with psychoses that complement their skill. They both throw nasty stuff, and neither is afraid to go way up and way in on a hitter if that's what it takes to prevail.

Even more vital to the Cubs' resurgence is La Russa's counterpart, Dusty Baker. He's in his first season with the team; last year, he led the Giants to the National League Pennant. When Baker became available, La Russa was hoping that he would move over to the American League so that he might have to face him only in a World Series. But Baker dashed those hopes completely by settling in with *the Cubs*. Baker may not be the greatest strategist, but the way the sport and its players are evolving, La Russa also knows that how one manages during a game is becoming less important. What Baker is good at — superb at — is interacting with players. He can handle a ballclub as well as he handles the ever-present toothpick in his mouth; he knows better than anyone else in baseball how to manage the space between a player's ears. He is also masterful at deflecting attention to himself. He lets blunt and controversial remarks spill out of his mouth. But on closer analysis, they seem purposely designed to keep the media swarm buzzing around him. Better for him to get stung by clearly calculated outrageousness than his players.

The upshot is that the Cubs haven't done their annual cuddly collapse in the Friendly Confines. And the Astros, buoyed by the oak-barrel reliability of Craig Biggio and Jeff Bagwell, haven't fallen back either. On this last Tuesday in August, the Central Division standings reflect a race that's neck and neck as it heads into the summer embers:

ST. LOUIS	68–62	.523
HOUSTON	68–62	.523
CHICAGO	67–62	.519

By winning two of these next three games, the Cubs can overtake the Cardinals at a pivotal moment. Beyond that general worry are a lot of smaller, more specific concerns. Aside from the punk duo of Prior and Wood, there's the dark horse Carlos Zambrano, slated to go against the Cards in Game 3. Although few outside of Chicago know much about Zambrano, he is pitching better than Prior and Wood. He has, in fact, been the best pitcher in baseball the past month.

La Russa worries about how he will counter this trio with his own trio: Garrett Stephenson in Game 1, Woody Williams in Game 2, and Matt Morris in Game 3. It's not a shabby trio by any means; nor is it accidental that they'll be pitching in this three-game series. More than a month ago, La Russa and Dave Duncan mapped out their rotation all the way to the end of August to ensure that these would be the pitchers who went against the Cubs now. La Russa and Duncan purposely decided to backload the three-game series, sending the weakest of the three pitchers out first. As one of the many philosophies they have developed during two decades together, they would rather finish the series strong than begin it strong.

La Russa likes this rotation, but he doesn't love it. Each of his pitchers is hauling baggage. Stephenson has some kind of bipolar disorder on the mound. Williams, the staff workhorse, has hit a winless trough after an All-Star first half and may be mentally exhausted. Morris is still recovering from a recently sprained ankle that could well prevent him from pitching with any sustained effectiveness.

La Russa also frets over his hitters, particularly the top of the lineup, with two unpredictable neophytes. He's worried about Rolen's shoulder and neck, which have been hurting him ever since he slid headfirst into home plate at Fenway Park two and a half months ago. The injury restricts his mobility to get to certain pitches, not to mention that it's also painful. La Russa needs to give him a day off. But he can't give Rolen a day off, at least not for this series, anyway; even with a bad neck and shoulder, Rolen at third is still better than any other third baseman in the league, both defensively and offensively. La Russa is worried about Edmonds in center, whose shoulder has been cranky ever since the All-Star game in Chicago when he apparently did something to it during the Home Run Derby. La Russa is worried about Renteria at short, who collapsed in the shower with back spasms the previous game and will definitely be scratched from Game 1. La Russa worries too about the Cubs' lineup. There are Sammy Sosa and Moises Alou, the obvious game breakers, but he's even more worried about three ex-

Pirates who have given the Cubs enormous value down the stretch: Aramis Ramirez at third, Randall Simon at first, and Kenny Lofton in center.

As La Russa refines the little cheat-sheet cards in his tiny hiero-glyphic handwriting, he spies a glimmer or two of possibility. The Cubs' starters make a lot of errors, and maybe it's an Achilles' heel he can exploit by bunting more than usual. And Prior, despite his prowess and his puffed-up attitude, still has never beaten the Cardinals. But La Russa takes little relief in any of this. Like most managers, he lives by adages and aphorisms, and the one he applies here resounds with his trademark joy: *Hope for the best; prepare for the worst.*

2

LOCKED IN

I

● ● ● WITH BATTING PRACTICE and the meetings that take place before every new series still a good hour away, the players mill about the clubhouse with an ease born of privilege. They pad across the carpeted floor in white slippers. They pass a little round table where a red batting helmet, destined for an army sergeant in Iraq, awaits their signatures. They tend to their bats, examine them for scuffs and imperfections, or in the case of Eddie Perez, strum the barrel of them like a banjo to ensure that they have the right pitch.

Other players scan a whiteboard just inside the entrance to see where their names are for batting practice, the groupings carefully constructed in terms of who gets to bat when and with whom, Pujols and Rolen getting to go last in the final embers of the afternoon, when the glare of the sun isn't so severe. At the opposite end of the clubhouse, past the little facsimile locker containing Stan Musial's itchy uniform and shoes that seem too small and flimsy for someone that fierce and good, players cluster around an oversized sheet that shows each team's lineups for tonight. Before game time, bench coach Joe Pettini will remove the sheet—now taped to a whiteboard—with a curator's care and retape it to the far corner of the dugout where La Russa resides. During the game, as players enter and exit, the sheet will precisely reflect their movements so La Russa can keep track of who is available and who has been excommunicated. By the last out, it will reflect a frenzy of activity:

crossouts, write-ins, cold diagonal lines through the first letter of a player's name, meaning that he's been rendered unavailable. But for now, the sheet is clean and pristine. It exudes hope, the vain suggestion that everything will proceed with ease and order.

A bit of adventure is always involved as the players scan the lineup sheet to see who is in tonight for the Cardinals, whether La Russa's analysis of the matchups has produced any last-minute surprises. Dusty Baker's not quite as itchy, but it's still an opportunity for the players to see whether he has any tricks of his own:

ST. LOUIS CARDINALS		CHICAGO CUBS	
Original Position	Change	Original Position	Change
Robinson RF		Lofton CF	
Hart 2B		Martinez 2B	
Pujols LF		Sosa RF	
Edmonds CF		Alou LF	
Rolen 3B		Simon 1B	
Martinez 1B		Ramirez 3B	
Cairo SS		Gonzalez SS	
Widger C		Bako C	
Stephenson P		Prior P	

ST. LOUIS CARDINALS　　　　**CHICAGO CUBS**

Available Position Players

Left-Handed	Switch	Right-Handed	Left-Handed	Switch	Right-Handed
Palmiero		Perez	Goodwin		Glanville
		Matheny	O'Leary		Karros
		Taguchi	Womack		Miller
		Renteria			

ST. LOUIS CARDINALS　　　　**CHICAGO CUBS**

Available Pitchers

Left-Handed	Right-Handed	Left-Handed	Right-Handed
Kline	DeJean	Guthrie	Alfonseca
Fassero	Isringhausen	Remlinger	Borowski
	Eldred		Farnsworth
	Simontacchi		

Tonight, for Game 1, the Cubs' lineup is straightforward. Sammy Sosa and Moises Alou, batting third and fourth, form the center of gravity, with forty-nine homers between them. Sosa's had a split personality this season, almost helpless the first half and now hitting with venom the second. Alou in particular is a Cardinals killer, so much so that Dave Duncan believes that they need to completely rethink how to pitch him: Simply stop feeding his first-pitch addiction. Alex Gonzalez, in the seventh hole, has seventeen homers. He strikes out a lot: 105 times already. But he likes to be a long-ball star, and he is the kind of dangerous low-end-of-the-lineup hitter who will kill you if you get lazy with him and let him be too comfortable, give him something too fat on the outside of the plate, something he thinks he can simply reach over and loose a swing at. Paul Bako, in the eighth spot, can't hit a lick: .213 coming into tonight. He's played with so many teams already in his brief career—this is his fifth in four years—he might as well keep his belongings in storage rather than risk the disappointment of setting down roots. He's in for his defense, a tough and uncompromising handler of pitchers that the Cardinals starter Brett Tomko distinctly remembers from their days together in the minors when he called time and came out to the mound to have a word with him.

"Are you really trying out here?"

"What do you mean?"

"Because your stuff is horrible today and if you don't try a little harder, you're not going to make it out of this inning."

The three Pirate expatriates—Lofton and Simon and Ramirez—have been equitably interspersed in the one-, five-, and six-holes, and it isn't pretty: A look at the matchups makes La Russa briefly wonder whether they'd been brought over from Pittsburgh specifically to torment Garrett Stephenson in Game 1. Against him, the three players are an aggregate 19 for 42—almost .500—with two home runs.

LOFTON	6-12-1	
SIMON	8-18-1	
RAMIREZ	5-12-0	

As for the Cardinals' lineup, it's a patchwork because of injuries. Still, it features Pujols and Edmonds and Rolen in the thick of it, the best-hitting threesome in baseball right now. They have ninety home runs among them through 130 games, and each of them may well drive in more than a hundred runs. Despite a recent bout of the flu, Pujols has been in the stratosphere all season, contending for the Triple Crown and fresh off a thirty-game hitting streak. Edmonds has had stratospheric moments as well. If his shoulder hadn't turned cranky, he could have forty home runs instead of thirty-two, and he continues to play center field as if he's at the nastiest Texas Hold 'Em table at Binion's, betting the pot on every catch. Rolen, who is from a small farming town in southern Indiana and likes to draw as much attention to himself as you would expect from someone who is from a small farming town in southern Indiana, is humming along with typical incandescence. In the field, he doesn't have the gambler flair of Edmonds. Rolen's far more self-effacing, his style gritty and as determined as a linebacker without a single whiff of hey-look-at-me; it's easy to forget that he's already won three Gold Gloves and in all likelihood will win a fourth this season. As for his performance at the plate, he's once again on his way to another year, his fourth of seven in the major leagues, in which he will hit more than twenty-five homers and drive in more than a hundred runs.

These three players provide meat in the middle, but La Russa also likes danger at the top: a hitter in the one-hole who can get on base whether by hit or walk, followed by a hitter in the two-hole who can uncork power. He's felt that way at least since the early 1980s when Carlton Fisk came over to the White Sox from the Red Sox. In 1983, La Russa started putting Fisk at number two even though he was a prodigious home-run hitter. For virtually all his career, Fisk had hit in the three-, four-, or five-spot, and he didn't like the change in stature much at first, shunted into the space universally reserved for the little get-on-base piccolos. Given his immense New England pride, he didn't appreciate La Russa for much of anything at the beginning of the 1983 season. When the White Sox brought up catcher Joel Skinner from the minors without telling him, La Russa and Fisk started screaming and yelling at each other during stretching exercises before a doubleheader against the A's in June. But there were other frustrations. He was hitting under .200 at the time, and it was shortly afterward that La Russa, in trying to figure out something to get him unblocked, put him second in the order. He did it because of his thirst for power in the two-spot. He also did it because he knew he could, with his lineup strong enough in the middle to still pack pop. Fisk started blossoming at the plate afterward. He ended up hitting twenty-six home runs, his career high at the time. Placed ahead of Harold Baines, Greg Luzinski, and Ron Kittle, the foursome became an unorthodox murderers' row in the two- through five-holes, combining for 113 home runs, 380 RBIs, and 309 runs scored as the White Sox ran away with the division by twenty games.

Later, when La Russa managed the American League in the 1989 All-Star game, he took his theory of danger a step further when he put Bo Jackson in the one-hole. La Russa once again had the luxury to do so, because just about everybody on the team was a dangerous hitter. But still, Jackson wasn't your prototypical lead-off hitter. He had great wheels, but he struck out a lot: a natural-born cleanup hitter. His power carried danger, though: the ability to change the dimension of a game right away. When Jackson hit a 455-foot home run off Rick Reuschel in the bottom of the first, La Russa again saw what that danger can do to an opposing pitcher: rattle him and keep him rattled. When the next hitter up, Wade Boggs, who had everything but power, homered off Reuschel, it only confirmed to La Russa why explosive danger at the top is a good thing.

Another reason for explosion at the top—stacking the deck early—is to capitalize on the starting pitcher's uncertainty. In the first inning, even the best hurlers are still evaluating the feel of their fastballs and off-speed, no matter how well they warmed up. (Starting pitchers generally agree that there is little correlation between how well they warmed up before a game and how well they actually perform during it.) Sometimes, in the absence of classic power, its catalyzing effects can still be manufactured. In 2001, La Russa had

Placido Polanco bat second for part of the season. He was hardly a power hitter, but he was a great hit-and-run man, and toward the end of the year, La Russa almost always had him hit and run, both to push for a run and also to keep defenses on edge. But there is no sudden explosion tonight, even of the manufactured variety.

Normally, the veteran second baseman, Fernando Vina, would hit lead-off and the right fielder, J.D. Drew, hit second. But Vina is just coming off a torn hamstring that sidelined him for three months. He's played a few games in the minors to get the timing of his stroke back, but he looks lost at the plate and isn't ready yet, which leaves La Russa with Bo Hart, a last name straight out of central casting given the way he plays. He's the poster boy of scrappy, listed at 5'11" and 175 pounds, although he doesn't seem even as big as that. He's twenty-seven years old but looks in his late teens, with his nubby blond hair and a chin vainly struggling to grow something, as if he's not quite ready yet to grow something. When he's in the clubhouse on the road before a game, he likes to play cards—*cards*—as sweet as it gets in baseball.

His play at second since coming up from Triple-A in June has been exceptional, really. Into the middle of July, he was hitting over .350, and it's clear that he's one of those guys with average skills and above-average heart and fire. La Russa can't help but love players like that, but he also knows that stories like his rarely end the way they begin. Since mid-July, Hart has cooled off considerably. He's hitting .283 coming into the three-game series. With 240 at-bats, he's not the virgin he was when he came up, and every pitch Hart takes in the major leagues is one more chance for pitchers to discover and exploit the places he's having trouble getting to.

His stroke is compact, a delayed swing in which he lets the ball virtually get to the plate before he goes to hit it. He has good punch for a player that small, like a pinball smacking off a lever. But he has trouble with the breaking ball, which surprises La Russa because a swing like that should allow him to recognize a curve ball and react to it. Hart also tends to get too aggressive out of the strike zone, resulting in a quick strike 1 to put him into a hole. All this makes him a perfect hitter in the eighth spot, where that aggressiveness and punch would be a definite plus, making pitchers pause before thinking that they can simply go after him with high heat. But it's another La Russa adage that you can't dwell on what you don't have and can take advantage of only what do you have, so Hart is starting and batting second.

As for Drew, capable of launching the ball as far as anyone in both leagues, he went on the disabled list nine days ago. He's injured again, as he was at the beginning of the season. It's the sixth time he's been on the disabled list since coming into the league in 1998, surrounded by more anticipation than any other rookie since Mickey Mantle. Perhaps never in his managing career has La Russa had a player more tantalizing in terms of talent and more difficult to unleash. But like many young players, Drew came in with the advantages that only plot against you if your goal is the realization of what God gave you: a long-term contract, too many early millions, a billboard mystique about him before he had taken a single road trip.

To La Russa, there is a certain bittersweet tragedy to Drew, the embodiment of the best of times and the worst of times in baseball. The best of times for players because there is so much money out there and the ability to control your future. The worst of times because the money corrupts and compromises, makes it easy to play under your maximum and to reject the daily commitment that wins awards and World Series rings, because you can still make a ridiculous living at three-quarters speed. "A lot of young players fall into this trap where it's uncomfortable to push yourself on a daily basis," says La Russa. "They settle for some percent under their max. If you have the chance to be a two-million-dollar-a-year player, they might settle for 75 percent of that. In the case of J.D., if you have the chance to be a twelve-million-to-fifteen-million-dollar-a-year player, you settle for 75 percent of that."

The irony for La Russa—and what an irony it is—is that Drew may be *too* talented, that it comes too easily to him. He plays with little outward passion for the game, gliding through because even when he glides through, he still gets enough hits and enough home runs to make about three and a half million dollars a year. La Russa knows that of all the qualities that a player possesses, outward passion is the most deceptive in terms of what it indicates. When Harold Baines played for La Russa on the White Sox and in Oakland, he had no outward passion. He said little in the clubhouse and even less to reporters; once, after hitting a prodigious home run to win a game, his answer to the standard question "Guess you got a piece of that, huh, Harold?" was expressed in one word: "Evidently." But Baines was also a great competitor—one of the best late-inning clutch hitters that La Russa has ever managed—with no correlation between outward temperament and inward passion for the game. La Russa doesn't feel the same about Drew.

He still believes in him, but he's also had ample opportunity with him, and he wonders whether it would be better for someone else to open himself up to the seduction of his limitless talent, find what he never could.

When he thinks of Drew, La Russa inevitably thinks of another player he once managed in the 1980s, Jose Canseco, the charming, self-destructive, preoccupied poster boy of distraction. Once the multiyear contract came Jose's way—once the money got into the heavyweight millions—playing every day became nostalgic. "I'm a performer, not a player," said Canseco, which in a lifetime of incredible comments from players, may well be the most incredible one ever spoken to La Russa. But the comparison between the two players goes only so far, because Canseco did work for the advantages he eventually got. He did turn in that MVP year with the Oakland A's in 1988 when he became the first player ever to hit forty or more home runs and steal forty or more bases. He loved hitting with two strikes—half of his home runs that year were with two strikes—which is about the discipline of getting a little wider and not striding as much and working on reflexes through tedious short-toss drills during early batting practice. Canseco had competitive passion before he pissed it away, only to have his body betray him when he tried to recover what had once made him.

That leaves La Russa with Kerry Robinson in right field batting first, and La Russa has significant concern about being left with

Robinson in right field batting first. It's the classic tension between manager and bench player: how much Robinson thinks he should be playing versus how much La Russa thinks he should be playing. Robinson aches and itches to be in the lineup every day. He sees himself in the same category as the Marlins' Pierre, who is on his way to stealing sixty bases this season, whereas Robinson is stuck on the bench most of the time. That's the way he feels about it — *he's stuck there* — and that infuriates La Russa, given his team-as-puzzle theory. He sees Robinson as a role player with a left-handed bat, good speed, and nice range in the outfield. All this means that Robinson can be vital in the right situations. But La Russa doesn't see him as another Pierre. As far back as spring training, he flat-out told Robinson that if he really thought he should be playing every day, he should go to the general manager, Walt Jocketty, and demand a trade. "Go find somebody who's going to give you the four or five hundred at-bats," La Russa said. "And I hope they're in our division so we can play against you."

Robinson accepted his fate; he had no choice. But he still doesn't like it, and he makes few bones about not liking it. He sulks when he is not in the lineup regularly — as when he sat on the outermost edge of the dugout by himself in Houston one day as if he were fishing off the end of a pier — and La Russa *hates* sulking. As for how Robinson will perform now that he is starting, La Russa doesn't really know. Robinson has played pretty well since replacing Drew — 8 for 14 in his last four games. He's getting it into the opposite field, which is a good sign, because it means that he's not trying to do too much by trying to power and pull the ball every time he's up. But as a lead-off hitter, Robinson is the antithesis of danger. He has no home runs in 165 at-bats so far this season and only three in his five-year career. Nor does he compensate for it with his on-base percentage, which is a meager .302.

The players continue to do what players do. They sit in front of their lockers and catch up on a little mail, which they never catch up on, given the torrents of letters that come in addressing them as "mister" and beseeching them with religious humility for autographs. They put on headphones because even they can't take the deafening sound of "P.I.M.P." stampeding through the locker room. They contend with the reporters already swarming, asking them the obvious so the obvious can be restated. They pad on those white slippers into the eating area, an oasis that provides not only sustenance but also a fine little hideout, as it is off-limits to the media. They make square little white-bread sandwiches from the trays of cold cuts. They help themselves to the private stock of ball-park hot dogs sunning on a metal grill. If they feel like having an omelet, an obliging cook will prepare one with fresh vegetables and finely diced cubes of turkey and ham and bacon. They read the sports pages of *USA Today* and the *St. Louis Post-Dispatch*, the other sections of the paper generally untouched by human hands. They grab from the plastic tubs of Butterfingers and Ding-Dongs and Twinkies and Kit-Kats and Snickers that have been laid out on a series of shelves. They dip into canisters of Bazooka and Double Bubble and individual sticks of Juicy Fruit that a clubhouse atten-dant has already unwrapped for them. They reach for the little packages of David's sunflower seeds that now come in four flavors: original, toasted corn, barbecue, and jalapeño hot salsa, for those who may need a little pick-me-up in the late innings. When they leave the kitchen, some go into the weight room to lift weights or to ride one of the stationary bikes. Some go into the training room where arms, in particular pitching arms, are salved and stretched and iced, in vain efforts to shield them from the inevitable attacks of time and extended use.

A steady flow of players leaves the clubhouse altogether and goes in two different directions. A trickle heads for the indoor cage to work on various drills: One is the basic hitting drill off the tee to hone the swing; a second is the short-toss drill in which batting coach Mitchell Page kneels about 15 feet away on one knee behind a screen and gets it in there with enough velocity and varied loca-tion to allow hitters to work on their two-strike reflexes as well as laying off the sinker or the high fastball; the third is a drill, invented by Pete Rose, in which first-base coach Dave McKay tosses the ball but the hitter purposely doesn't swing, instead simply watches the ball over and over as it comes in, to gain further intimacy.

A trickle heads through a nondescript red door. Inside is a dark little submarine of a room overstuffed with televisions and video consoles and satellite feed boxes and cable boxes and two computers and wires as criss-crossed as dreadlocks. Pipes leak in a corner, and several holes in one wall suggest something serious to do with rodents. Given that the Secret Weapon resides here—La Russa's own term for him—the place should have a little more flair, a little more style. Then again, Chad Blair doesn't look like much of a Secret Weapon, so maybe it's the right fit, after all.

Blair's standard-issue uniform—a T-shirt and shorts just above the cusp of some raw and ugly knees—gives no inkling of the contribution he makes. Nor do his glasses or his sweet, shaggy-dog voice. His physique is small and unimposing, entirely out of place beside those he works with. Blair also looks bleary-eyed *all* the time, maybe because his wife and he just had a baby girl, or maybe because his professional life is spent staring at grainy images, searching for the tiny differences that draw an unforgiving line between those who can and those who sometimes can and those who never will.

II

BLAIR IS the Cardinals' video coordinator, a vocation he stumbled onto in the early 1990s, when he was a freelance cameraman in the Bay Area and the Oakland A's built a video room for $100,000. It looked nice and had fancy equipment, but the team had no idea what to do with it, so Blair was asked to run it. It's been his life ever since: the compilation and dissemination of bite-sized chunks of video. At first, only coaches studied film, but it has become essential for players as well, or at least those players who want to remain competitive. Of all the changes in baseball over the past decade, the rise of video is the most significant. It has transformed the sport, showing hitters and pitchers how to refine their craft so minutely that their profession is no longer merely a game of inches. Now it's a game *of an inch* because of the ability of video to alert players and coaches to the slightest imperfections, and many franchises are spending millions for the latest in razzle-dazzle imaging technology.

Blair's Lair dazzles nobody. It's all of 750 square feet and has only one computerized editing system. It's dark even with the lights on. Its array of machines and screens has clearly been cobbled together since its humble start in 1996, when there were only two tape decks and a TV monitor. Now Blair can pull in cable or satellite feeds from virtually every team in both leagues; he can compile video on every player in the game. But it isn't simply the diligent collection of footage that makes Blair special; that's a technician's skill. He also has microscope eyes that can discern subtle patterns in the opposition. For Cardinals hitters, it's about identifying the repertoire of an opposing pitcher beforehand, seeing what he throws and how he throws it and where he throws it, so they can seize on a pitch when it comes or lay off of it. For Cardinals pitchers, it's about finding the hole that every hitter possesses somewhere in his swing and avoiding the wheelhouse.

Blair isn't a substitute for any of the coaches. He never says anything unless asked. But he's another detective on the never-ending trail of clues to how opponents can be exploited. Despite his ugly knees, players love the sharpness of his eyes and respect his analysis. They *listen* to him. So do La Russa and Duncan, no small acknowledgment from two men who between them have close to seventy-five years of experience in the game.

Blair's job imposes weird demands and limitations. As part of his duties, both at Busch or on the road, he charts pitches during the game by virtue of a center-field camera that feeds into a little video monitor in whatever clubhouse he happens to be in. It means that he is present for every game of the season yet never gets to see one in the flesh. His whole life is subterranean, spent beneath the steel skeleton of something. He is always squinting at something: a television monitor, an editing machine, a computer screen. He knows pitchers and he knows hitters solely by those pixilated images that come at him day after day, as if this is the only way baseball exists. It seems as though it should all blur together after a while: the difference in movement between one fastball and another too imperceptible to matter, one hitter's sinker hole no different from a dozen other hitters' sinker holes. But Blair's eyes are just *different*. Sinker holes are like fishing holes, each one unique and worthy of discovery. As for pitchers, he picks up on the slivers of gradations that make home plate, relative to its size, the most hotly contested piece of real estate mankind has ever known: a million battles fought over terrain that measures 17 inches across at its widest point.

As part of his preparation for a three-game series earlier in the month, Blair watched Dontrelle Willis of the Marlins and noticed that his high herky-jerky leg kick, beyond being something cute for broadcasters to talk about, is an essential factor in his remarkable success this season as a rookie. Blair realized that it enables him to hide the ball up to the moment he delivers it, which gives him one of those fastballs that sneaks up on hitters, gets in on them real quick so that a pedestrian velocity of 92 mph seems a lot faster when a hitter tries to catch up with it. He watched the Marlins' Brad Penny and noticed that it isn't only his 95-mph fastball that kills a hitter but also the way Penny plays havoc with the hitter's line of sight: the high-heat fastball traveling the ladder up and the big-break curve ball traveling down.

Before every three-game series, the Secret Weapon creates three basic sets of videos. For the Cubs series, he first compiled recent performances of Cubs hitters for Duncan and bullpen coach Marty Mason to dissect and then disseminate to the pitching staff before Game 1. Blair chooses only a handful of at-bats per hitter, because Duncan and Mason don't need more than that to make their findings. Another compilation features the Cubs starting triumvirate against both the Cardinals and other recent opponents. The third features pitchers with styles *similar* to this series' Cards' starters who have done well against the Cubs. Certainly, the Cardinals hurlers can look at videos of their own performances. But the theory behind this compilation is that it helps pitchers enormously to see other examples of success besides their own.

With game time about three hours away, more players file in to Blair's Lair. They sit on gray-backed swivel chairs, staring at a row of four Panasonic monitors on a black Formica table. They prop their feet up and thumb little remote controls to push the tapes back and forth. They settle in comfortably before the TVs: potato chips and beer the only things missing. Some stay for only a few minutes. Some like to linger. Pujols, in a swivel chair at the end, is a lingerer. So is Mike Matheny.

Matheny typically lingers so much in Blair's Lair before a game that he often takes on the same bleary-eyed look as Blair himself: a head too full with video snippets. He is inordinately hard on himself—too hard, in La Russa's judgment—beating himself up for failure when teammates will tell you that he is as diligent and rock-solid as any player in the game today. When you see him in the video room, it's clear that he is simply watching too much of the stuff: a digital overdose. Even he admits that he watches too much of the stuff, until you consider that Matheny's job—catcher—is the most demanding in all of sports and maybe the worst. It's the equivalent of going both ways in football, because of the offensive demands of it and, in the eyes of La Russa, actually more important defensive demands of it. La Russa places a high premium on what a catcher does behind the plate: not only blocking it and preventing pitches from going wild but also the very style with which a catcher calls a game, the ability to be creative within the context of knowing what his pitcher is capable of and what opposing hitters are incapable of. It's an act of tremendous balance and feel and intelligence, so much more than simply throwing down fingers behind the plate and hoping for the best.

By these exacting standards, Matheny is as conscientious as any catcher La Russa has ever had. His contribution behind the plate is so valuable that La Russa couldn't care less if he hit .000. But Matheny cares profoundly about his defense *and* his offense. So he screens more video than any other player. He watches it from both perspectives, fretting over what pitchers are likely to throw at him, fretting over what opposing hitters are hoping to see. You can feel his burden, click, rewinding, then playing a snippet of video again, click, rewinding, then playing the snippet again, click, rewinding, then playing the snippet again until all the swivel-backed chairs are empty except his.

· · ·

The players trot out of Blair's Lair around 4:15 P.M. They leave the clubhouse and work their way through the tunnel that leads to the dugout and the field beyond. The tunnel is carpeted with artificial turf so splotched and stained it looks like the product of a kindergarten painting class. They pass an ancient floor fan that vainly tries to cut the St. Louis heat so thick that even the Mississippi wilts. For men who among them make over $80 million a year, it's an incongruously low-rent backdrop. Around the corner and down another hundred feet, they come to the back end of the dugout. Inside the tunnel by the dugout entrance, several rows of cubbyholes resembling old-fashioned mail slots hold batting helmets. A bat rack underneath has also been divided into cubbyholes so nobody gets confused and picks up a bat that isn't his. It's all once again hierarchical; the bench players and the on-the-cusp players leave their equipment here, and the regulars put their tools in compartments located in the dugout itself.

They hit the field for batting practice, wearing bright red warmup jerseys: cherries baking in the sun. Stephenson goes first because he's tonight's starting pitcher. He gets five minutes. Then he slips back into the clubhouse for the pitching meeting with Duncan, perhaps the most important element of Game 1, although the game itself hasn't even begun.

3

"I'M GONNA KILL YOU!"

I

● ● ● DAVE DUNCAN IS the kind of man who in the storm at sea would simply lash himself to the mast; he'd wait out the hurricane by reading the paper, hold the putter steady in the tornado. His nothing-gets-to-me look is the same in the dugout whether the Cardinals are up 5–0 in the top of the ninth with the bases empty or 1–0 in the top of the ninth with the bases loaded. La Russa wears tension like a catcher wears a face mask, but Duncan wears nothing on his lean Texas-flat features except that deadpan. It makes him a source of reassurance to pitchers and La Russa alike: the coach who won't crack.

In twenty years together in the claustrophobic hothouse of the dugout, Duncan and La Russa have never once argued; they have yet to share a bad vibe, except when La Russa gives some stock complaint about ineffective pitching during a game and Duncan studies him and says, "Here we go again." The two men know each other as well as any two men possibly can, honoring the boundaries of each other's baseball knowledge and the equally vast continents of their silences. La Russa gets through to Duncan whenever it's necessary. But there is something eternally inscrutable about Duncan—a safe that can't be cracked—hours spent before his computer with a pinch of Skoal in his cheek as ample companionship. Words emerge from his mouth like reluctant bubbles that barely ping the surface. You can sit in the same room with him for sizable stretches and he'll utter nothing beyond, "How's it going?" The only reason he'll divulge this much is that someone has said, "Hey, Dunc," and courtesy dictates saying *something* back. When he does expound into a sentence or two in his slivery voice, it's never for pleasure, which is maybe why one of his prize pupils, Todd Stottlemyre, refers to him as "The Deacon" and calls his words "biblical."

In addition to the two decades Duncan and La Russa have shared in the dugout, their history goes back another twenty years before that when they were teenagers coming up in the Kansas City A's organization. They first played together in the winter instructional league in Bradenton in 1964, then in the minors over the next three years. Most of the players on those teams were still "kids," as La Russa put it, still "trying to figure it all out." But Duncan was different, with a steadiness and maturity even in his late teens and early twenties. Advancing through the A's system as a catcher, making it to the major-league team in 1968, he also displayed another quality: bullwhip bluntness, regardless of the repercussions.

In the 1972 World Series, Duncan caught Game 7 for the A's against the Cincinnati Reds, not the least bit nervous even though this was his first start. In the bottom of the ninth, baseball's top reliever, Rollie Fingers, got two outs to bring up the Reds' Pete Rose in a last-chance gasp with the score 3–2. When A's manager Dick Williams headed for the mound, Duncan knew his intent: to replace Fingers with starter Vida Blue and turn the switch-hitting Rose around from the left side to the right. Duncan thought that it was a bad idea, putting Blue into a situation he wasn't used to, taking Fingers out of a situation that he conquered better than any other reliever in baseball at the time. He more than thought it was a bad idea: Joined by A's captain Sal Bando on the mound, he told Williams that it was a *bad idea*, even though he was a twenty-seven-year-old catcher and Williams was a forty-three-year-old manager with 793 games of experience. Williams did what Duncan suggested: He left Fingers in, then watched along with the rest of

America as Rose hit a shot toward the outfield wall in left center. Now Duncan got *nervous*, proof of the existence of blood in his veins. But Joe Rudi snagged the ball to save Duncan and the series.

After the season, the irresistible force of A's outfielder Reggie Jackson went against the immoveable object of A's owner Charley Finley in a salary dispute. Duncan publicly sided with Jackson, which led to a predictable reaction, equal parts cheap and cantankerous, from Finley: He traded Duncan from the world champion A's to the arctic outpost of the Cleveland Indians.

Duncan became the bullpen coach for the Indians after his playing days were over. In 1982, he moved to the Seattle Mariners as the pitching coach with Rene Lachemann as the manager, taking a weak and watery staff and turning it around to finish second in the American League in strikeouts and saves. He thought he deserved a $5,000 raise for his efforts, but the Mariners' owner thought otherwise, so Duncan quit and joined up with La Russa on the White Sox.

Over the years, La Russa has found that a lot of hitting and pitching coaches are ineffective because they refuse to put themselves on the line. They don't want to tell a player what to do, in case it backfires. So they deal in open-ended aphorisms or dish out moral support, a steady stream of claps and "C'mon, baby" from the dugout. But that's not Duncan: the brevity of a news bulletin, maybe, but never reticent. He has the laser eye for mechanical flaws and where to make adjustments. He has given performance makeovers to dozens of pitchers over the years by adding a pitch to the repertoire or modifying one. Just as important, he bases his ideas not on ethereal wisdom but on hard data that he continually examines: breaking down video of opposing hitters, analyzing by computer to further ferret out the best pitch to throw in the best situation, and compiling his own legendary pitching charts.

La Russa cedes little territory to his coaches. He takes their input, but he shoulders the decisions. The one exception is Duncan; if La Russa approaches anyone during a game, it's almost invariably him. He knows of Duncan's penchant for solitude, to work out problems on his own. But he will never confuse his deadpan for inaction. When Duncan caught for the A's, his nickname was the

Quiet Assassin, and it still rings true today. When pressed for proof, La Russa gets a little Cheshire cat smile on his lips, clearly recalling one of his most beautiful baseball moments ever: George Bell of the Toronto Blue Jays charging one of Duncan's pitchers, and Duncan leaping out of the dugout and chasing him around the field, screaming, "I'M GONNA FUCKING KILL YOU!!!!"

Duncan's attitude toward his pitchers is fatherly: He protects them against attack, and he holds himself responsible for their improvement. He gives his starters detailed plans for dealing with every opposing batter in the starting lineup. He teaches his pitchers to think differently on the mound; he'll lessen the burden of a bases-loaded-and-one-out situation by going to the mound and pointing out to the pitcher that he's *one pitch* away from getting out of the inning with a double-play ball. He specializes in rescuing pitchers at precarious points in their careers, pitchers who are on the skids and have bounced around too much or have lost too much confidence or have broken up with a pitch they need to woo back. He did it with Dennis Eckersley, whom nobody wanted in 1987 when the A's plucked him from the Cubs after a season in which he'd gone 6 and 11 with a 4.57 ERA. He did it with Mike Moore, who went 19 and 11 with Oakland in 1989 after two seasons with Seattle, when he'd been an aggregate 18 and 34. He did it with Stottlemyre, a .500 Blue Jays pitcher who went 14 and 7 in his first season with Oakland. He did it with Kent Bottenfield, who had gone from one mediocre season to another before he won eighteen with the Cardinals in 1999, equaling his total number of major-league wins until that point. He did it with Darryl Kile after a disastrous season in Colorado, where he'd gone 8 and 13 with a 6.61 ERA. La Russa told Kile to "place his career in Duncan's hands," and Kile did so, building a record of 20 and 9 the next year.

Most notably, he did it with Dave Stewart, out of baseball altogether in 1986, when the A's picked him up as little more than a curiosity. Stewart had played around with a forkball for a little bit during his career, but in Texas and Philadelphia, he had been discouraged from using it amid the widespread belief that throwing a forkball could hurt your arm. But Duncan encouraged him to rediscover it, convinced that Stewart needed a change in style. Duncan understood that the pitch had to be executed properly, and he showed Stewart how to throw it with the right motion, retaining a loose wrist. Duncan got him to stop making mistakes that caused it to go up. It didn't take long before Stewart was throwing a filthy little forkball. It became his second-best pitch after his fastball, pushing the slider to third, and suddenly Stewart *was* a different pitcher. He finished the year 9 and 5. Over the next four years, from 1987 to 1991, Stewart won twenty games or more each season. His forkball was a hitter's temptress, slow and sweet before the bottom went to hell.

II

TONIGHT, DUNCAN'S TRYING to do it with Garrett Stephenson. Stephenson has tools. Because he's a major leaguer, he has tools, and his one breakout season, in 2000, shows what he can do with them:

W	L	ERA	G	GS	IP	H	HR	BB	SO
16	9	4.49	32	31	200.1	209	31	63	123

This season, going into tonight's game, the numbers are different:

W	L	ERA	G	GS	IP	H	HR	BB	SO
7	12	4.41	27	25	159.1	148	26	57	83

Obviously, they reflect a losing record, but they also reflect Stephenson's schism: He has given up fewer hits than innings pitched, an increasing rarity among starting pitchers. At this point in the season, he has an even better ERA than he had in 2000. It means that he has pitched at certain moments with effectiveness this year. But the numbers also reflect that he has given up twenty-six home runs, a horrific number. Which means that there are times when he ends up challenging hitters with that fastball that simply doesn't pose enough of a challenge, particularly when he throws it high.

He lacks one of those Bugs Bunny sliders that stops at home plate, catches some bennies for a split second, and then exits in a vapor. He doesn't have one of those wicked Mariano Rivera cutters that against lefties should be declared a WMD. As a result, he has the problem shared by many starting pitchers: a macho refusal to accept that pitching is not only about speed. Speed is considered God in baseball. Speed sells in baseball. Virtually every scoreboard now has a little square section showing the velocity of each pitch. Fans ooh and ah, nudge each other in the ribs the faster a pitch gets. But it's a false God, in La Russa's eyes, a fastball in the high eighties with movement and location far preferable to a flat fastball in the nineties. Speed alone can kill, at least kill a pitcher's performance. To offset this obsession, La Russa once ordered the speed section of the scoreboard juiced up a few miles per hour because he could tell that his pitcher was paying as much attention to it as the fans were.

To make the best use of his tools tonight, Stephenson *has* to mix location and mix speeds. He needs to use his lumbering fastball almost as a flirtation, to get the Cubs hitters looking for it, craving it, only to confound them with his off-speed curve and changeup on the edges of the plate. It's a mental art as much as it is a physical one, every pitch a product of conscious deliberation: *What am I going to throw and where am I going to put it?* It's exhausting to have to concentrate this much, far easier simply to get up on that mound and wing it. And sometimes, Stephenson likes to do just that: be a macho man, dare opponents to hit his fastball. Which they often do.

Using a little portable DVD player, Duncan has spent several hours reviewing the disc of Cubs' hitters that Chad Blair made for him. He has seen the Cubs nine times already this season, but Duncan is looking for the slightest little slice that may be new, ways they may be covering the plate better or adjusting to inside pitches better or handling curves in the strike zone better. He's also patrolling for new weaknesses that might have developed in making those very improvements, every tiny patch creating another tiny hole. He also has a red binder in front of him. This particular one is marked "Cubs," but he has one for every team in the league. He stores them in a red steel case that goes on the road with him. It looks a little bit like a vault on wheels, maybe because the knowledge it holds is priceless.

The binders contain his charts, a packet for every opposing player, a remarkable Rorschach in which he has tracked every pitch each batter has been thrown by his pitchers and what that batter did with it. Using a system of grids, three up and three across dividing the hitting zone into nine sections, he has made small notations that record the type and location of every pitch. The charts also track any trends that have emerged in particular situations— where a Cardinals pitcher has given up first-pitch hits and where he has gotten first-pitch outs, where he has given up hits with two strikes, and where he has gotten outs with two strikes. Duncan is looking for patterns, a cluster of notations together in a certain spot, almost like tiny cracks in a frozen lake, to detect spots that a given hitter is getting to.

He sees those clusters with the Cubs hitters. They tell stories, much like La Russa's matchups tell stories. In the quiet of the clubhouse, he is trying to make Stephenson heed the morals of what they say, the same as he does with every starting pitcher and catcher two hours before the start of every game.

The meeting takes place in the room that Duncan uses when he is in the clubhouse. It's next to La Russa's office, with a common doorway in between, affording the two men easy access to each other, although each stays in his own sphere. The room is small and Spartan: a bookcase filled mostly with the current media guides of opposing teams, a rudimentary copier, several utilitarian desks of beige metal favored by police stations and mental asylums. Its only function is the microscopic grist of baseball, the captivating and strange science of pinpointing pitches, anything else an unwelcome distraction.

Duncan respects his pitchers and knows that they have their own set views on how hitters should be handled. He appreciates that they have earned their opinions the hard way, out there on the mound, the most isolated spot in sports, even when things are going well. He also has his own back story, the handling of six Cy Young pitchers between his playing days as a catcher and his years as a pitching coach—Catfish Hunter and Blue and Jim Palmer on the playing side and La Marr Hoyt, Bob Welch, and Eckersley on the pitching side.

He wants to hear from Stephenson on how he wants to handle the Cubs hitters. "Okay, Garrett," Duncan says, and Stephenson starts in with the lead-off hitter, Kenny Lofton. He talks about mixing it up and using both sides of the plate, then quickly repeats the part about using both sides of the plate. "Can I make a suggestion?" interrupts Duncan. Based on his charting, he has made the analysis that most of Lofton's hits off Stephenson have come on "sloppy breaking balls" that were either up or over the plate, whereas most of the outs he has gotten have been on changeups down in the zone after fastballs. From this moment on, with that voice even softer and lower to the ground than La Russa's, Duncan takes over the meeting.

He points out a general truth: Almost all the Cubs hitters tonight are aggressive. They have a tendency to seize on pitches early in the count, so more than normal attention has to be paid *not* to put the ball over the plate. Which means, as another general truth, that Stephenson must establish the inside on hitters. Going inside has two purposes. The first is that it marks Stephenson's turf, making the Cubs "inside conscious" to prevent them from effortlessly reaching to the outside for pitches. The second is that it will intimidate them by playing on the understandable fear all hitters have of getting jammed.

If he doesn't establish the inside on Lofton in the lead-off spot, Duncan predicts, "he'll just hang out over the plate." Stephenson must do it with Sammy Sosa in the third hole for much the same reason, because it's the only way of rearranging Sosa's focus so he's not totally locked on getting something up over the plate. He needs to do it with Moises Alou, because Duncan's charts on Alou show a first-pitch jackpot against Cardinals pitching—first-pitch slider for a home run, first-pitch middle-high fastball for a home run, first-pitch high-away fastball for a home run, first-pitch sinker high middle for a home run. And he needs to do it most of all with Randall Simon, the greatest of Stephenson's three ex-Pirate nemeses.

"This guy *kicks* my ass on off-speed," says Stephenson in a gust of frustration. "He hits every off-speed I've *thrown*." It doesn't matter whether Simon gets three good inside fastballs in a row, Stephenson notes. Presumably, the steady stream of those fastballs and their location should speed up Simon's bat enough, make him expect the fastball enough, so that when Stephenson comes with something slower, Simon's timing should be completely off. But he *still* gets to it.

Duncan, based on his charts and Blair's DVD, has another explanation for what ails Stephenson: *location*. It's not what he's throwing or what sequence he's throwing it in as much as it is *where* he's throwing it.

"Garrett, let me make this real simple for you," says Duncan, using the past history of his charts as potential prologue. "Hit: high-and-away fastball. Put in play: high away. Struck him out: low and in. High and away: base hit. High and away: base hit." The point is obvious.

"Everything that he has hit against you has been up."

So Duncan's first lesson for Stephenson is not to give Simon anything up, even on the outside, because video analysis has shown that Simon has an ability to get to these pitches, especially if he doesn't think he has to worry about the inside.

"First time up," Duncan advises, "I would pound this guy [inside] with every pitch."

On it goes like this for about ten minutes, Duncan providing Stephenson with a concise MapQuest on how to get past each Cubs hitter. Stephenson listens intently; he wants to do well. But Duncan has had such meetings with Stephenson before, when he seemed to be listening. La Russa has had some as well. And then . . .

It came to a head in July, after Stephenson gave up a home run and double to the Dodgers' Hideo Nomo—a pitcher, for God's sake—out of what Duncan termed sheer "carelessness": You can't simply roll it out there even if it is the *pitcher*. Stephenson was demoted from the starting rotation and sent to the bullpen. He was indignant, blaming poor run support and lousy defense for his misfortune.

La Russa was indignant at Stephenson's indignation. In a closed-door meeting, he adopted the increasingly frequent role of psychiatrist, telling Stephenson that the only way he could be an effective major-league pitcher—get back to the groove of 2000—would be to concentrate better and stop blaming everyone around him for his problems. La Russa complimented his fearlessness, his conviction that "whoever the guy is, you can pitch to him." He liked that Stephenson had the guts to keep hitters inside conscious, as many pitchers don't like to throw inside, for the very reason that they may hit someone. But, La Russa pointed out, Stephenson had started challenging people at the wrong time with that fastball of his, which never rose above the high eighties. Like Brian Giles of the Pirates, whom Stephenson treated as if he hadn't hit a single dinger this season, when he'd hit thirteen of them and was the ultimate aggressive fastball hitter. Then there was Stephenson's general failure to respect the bottom third of an opponent's order, feeding them too many fastballs on the plate, giving these guys an undeserved feast. He had been careless all season long about keeping the ball down, and La Russa advised him rather strenuously to stop worrying about defense and run support and to pay attention to the only thing he could control: his pitching.

The result was a 3–1 win against the Braves in early August; Stephenson kept the ball down and went all the way into the eighth. Five days later, he gave up only one earned run in eight innings against the Pirates. Based on those recent performances, it's likely that he *can* keep the ball down. He *can* use his fastball to set up the curve and change, hit those edges. He *can* go inside. Duncan still believes in him—tells him as much—as the meeting nears an end.

"If you concentrate and really just get locked in out there, you'll pitch good against these guys. If you get careless—that's what they are—they're mistake hitters. And we need a game, so get your game face on and be ready to stick it in their ass."

As Stephenson heads out the door, Duncan leaves him with one final thought: He reminds him that the most successful pitchers are not mistake free—because every pitcher makes mistakes—but are those who don't fall apart after they do make one.

"And hey, don't get frustrated out there if something doesn't go right. Don't lose your concentration and make a couple of bad pitches before you get it back."

III

THE PLAYERS finish up batting practice around 5:45 P.M. and travel back through the tunnel to the clubhouse. As a matter of league rule, the clubhouse is now closed to outsiders, so none of the players find themselves hopelessly outnumbered by the wolf pack of print and television and radio reporters who were there before batting practice. Back in the clubhouse, they immediately pump up the sound system, and they continue to loiter, loose and carefree. But the music soon gives way to two meetings. The first is for the relievers, in Duncan's office. It's run by Marty Mason, in an Alabama treble of such perfect down-home pitch, you long for the Confederacy even if you're from the North. The information is largely the same as what Duncan went over with Stephenson but with a slightly different emphasis. Relievers, unlike starters, almost never face a batter more than once, so they are much more inclined to go with their strength rather than try to whittle away at a hitter's weakness. La Russa is there, his chair straddling the open door that connects his office to Duncan's. He says little, except when it comes to Aramis Ramirez in the sixth hole and the terrible price you might pay for giving him a breaking ball in the strike zone: "He'll launch it."

The meeting is followed quickly by a gathering of the hitters in La Russa's office. Hitting coach Mitchell Page goes through the Cubs pitchers, beginning with Mark Prior. "First thing you gotta do, boys, lay off the high fastball," he offers, admittedly easier said than done. The meeting has more of a war room feel as hitters trade their own intelligence back and forth. The consensus on Prior's fastball, as Orlando Palmeiro puts it, is that it's "sneaky," exploding in on you at the last moment. The hitters also trade tidbits about the Cubs relievers. How Joe Borowski, the closer, isn't above a back-door slider; how the lefty set-up man, Mike Remlinger, has no fear when it comes to his changeup and will throw it in any situation to any hitter, righty or lefty. La Russa speaks only at the end, urging his hitters to work up the pitch count on Prior, so Dusty Baker is pushed earlier than he would like to where La Russa wants him: the tender meat of the Cubs' bullpen.

"It's the end of August. I don't think Baker is going to let Prior throw a bunch of pitches like he would at the end of September. Make him work for every out he gets."

The players trickle out of La Russa's office after the meeting. There's now about a half hour left until the start of Game 1. The music ignites again, "Shake Your Tailfeathers" from the soundtrack of *Bad Boys II* spewing fury and testosterone. Jeff Fassero sits in front of his locker, reading the paper. Tino Martinez, so struggling at the plate in the shadow of his former Yankee self that it's become a perpetual cloak, adjusts his uniform pants. Scott Rolen emerges from the shower, then goes to the indoor cage for one final run-through. Jim Edmonds, typical of his Hollywood roam in center field, dons a series of bright red wristbands like strips of neon. From the two television consoles that hang from the ceiling of the locker area, video loops show Prior's most recent outing against the Cardinals in early July. Bo Hart watches raptly, so hungry for improvement, joined by Eddie Perez, who gets there just in time to see the three-run bomb he banged off Prior in the second. "That was so much fun!" he says, then trots off with a beatific smile.

With twelve minutes to game time, after most of the players and coaches have already left for the dugout, La Russa puts on his uniform shirt and pants and begins his ritual. He closes his closet door. He neatens up his desk, moving wayward papers into right angles. He gathers up the information that he has carefully inscribed on the fronts and backs of several scorecards: the matchups as well as an additional reference guide to the Cubs hitters and how they should be pitched, in little two- or three-word capsules. He folds and creases them so they make that perfect fit in his back pocket. He adjusts his cap. He turns off the lights. And then he strides out toward the dugout and Game 1.

4

THE PEEKER

● ● ● KENNY LOFTON leads off for the Cubs. He is what he is: a sneaky pest with good speed and a veteran hitter's instinct for survival. No shame in simply staying with the ball and slapping it to the opposite field for itsy-bitsy singles if that's the best a pitch can offer. A single gold chain nestles neatly under the collar of his gray uniform. "CHICAGO" wraps across his shirt in bright and muscular red. His hands, swathed in white gloves, heft a black bat. He gently taps it on the plate as if it's a divining rod in search of water —plentiful abundance around that plate if he can just find it.

Cheers go up from the thousands of Chicago fans who have made the pilgrimage for the three-game series and taken over downtown St. Louis like Cossacks in Cubbie Blue, overrunning hotels and restaurants with their meaty fists and happy beer bellies and this-is-our-year swagger. Unlike his teammate Sammy Sosa, who enters the batter's box with a puffed-up presence so grand he might as well be the pope, Lofton draws no particular attention to himself when he settles in. It's more a glum matter-of-factness, a business, the business of batting—*hey, been there, done that*—with just the slightest oregano of arrogance, the implication that he knows he has Garrett Stephenson's number and has no reason to get all herky-jerky and hyperventilated.

The first pitch is a fastball on the far side of the plate. It's a smart pitch: not too fat, not too fine. It carries the outside corner for a strike as Lofton looks it in with curiosity, as if a car of make and model he's not sure he has seen before has just sped by him. Dave Duncan has to be smiling inwardly, because it abides by his belief in the power of the first-pitch strike. Of all the pitches in a given at-bat, it is by far the most important, and Duncan has more than merely sentiment on his side. In addition to his binders full of pitching charts, he does his copious computer analyses, inputting every pitch a Cardinal throws to see what kind of predictors emerge beyond hunch and gut instinct. He's looking for trend lines, just like mutual fund managers look for reliable indicators of a stock's performance. Based on that analysis, the value of a first-pitch strike is so overwhelming he calls it "almost goofy." During spring training, Duncan trotted out his theory of the value of strike 1 for pitchers. To make the point, he was equipped with statistics for several past Cardinals seasons in which he had tracked each opposing batter faced, roughly 6,100 per year. His analysis showed that in 2002, for example, Cardinals hurlers threw first-pitch strikes 59 percent of the time. Of that number, 17 percent were put in play, with the actual yield of hits equivalent to a batting average of .059.

The first pitch also ignites the game's smallest subplot and one of its more intricate ones—what La Russa is fond of calling "the war" of each at-bat. As Duncan's stats demonstrate, who draws blood first forms a remarkable barometer of who will win this little war: a pitcher who goes 1 and 0 now peering at a plate with a smaller-than-ever margin of error because he doesn't want to fall even further behind, and a hitter who goes 1 and 0 getting pumped because nibbling has just been curtailed. Like everything else in baseball, the barometer isn't foolproof. There are exceptions that define greatness, pitchers such as Greg Maddux and Curt Schilling, who still have the confidence to work the wisps of the plate even when the count is 1 and 0, and hitters such as Pujols, who even when they fall behind 0 and 1, refuse to chase in the face of a strike zone suddenly widened by the pitcher's advantage.

Duncan has come to conclude that many pitchers pitch backward, try to be too *fine* on that first throw—aim for something perfect on the elusive black of the plate—because they think that they have some room to maneuver with a virginal count. But once they get behind, they have no choice but to come with something too fat over the plate. In Duncan's experience, the exact opposite approach is the most effective: Don't be too fine. Instead, use a portion of the plate to get that first strike. If the hitter puts it into play, so be it. If he doesn't, the pitcher still has an enormous advantage: Now he can nibble at the black without pinpoint precision, as hitters, made nervous by their 0 and 1 deficit, are far more inclined to go after pitches that aren't strikes.

Baseball is a game primarily of firsts in terms of who wins and who loses: getting the first strike in an at-bat, getting the first out of an inning, scoring the game's first run to gain momentum and tempo. Like Duncan, La Russa believes fervently in the importance of firsts, but the game's first first doesn't comfort him. He's nervous, anxious for a zero here because the worst thing you can give a pitcher the caliber of Mark Prior is an early lead, the aura of intimidation that surrounds him to begin with now a full galaxy. So he's obsessively watching Stephenson to see whether he's doing what he needs to do, not being some heavy-metal rocker out there with an instrument that's strictly acoustic.

In the dugout, La Russa stations himself near the entrance to the tunnel, so far to the left that he sometimes spills over into the concrete square reserved for the cameras that televise games locally on Fox SportsNet. He is standing alone, with a hand on the railing of the steps that lead up to the field. Some managers like company during a game. They like to chat back and forth, if nothing else to deflect the anxiety onto someone who at least can provide a little companionship. Joe Torre of the Yankees has had his Pagliacci, Don Zimmer, for years. Bobby Cox of the Braves has pitching coach Leo Mazzone, their jowls working in unison. But except for the occasional whisper to Duncan, La Russa refuses such relief. Instead, he occupies a self-imposed foxhole, big enough for only one, in which he alone must fend off all present and future crises. Even after one pitch, his face is clenched and closed off.

With the count 0 and 1 to Lofton, he's not inspecting only Stephenson for signs of which persona is on the mound tonight. He's also eying Lofton, the pesty part of Lofton, the shameless part of

Lofton that would steal first if it were legal. Lofton isn't above trying a bunt to third base. Both Duncan and Marty Mason discovered the trend of it when they broke down the Secret Weapon's
DVD, so La Russa is making sure that Rolen is sufficiently guard-
ing against it at third. La Russa also knows that Lofton, like most
hitters, is a creature of irresistibility, who can be brought down
through his chase hole—the spot he thinks he can get to but can't.
La Russa hopes that Stephenson will recall Duncan's advice to go
above the strike zone for Lofton's chase hole—the high fastball.
When the next pitch is a fastball in, La Russa is encouraged even
though it's a ball. It's still a smart place to spot a pitch, particularly
effective against hitters such as Lofton, who has a tendency to
make a big fuss when the ball is inside. He makes no bones about
the indignity, glaring at the pitcher, beseeching the umpire with a
look—*Did you see what they just did to me?*—his histrionics guaranteeing only that he's going to see even more pitches inside than
usual for the very reason he makes such a show.

Stephenson throws another fastball, this time down and away.
La Russa thinks that the location is good, *really good,* another
smart pitch: three in a row, if you're keeping score at home. Lofton
simply slaps at it, stays with it just enough to hit an easy two-hopper
to short.

La Russa does say repeatedly that baseball is a cruel game.
Much of that has to do with decisions you make as a manager that
seem like no-brainers and still devolve into disasters. But the ball
itself is sometimes cruel, not simply a benign layering of twine and
rubber and leather but a little organism with a perverse love of tur-
moil: *Where can I go to create the most disruption? Who needs to be
tested right away?*

Edgar Renteria usually plays shortstop. He was a Gold Glover
last year and will probably get another one this year, so this would
be a routine play for him. But two days before, after a grinding 3–0
win against the Phillies in which he made several wonderful defensive plays, he hobbled into the clubhouse. It was suddenly cleared
of all outsiders, even reporters on tight deadlines—an unheard-of
step. In the dignity of privacy, Rolen and Edmonds each wrapped

an arm around their teammate and helped him out of the shower; wrenching back spasms prevented him from walking by himself. By now he has partially recovered, but he's still unavailable.

In Renteria's place at shortstop is Miguel Cairo, a consequence of consequences, as Cairo, a valuable utility infielder, has little experience at short. Which is why the ball determinedly seeks him out on the very first play of the game. It bounces directly to Cairo, and he scoops it into his glove. But his throw to Tino Martinez at first is off target, lacking assurance. It comes to Martinez on a hop far more devious than the one that settled into Cairo's glove. Although he's thirty-three, Lofton still has a sweet set of wheels. He's hustling, really hustling, his hustle suggesting what it usually suggests in players who have had rocky mood-swing careers regardless of prodigious talent and impressive numbers: It's the free-agency year, and good behavior has far more rewards than American Express. Martinez tries to keep his right foot pinned to the corner of the bag as he fields the hop. But he can't.

Lofton is safe at first. Instead of one away in the top of the first, there is only potential chaos in the top of the first.

Lofton is nowhere close to the golden season he had with the Indians in 1996, when he led the league with seventy-five stolen bases, but he is still a threat to steal second. He's already stolen nine bases since he came over to the Cubs in mid-July, and the mere suggestion of it sets all sorts of plot subtexts in motion. He's jittery at first, not a huge lead. One arm is folded, and the other hangs between his knees. He's being coquettish, a professional flirt, what he may *not* do as important as what he *may* do: *Will he or won't he?*

The plot turns on the speed of Stephenson's delivery to the plate. Joe Pettini, the bench coach, is timing it with a stopwatch, and the results are pretty good. It's taking 1.3 seconds from the start of Stephenson's wind-up to Chris Widger's getting the ball in his catcher's mitt. It's the Maginot Line of base stealing, 1.3 seconds or less making it difficult for a gifted runner to steal with any smugness.

He's going to have to factor in at least six other complexities:

the arm strength of the catcher, the quality of the pitcher's move to first whether it's a snap throw or long-armed, the hardness or softness of the base path, whether the pitcher is altering the timing of his delivery from one pitch to the next, whether the hitter is right-handed or left-handed—since a left-handed hitter shields the catcher's line of sight to second—and the pitcher's repertoire—since a forkballer or sinkerballer forces the catcher to drop his mitt low for the pitch and therefore have a more difficult throw.*

If video is the greatest revolution in baseball over the past twenty years, the running game is its greatest crushed revolution. In the 1960s and 1970s, Wills and Lou Brock each stole more than a hundred bases in a season. Into the 1980s, when La Russa was cutting his teeth as a manager, Rickey Henderson stole a hundred or more bases in three different seasons. All over both leagues, good base stealers were running wild, out of control, taking second base like their birthright. Except against teams managed by Gene Mauch. Legendary for his strategy, acclaimed by his peers as the shrewdest tactician to grace the dugout in modern times, Mauch had gotten tired of the base-stealing revolution; he became determined to quell it once and for all.

La Russa saw that Mauch's pitchers weren't going to the plate in what was the standard threshold then: 1.4 or 1.5 seconds. They were going even more quickly—1.2 or 1.1 seconds—in an effort to make stealing second a far more risky venture. La Russa also noticed that Mauch had gone a clever step further. Good base stealers try to pick up a pitcher's pattern in his delivery—the so-called mind switch—the moment when his attention shifts from the base

---

* Altering the playing surface to dampen fast runners and base stealers is not nearly as common today as it was when La Russa first came up as a player in the early 1960s. When the Dodgers came to town, groundskeepers would give the dirt in front of the plate and on the base paths between first and second a healthy soaking to make it soupy and beachlike, to help prevent Maury Wills and Willie Davis from simply slapping the ball high to get on first and then stealing second. Conversely, the Dodgers packed their own surface to resemble concrete, to make it as easy as possible for Wills and Davis to slap the ball high to get on first and then steal second.

runner on first to the batter at the plate. Base runners are taught to look for it, and the great base stealers, such as Henderson, had developed a feel for it that let them get a good jump and steal regardless of how quick the delivery.

So Mauch worked with his pitchers to break their patterns. One way was to simply hold on to the ball or make a throw over to first or step off the rubber. All this made it more difficult for a base runner to pick up the mind switch, and eventually, Mauch countered the base-stealing revolution. La Russa copied Mauch's tactics. So did other managers, and by the 1990s, the stolen base had lost much of its impact as an offensive weapon.

Lofton obviously knows that Stephenson isn't going to display an easily recognizable pattern. Also, Lofton is a "peeker," and "peekers" do what the name implies. They are voyeurs—alleyway window watchers—peeking from first at the catcher as he puts down his signs and trying to figure out the one for the curve ball, a better pitch to steal on than the fastball because it takes longer to get to the plate. Which means that from the dugout, La Russa is instructing Widger to put on all sorts of decoy signs to make sure that the one for the curve ball is sufficiently buried.

Lofton continues to flirt off of first. He's still jittery: *Will he or won't he?* But he isn't going anywhere. Stephenson is maintaining the essential benchmark of delivering to the plate in 1.3 seconds. As a further impediment, Stephenson is also throwing fastballs to the number two hitter Ramon Martinez instead of slower off-speed stuff, the last a nasty jam that he hits harmlessly to Kerry Robinson in right field for the first out.

It brings up Sosa, who, much like Stephenson, has been suffering from a bipolar disorder this season. When the Cards faced him in May, it was pretty clear to Duncan and Mason, watching the DVD on him, that he was going through *something*. He was flinching on curve balls as if he were afraid he might get hit, and he began to develop a sizable hole in his swing on pitches down and away.

To La Russa, the explanation was embedded in human nature. In May, Sosa had gotten beaned by a pitch, his batting helmet splintering like a dropped glass of water. It was clear that he had gotten tentative after that, with good reason. Few things in sports are more terrifying than a pitch hurtling at a hitter's head with no time for reflexes, the incident only reinforcing to La Russa the urgency of the commissioner's office to stop ignoring the increasing problem and do something about it, such as an automatic three-week suspension for the pitcher involved.

Sosa had become intimidated, as every hitter in the history of the game has become intimidated, after such a frightening moment. He suffered a lapse of courage, and the question was how long it would last, since La Russa has seen such varied reactions: It could be an at-bat, a game, a series, a season, even, in some cases, an entire career.

When Sosa drives the ball into center and right center, it means that he's getting to balls away. But after he got hit, he became reluctant to dive over the plate to get to them. One of his hitting strengths is good plate coverage, but he was almost turning from the ball, as Duncan and Mason had discovered. Over the past several weeks, however, the old Sosa has re-emerged. It's the one who "sticks his nose in there," as La Russa puts it, staying on the ball wherever it is thrown, once again showing the courage that all great hitters possess. The result has been thirteen home runs in July and another seven in August to give him thirty for the season leading up to the three-game series. He's also made an adjustment: He's moved his stance closer to the plate because once the word was out that Sammy wasn't the same Sammy anymore—couldn't get to it anymore unless it was down the pipe where anybody could hit it—he had been fed a steady diet of pitches away.

He gets three fastballs from Stephenson. All of them are high. The count goes to 3 and 0. But that's okay, because Sosa has a chase hole up, and there's also no point giving him something in his wheelhouse that he can turn on. Widger sets up outside on the 3-0 count. Sammy, still being Sammy, has the green light to swing. He hits the pitch with power, but he gets under it a little bit, and the result is a high fly to Robinson in right for the second out.

Lofton is still at first when Moises Alou comes up in the cleanup spot with two outs. Lofton has been effectively hog-tied there, enabling Stephenson to focus on Alou and try to avoid the first-pitch pitfalls that have made him so dangerous. Stephenson comes in with a fastball. Alou goes for it in his unbridled aggressiveness. He gets a swing on it, a pretty good swing—a damn good one, actually. He fouls it straight back, meaning that he missed driving it by a matter of only inches. Stephenson throws another fastball, this one better located on the inside. Alou gets a swing on it, a pretty good swing—a damn good one, actually. He hits it sharply to third. Rolen backhands it, his reflex action so sublimely quick, it seems like a natural extension of him—the way the rest of us pick up a fork to eat—and makes one of his lightning-bolt throws to first to end the top of the first.

It's a twelve-pitch inning for Stephenson. Every pitch he has thrown has been a fastball, which could be a recipe for implosion if he keeps it up and doesn't mix his pitches. And maybe it means that not a word of what La Russa and Duncan have preached to him all season has sufficiently spread through his 6'5" frame. But Stephenson, like many pitchers, tends to rely almost exclusively on the fastball the first time through the lineup. And La Russa has no problem with that, particularly if it means that he's using the fastball as a setup for something else, lulling the Cubs batters into complacency, getting them to chirp up and down the gossipy line of the dugout that all he's throwing out there is fastballs, only to shut them up with off-speed.

In every game that La Russa manages, he conducts a running conversation with himself, a *Waiting for Godot* dialogue to keep the pressure on and make sure that he doesn't miss anything, mining for gold even though it's the top of the first, because sometimes, it's those little nuggets that can win a game. Lofton didn't go anywhere, which is good. Sosa's ego on 3 and 0 caused him to try to drive an outside fastball, which is good. Stephenson threw first-pitch strikes to three of the four batters he faced, which is very good. And he likes what he is seeing from Stephenson, the fearlessness and big balls folding into a pitcher tonight, glimpses of that 16 and 9 season in 2000 returning.

Between halves of the inning, La Russa retires to the dugout bench. He sits by himself. He's still nervous, because he's always nervous and his patented glower is not some pose. The stakes are high in every game, since one game can prove the difference between the playoffs in October or golf in October. The best managers—the ones La Russa has modeled himself after—ground their way through every at-bat, unlike some others he knew who believed that their job really didn't begin until the last three innings, when moves became more readily apparent. La Russa's inability to smile also goes to the very nature of the game: capricious, mean, sneaking up on you with accumulated vengeance if you let down even for a moment. "Unless you pay it respect, it's gonna spank you, and the fact is that even when you do pay it respect, it's gonna spank you, just not as often or as hard," he says. The feeling he wants after every game, whether it's a 1–0 win or a 10–0 loss, is that everything he had was left in the dugout—he had nothing else to give. It's his nature, what comes with the territory when you spend so much of your life alone in a dark and subterranean place. But whatever fear he feels, whatever anxieties envelop him, there's a supreme confidence to the decisions he makes, probably because there's no way he could have survived for almost a quarter century if he weren't.

It was different at the beginning. When he started his managing career with the White Sox in the middle of the 1979 season, the prevailing sentiment was that he had been hired by owner Bill Veeck because he came cheap; his only experience was a little more than a year of managing in the minors with Knoxville and Des Moines. He was thirty-four years old and scared for his life. Self-doubt rattled through him—*Do I really know what I'm doing?*—and he became a whipping boy for the radio broadcast duo of Harry Caray and Jimmy Piersall, who offered the almost daily critique that he managed with his head squarely up his ass. In the insular world of baseball, where newness was anathema and crustiness a work of art, La Russa was a typical Veeckian choice, playing so far against type that he could have been sold as a novelty at the concession stand. His general manger, Rollie Hemond, tried to warn La Russa that few in the game were rooting for him.

"You have five things going against you," Hemond told him. "You're young. You're handsome. You're smart. You're getting your law degree. You have a nice family —

"I don't think you're going to last very long."

Given that La Russa was also bilingual in English and Spanish, as well as a strict vegetarian in a church of meat eaters, there may well have been seven strikes against him. La Russa also from the outset showed a streak of defiance, stubbornness in the face of a second guess. Early on in his career against the Yankees, he tried a hit-and-run in the top of the ninth with a man on first and no outs and the White Sox losing by a run. Goose Gossage was in his prime then. He threw 95-mile-an-hour fire, fire that exploded high, making it impossible, in La Russa's estimation, for a hitter to successfully bunt the runner over to second. Few things in baseball are more difficult than trying to bunt with heat like that rising up on you. So he went with a hit-and-run. The runner on first tipped off the play with his lead: The Yankees pitched out and nailed him, killing any chance to tie the game. Predictably, Caray and Piersall went nuts in the broadcast booth. Within the same series he had the exact same situation and did the exact same thing: a hit-and-run that also failed when the batter popped out. Caray and Piersall went nuts again, prompting Charley Lau, then the hitting instructor for the Yankees, to remark, "I don't know if you have enough brains to be a manager, but you have the balls."

La Russa finished that first season of managing in 1979 by guiding the White Sox to a .500 record, twenty-seven wins and twenty-seven losses. It was a nice performance given that the team was in disarray, still feeling the effects of the single worst promotion in baseball in the considerable history of them, the so-called Disco Demolition night. Intended as a gentle condemnation of disco in which fans were encouraged to bring disco records for destruction in between games of a doubleheader, it turned instead into a full-scale riot. Thousands of White Sox fans poured onto the field and began to tear it up. Genuine revulsion of disco no doubt had something to do with how the fans reacted. But after twenty years of watching the Sox without a pennant in the grime and gloom of old Comiskey Park, where the sightlines in certain places were worse than in the Cook County jail, this was their liberation. Sharp-edged vinyl discs were lasered across the field, perhaps intended only to insult disco but injuring many fans in the process. The collected waft of marijuana became a nuclear cloud over the South Side. The White Sox were forced to forfeit the second game, and soon La Russa was put in to finish out the rest of the season.

When it was over, Hemond made a point of taking La Russa to the World Series: the Pirates versus the Orioles. It was the first World Series that La Russa had ever attended, and he suddenly found himself in the company of all these men, all these *baseball men,* who knew more about the game that he could ever hope to know. They all rode in a bus together from the hotel to the game. They took the same bus back to the hotel afterward and congregated for a party. There were managers—Gene Mauch and Sparky Anderson and Whitey Herzog—and gun-slinger scouts—Hugh Alexander of the Phillies and Bobby Mattick of the Blue Jays. On the bus back from every game, they were already taking a blowtorch to how Earl Weaver had managed the Orioles and Chuck Tanner had managed the Pirates—*Weaver gave Flanagan too early a hook when he took him out after six down only by a run; Tanner put his ass on the line when he brought in Blyleven in relief for four*—evisceration, condemnation, and, of course, *what they would have done instead.* Nobody, nothing escaped their attention. They were brutal in their critiques. They were passionate, so unbelievably passionate, the game their animus, and the sound of it to La Russa, with his fifty-four games of major-league managerial experience, was gorgeous. "I mean, it was beautiful baseball," he remembered, that favorite phrase again. He was in awe, but he was also slightly terrified. If they were doing this to Weaver and Tanner, two legends who between them had won 1,871 regular-season games, what would they do to him if he ever made it to the postseason—hardly a legend—and even worse, *a vegetarian, a vegetarian with a law degree?* He honestly wasn't sure he could stand up to the scrutiny.

But as critical as the grand masters were, many of them were also benevolent. Managers such as Anderson and Tanner and Dick Williams and Billy Martin and John McNamara adopted an almost paternalistic stance toward La Russa—as did Earl Weaver, after a probationary year to see if the neophyte had any real clue. On the field before a game, when La Russa started in with his incessant riff of strategic questions, they took the time to answer. Along with the steady patience of new White Sox owner, Jerry Reinsdorf, who stood by La Russa as the team continued to chug and churn in the early 1980s, he somehow survived.

In 1983, he did arrive in the Promised Land—he took the White Sox to the playoffs for the first time in his career, against the Orioles. No matter how kind the grand masters were, he also knew everything he did would still be subject to their not-so-tender postgame party mercies. He emerged with an undesirable conclusion, a loss of three games to one to Baltimore. In the last game, he made a typically controversial balls-to-the-wall decision by taking his starter, Britt Burns, into the tenth, when he finally faded, and the Orioles broke through a drought of nine scoreless innings for three runs and the victory.

But even in the aftermath of his loss, La Russa found something valuable within himself. He realized that he had passed a test, withstood the scrutiny of those he cared about the most, by traveling deeply into the psychic tunnel of the dugout, so locked on the game that he had been oblivious to everything else—the fans in the stands, the millions watching on TV, even the very baseball men he knew were riding back to the postgame party to machete his every move. *Burns? How could you stay with Burns in the tenth? What's he thinking there? It's a damn good thing this guy got his law degree, because he's gonna need it.* He wasn't brilliant or close to brilliant—he didn't have every answer no matter how much he tried to act outwardly as though he did—but he had achieved the crucial art of hearing only his own voice. He learned that the variables of the game can overcome you, overwhelm you, if you don't figure out a way to slow it down. He developed a catch phrase for himself, a way of mental discipline:

Slow it down by staying ahead of it to stay on top of it.

It was the mantra he repeated to himself after every half inning. The mantra he used then and the mantra he uses now. *Slow it down by staying ahead of it to stay on top of it.* A minimum of seventeen times a game. The dual responsibility of focus on the present and anticipation of the future, sometimes playing out scenarios a full inning or two ahead so nothing will take him by surprise.

He pulls the little cheat sheets from his back pocket and looks at them even though they can't give him much advice so early in the game. Thoughts travel through his mind in those little Godot blips.

Does what he normally does, which is throw a lot of fastballs early . . .

Showed good command . . .

Got the ball inside good . . .

Away pretty good . . .

There should be some relief in those blips; they suggest that Stephenson's got game tonight, the head rejecting the heart. But La Russa feels no respite, because of what awaits the Cards: the most talented pitcher in baseball right now.

5

THE PITCHER'S TALE

I

● ● ● IT'S MARK PRIOR, standing on those thick redwood legs, peering at the plate with that blank stare of beneath-me contempt. But Prior's stuff is what gives La Russa the most trouble. Because Prior has the stuff—first and foremost a nasty fastball with what hitters call "late life." It has a little extra *pop* at the end that makes a really good fastball far more than simply a function of how fast it measures off the radar gun.

Orlando Palmeiro, who spot-starts and makes a careful study of pitchers, will tell you that there are some fastball pitchers who barely get out of the eighties. But that *pop,* that little point underneath the exclamation, makes them difficult to hit. But Prior *does* throw in the nineties. And he brings it smoothly and effortlessly all the way up from those redwoods, like the steady spout of water from a fountain where you can't quite grasp the mechanics of how it can flow so easily yet so forcefully.

And it's not only his fastball. He's got that curve with the nice tight break. If he ever gets that changeup going—the last dab of paint in crafting the perfect portrait of a power pitcher—the demands on hitters will become impossibly intense, forced to respond to the middle nineties on one pitch and the low eighties on the next, without knowing when the downshift is coming and having four-tenths of a second to react to it.

Kerry Robinson enters the batting box to begin the bottom half of the first. He's overmatched here, as is every Cardinal tonight except the great Pujols. Prior gets the sign from Paul Bako. Prior shows no emotion—not a speck, no anticipation, no excitement —just the machinery of his motion, exquisite, almost without exertion.

He comes with a fastball to begin the night's journey. It sails high to give Robinson the comfort of a 1-and-0 advantage in the count. In his foxhole, La Russa paces back and forth a little bit. There's a distinct pattern to it: three paces out, three paces in, three paces sideways. Part of it is habit, and part of it is a highly developed sense of superstition, the belief that any break in the routine will bring a hex. Early in his career with the White Sox, he had to wear a flak jacket as the result of a death threat. The threat passed, but La Russa wore the jacket for another month because his team was winning.

There isn't much to learn from that first pitch. But the fact that it was high might indicate that Prior, despite his outward presence, is acutely aware of what's at stake in this series and is maybe overthrowing a little bit, a heart that does beat madly under pressure. So La Russa lets himself hope that maybe this first pitch bodes poorly for Prior, just like Garrett Stephenson's first pitch of the game, a fastball strike, was a good omen.

But Prior settles down after that. He comes in with two nasty fastballs down and away in the zone to push Robinson into a 1-and-2 hole. He comes with a fastball, his fourth in a row. It's high and inside; Robinson takes a cut at it and manages to foul it off. Prior comes with a fifth straight fastball, clearly thinking that he can dominate Robinson with his strength: no need to break up the pattern with anything off-speed. It jams Robinson. He puts a swing on it, but there's no authority to it, and the result is an easy liner near the bag at second for the first out.

It brings up Bo Hart, second in the ersatz lineup that injuries have forced on La Russa. Hart approaches the plate with an infectious earnestness, bouncing and bounding in: *Let's go, let's go!* The Cardinals fans, red-soaked in their own regalia to counterbalance the machine gun nests of Cubs supporters, love him for it, live through him; he treats his at-bats as they might if they were suddenly told to get in there and hit major-league pitching, grab a stick of wood and plug their ass off. His uniform is usually dirty and his body outstretched, diving for something, getting to something, fighting off something. Now the Cards fans cover him with cheers as he arrives at the plate, bellowing his name: *Hart.*

Prior throws a curve that catches him looking for strike 1. It's obvious that the Cubs have been studying their own video compilations; this is an area where Hart has been having increasing trouble. He swings through an inside-and-low fastball to make the count 0 and 2, and now he's in baseball hell, so helpless and lonely, the plate metastasizing because of the hitter's desperate impulse to flail at anything that might remotely get him out of his hole. Prior can feel the kill shot. He throws a curve that buckles down and away on the outside corner. In the parlance of the players, it's a *filthy* pitch. Hart has no choice but to swing at it.

He actually gets something on it. He hits it hard, and it skips past Prior's foot and past second base for a single. It's a sweet piece of hitting, a suggestion that Hart's War—his battle against the curve—will someday be won. Prior threw filth at him, and he spanked it right back.

Up comes Pujols, who takes two fastballs for an immediate 0-2 count. Normally, this *would be* baseball hell all over again, but neither Pujols nor Prior is normal, so the at-bat has just begun to have narrative. There is no better matchup in all of baseball right now: the perfect storm. Certainly, La Russa is eager for Pujols to emerge as the hero, but even he can't help but relish the mano a mano between the two, the beautiful game between pitcher and hitter.

There is Prior, as if he's been at it for a decade—in on the black, out on the black, up on the black, low on the black—trying to tempt with something nasty and offering nothing plump. As his performance shows tonight, he has exceptional location. He works both sides of the plate with his fastball. His curve, because of its tightness, doesn't hang like a fat apple on a tree. And he's smartly situational with it—with a "get me over" breaking ball early in the count for strike 1, and then a bounce-in-the-dirt breaking ball that a hitter will chase with two strikes. He isn't afraid to go inside, as many young pitchers are, either because they fear hitting someone or because they've been burned too many times by those springy aluminum bats that allow high school and college players to send even an inside pitch with authority to the outfield. But what is most prodigious about Prior is his combination of maturity and mechanics. Even before he had thrown a major-league pitch, one ranking had Prior fifth in efficiency after Nolan Ryan, Curt Schilling, Randy Johnson, and Roger Clemens.

As for his maturity, it isn't exactly the serene, modest, old-soul kind. He's cocky as hell, like many young athletes La Russa has seen in recent years who at the first sign of prowess are singled out by parents and coaches and teammates and lose all link to the grace of humility. His maturity has more to do with how he husbands his most precious resource: his arm. The fluidity of his delivery protects it, of course, but so does his attitude, his willingness to throw breaking balls in clutch two-strike situations instead of the more typical alpha-male fastball. Unlike most young pitchers, he does not believe that the solution to all problems is more juice on the ball. For now, his cockiness serves instead of impedes, never a sure thing in baseball.

Pujols also has an uncommon maturity, hitting as though he's been at it for a decade, with his own disciplined command of the strike zone, refusing temptation, trying to force Prior to throw the ball in a meaty part of the plate, where he can drive something with his own mechanically sublime stroke that *launches* the ball off the bat. Pujols comes into Game 1 with his statistical set and the heels of that thirty-game hitting streak:

G	AB	R	H	2B	3B	HR	RBI	BB	SO	SB	AVG.
125	473	110	171	43	1	34	108	54	50	1	.362

Prior comes into Game 1 with his statistical set, which has only gotten better as the season has progressed. In the last four games, he's given up two runs in thirty-one innings:

W	L	ERA	G	GS	SHO	IP	H	R	ER	HR	BB	SO	Opp. Avg.
12	5	2.54	23	23	1	159.2	134	55	45	11	37	179	.225

Pujols so far has Prior's number: unafraid and unabashed. He simply tags him, with a .556 average against him and two home runs. Prior, who considers Clemens and Ryan his role models, pitchers notorious for going up and in, is not about to back down by overtly pitching around him, an intentional walk without making it look intentional. Given that both players are still in their twenties, La Russa can sense the beginning of something memorable. "It's gonna be a war," was the description he once again used. There was a crease of excitement in his voice as he said it—not simply a manager's appreciation but also a fan's appreciation—something to look forward to in the way that DiMaggio versus Feller and Mays versus Gibson and Aaron versus Drysdale were something to look forward to, moments when the eight other players on the field might as well return to the dugout so they too can have the joy of watching.

So Pujols isn't going to wilt on the 0 and 2—go away with some halfhearted slap swing—just as Prior isn't going to wilt on it with some breaking ball in the dirt. Pujols is all steel, and Prior looks more impenetrable than ever. He's not afraid of Pujols—he's not afraid of anyone—which is the way every twenty-three-year-old should be.

You know he's going to bring it. He does bring it. And Pujols puts a swing on it. There is that sweet-sounding *crack* as the ball flies off the bat and launches into right with the speed of expectation. The red-drenched faithful come out of their seats, and so do the blue-drenched faithful, colors colliding all over the stadium. From his corner in the dugout, La Russa bolts forward a few steps, willing it with his eyes and a slight opening of the lips as if what he really wants to do is scream his head off—just bloody *scream* —savoring the prospect of a 2–0 lead in the bottom of the first off Prior, the anticipation on his face the anticipation he's had a million times as a manager when a ball starts off like lightning: Will it *carry?*

It's just a little too much off the end of the bat. Sammy Sosa in right makes the catch as it dies, and all that anticipation gives way to the reality that Jim Edmonds is up with two outs and Hart still on first.

Prior runs the count to 1 and 2. It puts Edmonds at a clear disadvantage, but the count also opens up a small sliver of possibility that La Russa may try to exploit. Because of the count in Prior's favor, La Russa figures that the next pitch will be one of two choices: a high fastball or a curve in the dirt, something out of the strike zone that still induces Edmonds to chase. He's also calculating that with the upper hand in the count, Prior's focus is going to be on Edmonds anyway, not paying attention to whether Hart tries to steal second.

As Prior goes into his wind-up, Hart takes off on La Russa's sign. It's a classic manager strategy, so classic that most managers now routinely look for a steal with two outs, on the theory that it's better to make the third out at second than at the plate. If the ball is a curve out of the strike zone, he'll probably steal it. If it's the high fastball, he probably won't, because of the greater velocity and the quality of Bako's arm. It's an aggressive play to try so early; other managers might wait for the game to settle in a little bit. But for La Russa, it meets the threshold of aggression with common sense. It's a push for a run with two outs in the bottom of the first against a pitcher who has thrown first-pitch strikes to the last three batters he's faced and has been virtually unhittable his last four games. It's the only way to deal with a pitcher this good: be proactive, *make something happen*. If Hart succeeds, he can now score off a single. That's obviously the preferred result. But if Hart is thrown out, it's not the end of the world, because it gives Edmonds a fresh count to start the next inning, a baseball mulligan.

Hart hauls down the line toward second. He's gotten a good jump and has decent speed. It still hinges on whether La Russa has guessed right that Prior will come after Edmonds with a curve.

It is a curve in the dirt. Edmonds doesn't chase, and Bako doesn't even bother to throw. An inning that seemed dead may have something left to it after all, particularly when Edmonds pushes the count to 3 and 2. Suddenly, Prior needs to make a pitch in the strike zone. He doesn't want to walk Edmonds, not with Scott Rolen up next and capable of hitting something for extra bases with his natural-born power. Because of the count, it's an obvious fastball situation, when a pitcher cornered like this goes to his strength. But Prior elects maturity instead. He comes with a curve, but it's not one of his best ones. It's middle of the strike zone, belt-high. From the dugout, La Russa can see its voluptuousness. It's such a peach for Edmonds, something he can drive. But he's not looking for it. His assumption, the common hitter's assumption, is that Prior is going to come after him with the fastball, which means that he has to adjust. It is virtually impossible to adjust to a fastball when you're looking for a curve, although it is possible to adjust to a curve when you're looking for a fastball. But Edmonds's timing is still off a little bit. He taps a three-hopper to first and the inning is over.

There is no particular tumult in the dugout as the first inning ends. Opportunities in baseball come and go all the time, and dugouts early in the game resemble luncheonettes where all the diners know one another and have formed little cliques and talk amiably until one of them has to go to work, and it may take hours before that even happens. Farthest right are the bench players, who may or may not get into the game. La Russa rarely ventures into this territory, perhaps because he may hear them talking about hunting or cars instead of baseball, which would drive him crazy, just as it drives him crazy when a hitter gets a single and starts chatting it up with the first baseman as if they're distant cousins at a family reunion. He shares the fan's view that it simply doesn't look good: Baseball is meant to be a game of competition, not a game of *whassup dawg?* In the middle are the starting pitchers who won't get into the game because, like an extended Sabbath, these are their days of rest. Stephenson sits on the bench in back, left alone to ponder the next inning, with Simon and Ramirez, the remaining two heads of the monster, due up. As Hart and Edmonds file back into the dugout to end the inning, Stephenson comes out of his reverie, gets his glove, and heads back out to the mound.

II

STEPHENSON THROWS a solid second inning. He gets Simon out
on a 1-1 fastball in. It's a good location pitch, banging Simon inside,
just like Duncan told him to do. Stephenson comes back from a 3-1
liability to Ramirez for an easy fly out to center. He uses his head
against Alex Gonzalez, working him in so he gets antsy that he better protect the inside of the plate, the *inside conscious* thing, then
works him outside and fools him so badly that he awkwardly lunges
at the ball for a weak foul out.

Prior answers in the bottom of the second with his own 1-2-3
dispensing of Rolen and Tino Martinez and Miguel Cairo in twelve
pitches. So far, La Russa hasn't seen anything from Prior that surprises him. He's spotting the ball well. He's showing excellent command. If there's anything that buoys La Russa, it may be the pitch
count. Rolen took a seven-pitch at-bat against Prior before flying
out. Edmonds went seven pitches in the first before that weak tapper on the stealth curve. Through two innings, Prior has thrown
thirty pitches, which would put him right around a hundred in the
seventh and maybe force Dusty Baker to consider the purgatory of
the bullpen.

La Russa watches Prior with professional admiration. But in
emotional terms, Prior gets under his skin. It isn't Prior personally
that bothers him but what Prior represents: the young player with
the big talent who instead of being circumspect his first few years in
the league routinely rises to the media bait so prevalent today and
gives answers to *everything,* when he hasn't been around long
enough to have the answer to *anything.* He doesn't like the intem-
perate out-of-the-blue comments Prior makes about the Cardinals,
how he hates them. He doesn't think he needs to make comments
about Barry Bonds, how he isn't afraid of him, when this is Prior's
first full year in the league and this is Bonds's eighteenth. *I think he
needs to be doing this a while* is the way La Russa thinks about it
when he watches him pitch. It's an old-fashioned comment, said by
a manager who believes in circumspection among young players
because that's the way he came up: Your first couple of seasons, no

matter how good you are, you should be in the corner, shutting up and soaking it in.

Prior can rank up there with Schilling and Maddux and Johnson by the time he's through. With his rare mix of stuff and smarts, he is that dominant. But he's also that young. He has the swagger that is the hubris of youth, taking his invincibility for granted when nobody ever should, receiving too much early attention and slathering in it.

La Russa has seen a procession of pitchers over the years who have broken down and busted out because of arm problems and high expectation problems and personal problems and, perhaps most of all, problems making the distinction between being a thrower and being a pitcher. He has seen young pitchers done in by their need for speed. He has seen pitchers done in by the fear of coming into the majors even though they have major-league-caliber stuff. He has seen young pitchers done in by being rushed to the big leagues, as every team is hungry for pitching. Time after time, he has seen the fall from the stratosphere, the burnup. No player in baseball is more vulnerable than a pitcher, the physical and psychic requirements for sustained success not only monumental but also fragile. The line between success and implosion is so terribly thin. Climbing a sheet of ice has more job security, as evidenced over the past thirty years by the number of number-one picks in the baseball draft who were highly touted, highly ballyhooed pitchers but flamed out without ever getting close to the majors.

And even when you do make it— even when the world seems sun-kissed, as Prior's world seems sun-kissed at this very moment as he mows down the Cardinals through two—something can happen, something you don't expect or could ever imagine. And La Russa knows it vividly.

III

THEY SIGNED HIM right out of high school, and pretty soon afterward the Cardinals brought him into Busch Stadium one Sunday so he could pitch batting practice, get a feel for what the big-league atmosphere was like, let him dress in the clubhouse and wear a uniform that bore his name.

A-N-K-I-E-L. It spread between the shoulder blades like neon. Rick Ankiel was eighteen. And he didn't seem to have a care in the world. The ball simply sizzled. It had that *pop* into the catcher's mitt, that sweet sound of a guy who was simply bringing it. And it moved—*oh, man,* did it move—the way it always seems to move a little bit more when a lefty is pitching. People gathered around the cage to watch this kid who had it. *Sizzle. Pop. Sizzle. Pop.* And nobody dared to say it then, because there's no way you say something like that about an eighteen-year-old kid. But here was *Sandy Koufax.*

He became the Prior of 2000, the kid with the golden arm. He came to the Cardinals, touted as the best young pitcher in the country. He was happy and carefree because there couldn't possibly be anything better than to be pitching in the major leagues at twenty-one. And he had good stuff, just like Prior three years later would have good stuff. He competed his ass off. He had a cool cockiness on the mound. And he was soaking up the game, learning it like a baseball prodigy, just as Prior would later learn it. Working almost exclusively with Mike Matheny as his catcher, he started with a fastball that smoked in the low- to mid-nineties. But then he developed a sinker that moved down and away from right-handed hitters. He threw it about four or five miles per hour slower than his other fastball. It was almost like a batting-practice fastball, but the change of speeds between the two pitches, combined with that sinking movement on the slower one, drove hitters to despair. They didn't know what was coming. They didn't know where it was coming. And they didn't know how fast it was coming. "He had a fastball that jumped up on you and he had that sinker that would get groundballs," La Russa remembered. He also had a curve ball that he wasn't afraid to use as an out pitch. With a little more refinement, the next pitch in the repertoire would have been a more consistent change, just like it would be for Prior.

In their twenty years together, La Russa and Duncan had seen their share of golden pitchers—La Marr Hoyt and Richard Dotson and Tom Seaver with the White Sox, Dennis Eckersley and Dave Stewart and Bob Welch with the A's, bulldog Darryl Kile and the eventual coming of Matt Morris with the Cards. Outward excitement is not something the two men would ever be confused with, Duncan the Quiet Assassin and La Russa always in the dark clench of his internal intensity. Riding in some Hertz Rent-a-Car together on the way to the ballpark five or six hours before game time, they spoke in short syncopation as if the other one weren't there — Duncan making some soft-as-a-feather short-sentence pronouncement as La Russa mumbled off into the windshield — yet both men understanding *exactly* what the other one was saying. They had the kind of relationship that men in baseball develop when they're together eight months out of the year for two decades. They spoke in the Morse code of the game: turbo sinkers, get-me-over curves, middle in versus middle away, nasty shit. They did *know* what each other was thinking without having to articulate it, so why bother to articulate it, and if you had to articulate it, why make some sloppy mess of it.

But when it came to Ankiel, they got excited. They got excited because of what he was doing on the mound, developing that nasty sinker to righties, watching him advance right past thrower to pitcher at such a tender baseball age. They got excited because a lefty like that comes up once in a millennium. He was the *real deal,* and the world, the entire world, was Rick Ankiel's, blowing away the game with that arm born and bred in the Florida sun, able to do whatever he wanted to do whenever he wanted to do it and nothing more Wild West in all of sports, a pitcher on a mound simply blessed with it.

Down the stretch run of the 2000 season in August and September, Stephenson's arm got sore and so did Andy Benes's knee. Pat Hentgen simply wore down. The rotation became a two-man show starring Kile and Ankiel, and Ankiel won his last four games to finish the year 11 and 7.

The Cardinals won the Central division. Their opponent would be the Braves, and before the playoffs started, La Russa made a decision that perhaps haunts him more than any he has ever made.

Aware that he had only two healthy starters and wanting to maximize their appearances, he discovered a potential edge in the playoff schedule. Ankiel needed four days' rest in between starts, but by pitching him in Game 1, he could still pitch Game 4 if necessary, whereas Kile, able to go on three days' rest, could go in Games 2 and 5. It meant giving two pitchers four of the five starts, and it meant that Ankiel would pitch that first game even though Kile, a twenty-game winner and the clear ace of the staff, would ordinarily get that honor. It also meant that Ankiel would be facing Maddux, who had gone 19 and 9 and would be starting his twenty-fourth playoff game, more games than Ankiel had started in his entire life.

Aware also of what that would mean in terms of media exposure and not wanting to subject Ankiel to any more pressure than there already was, he pulled a bait-and-switch with reporters the day before the series began. He had Ankiel do his pitching work and then got him out of the clubhouse. He then told Kile to go into the interview room to take the obligatory questions from the national media, as if he were pitching in Game 1. And Kile played the role perfectly, because although he acted as if he were pitching in Game 1, he never explicitly said that he *was or wasn't*. It was only after the interview ended and the reporters had left for the day that La Russa announced the switch. He did it to protect Ankiel, keep him away from the self-evident questions that are the bane of the professional athlete: *What about the pressure of facing Maddux in Game 1? How does it feel as a rookie to go against the best pitcher in baseball in Game 1? Any butterflies, Rick, any butterflies?* La Russa knew the media were pissed and had a right to be pissed. But his responsibility was to his team. And he had protected Ankiel. He had reduced the pressure on him, so all he needed to do was go out and pitch. Everything seemed to line up in Ankiel's favor, except for Mike Matheny's birthday.

The Thursday before the end of the regular season, Kile had won his twentieth game in San Diego. It was a strange and wild affair. La Russa got thrown out when he protested a balk call, throwing down his glasses and stepping on them, to the disgust of the umpire and the adoration of his players. He was in the runway behind the dugout, trying to manage with the Cards down by a run in the eighth, 6–5. He sent up three pinch hitters and each of them got hits and the Cards went ahead 7–6 and Kile, for the first time in his career, got to the twenty-game-win plateau.

It was a joyous moment, and it lasted until the next morning when La Russa was on his way to the ballpark and got a call from Barry Weinberg—always a bad sign when the trainer called like that. Matheny had cut his hand with a hunting knife he had gotten as a birthday gift. He would be out for the rest of the regular season and the playoffs.

The first playoff game took place in Busch Stadium. Right away, the crowd of nearly 53,000 could tell that something stunning was unfolding.

The Cardinals got *all over* Maddux in the first. Staying back on the ball, they countered the movement on his pitches by hitting to the opposite field: nothing fancy, no heroics trying to pull the ball for a home run. It was one of those days when the ball simply knew where to go, a grounder by Fernando Vina to the right side hitting the bag for a single, a broken-bat single by J.D. Drew, the usually seamless Andruw Jones muffing Edmonds's fly to left center, singles to center and right center by Will Clark and Placido Polanco. The score was 6–0 after the first. *Six runs* against Maddux. Could you believe it? *Six,* what La Russa called the "crooked number" when runs explode on the board rather than the usual trickle.

Ankiel had given up two walks in the top of the first to the Braves, as well as a single, but he got out of the inning when Brian Jordan popped up to Clark in foul territory. He began the second by striking out Reggie Sanders. Walt Weiss doubled on a 1-1 pitch, but then Edgar Renteria made a spectacular play on Javy Lopez's liner and flipped to Vina to turn the double play.

The score was still 6–0 when the Braves came to bat in the top of the third. The line score for that half-inning tells what happened:

Braves 3rd: Maddux walked; Furcal popped to Clark in foul territory; Ankiel threw a wild pitch (Maddux to second); Ankiel

threw a wild pitch (Maddux to third); A. Jones walked; Ankiel
threw a wild pitch (A. Jones to 2nd); C. Jones was called out on
strikes; Gallarraga walked (Maddux scored on wild pitch by
Ankiel; A. Jones to 3rd); Jordan singled to Lankford (A. Jones
scored, Gallarraga to 2nd); Ankiel threw a wild pitch (Galarraga
to 3rd, Jordan to 2nd); Sanders walked; Weiss singled to Lankford (Galarraga scored, Jordan scored, Sanders to 2nd; JAMES
REPLACED ANKIEL; Lopez popped to Vina; 4 R, 2 H, 0 E, 2
LOB. Braves 4, Cardinals 6.

With Matheny out with those torn tendons, Carlos Hernandez
was catching. He wasn't the defensive force that Matheny was, and
he also had a bad back, further limiting his mobility. Matheny's
strong and quiet presence had done wonders for Ankiel, as it had
for many pitchers. Despite his quiet, self-effacing exterior—no
bluster to be seen anywhere—he didn't take crap from pitchers.
He knew their foibles and petty pouts, how to a certain degree they
were spoiled prodigies who in truth had a far worse idea of what
they should throw and when they should throw it than he did. Or
sometimes they didn't pay attention to the signs he gave but instead
threw whatever the hell they wanted.

There had been slight bouts of wildness before from Ankiel, as
in the game against Cincinnati, when he had thrown four wild
pitches in five innings, or the time, two months later, when he had
thrown three in five innings, once again against the Reds. But Matheny's superb coverage behind the plate—nobody in baseball
could block the plate better—had minimized the impact of Ankiel's wildness and helped settle him down. They had a rhythm together, the same rhythm that Tim McCarver had when he caught
Steve Carlton with the Phillies and the same rhythm that Jorge
Posada had with Orlando Hernandez with the Yankees, even
though they seemed to be arguing most of the time.

But Matheny wasn't in the first game of the playoffs. And La
Russa, in trying to explain what will be forever inexplicable, wonders whether Ankiel began to panic without Matheny there to reel
in some of his errant pitches. And in panicking, Rick Ankiel began
to think about what he was doing and how he was doing it. What
had always seemed such a natural gift now seemed forced, as if he

had never done it before. The terror of self-consciousness set in and drowned out muscle memory. Because of the situation he had been thrust into—a rookie in the first game of the playoffs—he also had no experience to carry him through, no keys to draw on to determine whether what was happening was mechanical or emotional.

He laughed off the performance against the Braves at first, noting that, if nothing else, he had set a record for most wild pitches in a game in the history of the postseason with five, a record that he had actually broken in that one half-inning in the top of the third. He was loose and relaxed as the first wave of media buzzards started rubbernecking, smelling the burning rubber of a really juicy car wreck on the mound. And they were clearly enjoying themselves. There had been other mound meltdowns in baseball. Steve Blass with the Pirates. Mark Wohlers with Atlanta. But nothing this public, right smack in the playoffs. Nobody knew, or perhaps really wanted to know, the extent of what was happening yet.

The Cardinals ended up sweeping the Braves, and La Russa slated Ankiel to start the second game of the National League Championship Series against the Mets. His first pitch was a 91-mph fastball to Timo Perez that just missed beaning him. Of the twenty pitches he threw before he was taken out, five went to the backstop. And it was then that Ankiel, two weeks before described as a phenom and a wonder, began to have other labels applied to him by the media: *meltdown, crazy tosses.*

It was over after that. He came back the next season, and La Russa and Duncan did what they could to shield him from the rubberneckers determined to document every pitch of his ongoing disintegration. They had him work out at sunrise in spring training in the Cardinals' compound in Jupiter when it was cool and quiet and empty. Early in the regular season, they had him warm up in a tunnel underneath the stadium so no one could watch. Ankiel, who had initially reacted to his predicament with humor, now became hard and defensive and reticent. He turned down most interview requests, because who in their right mind would *want* to talk about something like that, but there seemed to be a joy among certain writers in goading him, seeing whether they could get to him:

C'mon, Rick, just a few questions about what it's like to crack up on the mound. And there was also a certain school suggesting that Ankiel had only gotten what he deserved—signing for too much money out of high school, hiring an agent in Scott Boras who always went for too much money, floating through life without the requisite suffering that they went through—*You want to know what pressure is, Rick, try writing for peanuts on deadline*—too damn golden for his own good with that fat contract and all those threats that he was going to go to the University of Miami if he didn't get the money he wanted.

In the Thursday afternoon sun at Busch in May 2001, Ankiel threw the final pitch he would throw that season against Pat Meares of the Pirates. The ball went to the screen, and Duncan went out of the dugout. Ankiel hung his head as he made the baseball equivalent of a perp walk, and then he put on his jacket in the dugout and headed down the tunnel toward the clubhouse.

He went to spring training a year later but was put on the disabled list with a sore elbow and did not pitch the entire year. He came back to spring training the season of 2003 with La Russa's hope that he could make the team as a reliever. It created yet another media deathwatch, the careful chronicling of his every pitch: how many were strikes and how many were balls and how many sailed wild and how many almost hit someone.

On a Thursday morning at the end of March in the clubhouse in Jupiter, Duncan came into La Russa's office to tell him that a decision on Ankiel's fate had been made by Walt Jocketty: how he would stay with the club until spring training broke and then go down to the minors where those in charge of minor-league development for the Cardinals would take over and determine the best course.

"How much influence do we have on where he's sent?" asked La Russa.

"I assume we'll have input," said Duncan.

Duncan wanted him to go down to Double-A, where there would be less pressure, but La Russa worried about the bus trips.

"He'll be fine," said Duncan. "There's less travel in Double-A than in Triple-A."

And then he added something else, perhaps what—in the best of worlds, where there is time to develop young pitchers physically and mentally and the economies of the game don't demand immediate results—should have happened all along.

"He's twenty-three years old. He should be in Double-A."

Two days later, the team left Florida to make its way north. There was a delicious sense of renewal and anticipation to it, the slate wiped clean, the arduous tedium of spring training over with its rote drills and games that don't count, every team in both leagues starting off fresh in first place with exactly the same record, each of them still believers in the beautiful delusion that it will come together. Two Bekins moving trucks pulled up outside the Jupiter clubhouse, and soon they were filled with the tools of the game: satchels crammed with batting helmets, canvas cylinders built for bats, red bags virtually overflowing with baseballs like a slot jackpot in Vegas, the trunk containing Duncan's pitch-chart binders.

The players and the coaches got onto two buses that would take them to the airport in Palm Beach, then off to St. Louis for the opener. La Russa was the last to get on. He was dressed in a black sport coat and blue jeans, a pair of sunglasses hanging by one of its stems out of the breast pocket. There was a smile on his face because it was finally going to start now, the season, the regular season, every question and anxiety about his ballclub to be answered now. In the rigid hierarchy of the team, he took the first seat of the first bus, and then off the team went. A clump of loyalists clapped as the caravan rolled through the black metal gate, and it was as American as America ever gets.

The clubhouse, relieved of its occupants, suddenly seemed sodden, flooded with the sad, slow weight of south Florida humidity, the constant chirp of ballplayers replaced by the void of departure. Lockers—once filled with uniform shirts and practice jerseys and bats and fresh batting gloves in shiny plastic packets and virginal hats without a crease and baseball cards to be signed and packets of protein powder—were now virtually empty, except for white plastic hangers and the nameplates of those who were now on their way north:

Robinson Renteria Pujols Drew Fassero Rolen Edmonds
Martinez Girardi Matheny Eldred Marrero Palmeiro Painter
Tomko Hermanson Perez Morris Cairo Isringhausen Simon-
tacchi Delgado Springer Stephenson Williams Taguchi

A box of scuffed baseballs stood in one corner, rejects that
hadn't made the cut. A stack of pizza boxes bore the pockmarks of
their half-eaten cargo. There was a FedEx slip on the carpet and a
picture of somebody's baby and a baseball card of the old Giant
great Juan Marichal with that leg kick poking a hole in heaven and
a stack of unopened fan mail and a twenty-dollar coupon for Guis-
seppe's restaurant. One player, Al Levine, a righty reliever cut
toward the end of camp, had even left behind a copy of his contract, as if the compensation he was receiving for being released,
$600,000, wasn't worth the paper it was printed on, probably be-
cause he knew he would find enlistment papers somewhere else.
The only people in the clubhouse were the attendants scurrying
about, throwing blue towels into metal shopping basket bins, col-
lecting soiled stirrup socks, removing peels of tape. And then Rick
Ankiel walked in to gather his things, as if he had waited for this
moment when no one would be there to see him.

La Russa still believes in Rick Ankiel. He still believes that he can
get it back if he's left alone for a little bit without the rubberneckers
smelling flesh, rediscover the muscle memory of what once was
there. "He still has it in him to pitch well," says La Russa.
    But whatever happens, there is the image of somebody trying to
make a comeback—not in his forties or fifties or even his thirties,
but at the age of twenty-three. Which is why, as La Russa watches
Prior on the mound in Game 1 with his impervious strut and thinks
to himself: *Maybe he needs to be doing this a while,* he's thinking it
as much for Prior's benefit as he is his own. Because nobody, no
matter how good you are already and how much better everyone
thinks you will become, is ever immune to the vagaries of what can
happen when your life depends on throwing a baseball.

6

PRAYING FOR CHANGE

I

● ● ● LA RUSSA FEELS gratified by Stephenson's performance so far. He's put two zeros on the board. He didn't float something up and over for Randall Simon. He used both sides of the
plate with Alex Gonzalez. He has kept the ball down.

It's too early to make predictions, but La Russa wonders
whether this might be a pivotal moment not only in Stephenson's
season but also for his career, the moment when a pitcher realizes
who he is and what he is and what he's capable of and drops the
action-hero pretensions that get him into trouble. Maybe it's like
the epiphany Todd Stottlemyre experienced when he came over to
the A's from Toronto in the early 1990s and placed himself at the
mercy of Duncan.

Stottlemyre, by his own admission, suffered from the big-balls
delusion. La Russa understood that attitude and to a certain degree
embraced it. He had been around pitchers enough to know what
egotistical creatures they had to be because of the very nature of
what they did, alone on that little hill with the outcome of the game
in lockstep with their performance. "They're starting pitchers," he
said. "They *need* to be heroes." Now he didn't even bother to ask a
starter how he was feeling when he visited the mound, as the only
one he had ever encountered in a quarter century who didn't flat-
out lie, admitted to being out of gas if he was out of gas, was Tom

Seaver. The rest said they felt great even if they no longer had any feeling left in their arms.

Stottlemyre was the ultimate mound warrior. But under Duncan, he harnessed his drive and competitiveness so that each batter became a potential out, not a rite of ego. He learned how to kill with location. He realized that if you toss in the right mix of pitches —think of yourself as a chef making a soufflé with varied ingredients—the hitter's timing, his most precious commodity, is stolen from him. Stottlemyre fell in love with command, which even when you don't have good stuff on a certain night can still get you through. He became something he had never really been before— a pitcher—and he credits Duncan for that transformation, the first pitching coach who taught him more than mechanics. The Deacon got inside his head because of the meticulousness of those charts, proved to him with hard-core data what he was doing wrong, and fixed the circuitry to turn him from an inconsistent .500 pitcher into a pitcher with a consistent winning record.

So maybe here's where Stephenson crosses the border from thrower to pitcher and never crosses back. He's had his moments before, moments when it's worked on all cylinders and moments, terrifying moments, when he himself has acknowledged that he has no idea where his fastball is going. Now would be a lovely time to do it, against a young gun like Prior with first place in the Central on the line. The only thing La Russa hasn't seen from Stephenson is off-speed. Twenty-seven pitches thrown through seven batters and all of them fastballs. But that's okay as long as Stephenson ultimately starts mixing in his curve and changeup. Also, with the eighth and ninth hitters coming to the plate in the top of the third before Kenny Lofton's up again, there's a little relief in the lineup. Given the way Stephenson is pitching, the third inning should be easier than the first two.

The catcher Bako leads off for the Cubs. He's hitting .213 with no home runs and eleven RBIs. Finally, Stephenson has a matchup that favors him; in four at-bats, Bako's never gotten a hit against him.

Stephenson comes with a low-and-away fastball that Bako

swings through to get the first-strike advantage. Stephenson's next pitch, his twenty-ninth straight fastball, is up and in for a ball to make the count 1 and 1. In the dugout, a queasy feeling comes over La Russa: *Where are the curve and the changeup? Where is the deception? Why give the eighth-place hitter who isn't hitting two and a quarter a gift like this by throwing nothing but fastballs?*

Stephenson comes with another fastball. He is hoping to locate the pitch inside, but he doesn't, at least not inside enough. Bako hits it sharply into right. Kerry Robinson reaches into the corner, cutting the ball off before it goes to the wall, and saves it from becoming a double.

Now La Russa begins to worry. Stephenson's bipolar disorder is showing definite signs of relapse. In the Cubs dugout, a vicious yet accurate rumor is no doubt spreading: *He's throwing nothing but fastballs up there.* No pitcher should ever let a hitter feel comfortable, and if Stephenson keeps throwing heat, the Cubs will come to the plate with a bat and a Mai Tai.

Stephenson faces Prior next and jams him, with the result a harmless pop-up to the infield. It gives Stephenson his first out, and maybe La Russa's agitations are the agitations of a man who agitates over everything, even the little crushed paper cups that procreate on the dugout floor: La Russa walks the length of the dugout, kicking them into neat little piles. The reality is that Stephenson, after working his way through the Cubs lineup, has given up only *the one hit,* to Bako. But La Russa still frets, waiting for the game to sucker-punch him, his only defense to *agitate.* He went into the inning hoping to catch a break. With the lowest spots in the order due up first and second, he harbored the expectation that Lofton, coming up with two outs and nobody on, would be neutralized. But that fastball to Bako has set off a potentially wicked chain, because Lofton now settles in with a man on first and only one out.

Stephenson digs himself a hole with three straight balls, then gets back into the at-bat with two strikes to make the count full at 3 and 2.

It's another sumptuous subplot: The hitter has an assumed advantage because of the likelihood that the pitcher will come with a fastball, rather than risk a walk with something too fine that will put runners on first and second. But La Russa and Duncan will often try to screw up that assumption if they figure it's likely that the runner on first is going for second off the 3-2 count. They encourage their pitchers and catchers to treat the situation as if the runner is *already* on second, with first base open, to lessen the usual tendency to give in to the full count with a fastball. Instead, they preach off-speed here; a walk that puts runners on first and second is still better than the hitter getting the fastball he thinks he is going to get. La Russa himself will further encourage the antifastball philosophy by conveying to the catcher through signs what pitch the pitcher should throw. But he makes no sign here. He believes that both Stephenson and Chris Widger have been sufficiently coached on fastball danger. He believes the pitch will be a curve or a changeup to muck up Lofton's anticipation.

It's a fastball. A *high* fastball. The kind of pitch that keeps Lofton in gloves and gold chains. He slaps it the other way into the corner in left, Pujols scampering after it. Bako scores easily from first. Lofton reaches second standing up. The Cubs lead 1–0.

The next batter, Martinez in the two-hole, singles on a fastball to drive in Lofton: 2–0 Cubs. That pitch was in but also up, the kiss of death. In the foxhole, La Russa's inner voice pleads with Stephenson: *Mix in something different!* Stephenson obliges with a changeup to begin the at-bat against Sosa. At this point, La Russa is almost shocked to see it.

Finally. But it's moot anyway, as Stephenson, after building to 0 and 2, loses Sosa to a walk to put runners on first and second with, still, one out. The last thing Duncan had told Stephenson in their meeting—the moral he left him with—was not to get frustrated and lose concentration if things started to go a little sour. But the back-to-back hits by Lofton and Martinez have obviously flustered Stephenson, and La Russa has the feeling that he is slipping away, a crooked number in the works with all that potential damage approaching in the four-, five-, and six-spots.

It's a great situation for Alou in the cleanup—he usually kills Cardinals pitching with his RBI aggressiveness—but he flies to left for the second out. There are still runners on first and second. Stephenson has given up three hits, a walk and two runs; he suddenly looks scraggly and rattled. It's been a bumpy inning, an ugly inning. Yet he can still walk away with minor scratches if he gets the next out.

The object that blocks Stephenson's escape from the inning is Simon, the very Simon who, Stephenson acknowledged, *kicks his ass*. This is the key at-bat of the inning, probably of the entire game, and La Russa's inner voice is succinct: *You get Simon out. You got a game.*

Stephenson knows it too. If he retires Simon here, it's the Cardinals who get the crucial psychological lift because the Cubs should have done more damage. It's also a crucial mental victory for Stephenson, a bad matchup that he turned in his favor, an at-bat that can propel a pitcher the rest of the way.

Simon offers no pretext of discipline. He plays the game the way Bernie Mac might play it: sweet and fun and just a wee bit devilish. His shirt billows like an America's Cup jib, his girth ample enough to scare Bigfoot. He likes getting up there, guessing the pitch, and then taking an El Niño swing. He has no clean stride into the ball, just a little baby step, and after he swings, he looks even more disheveled, as if he just exited from one of those roller coasters where you hang upside down.

His ebullience does sometimes get him into trouble. He has actually earned a little piece of baseball lore already this season, not for anything he did while playing but for using a bat to trip up an unsuspecting mascot dressed up as a bratwurst during the run-around-the-field race the Milwaukee Brewers put on at each home game. The poor bratwurst—it actually may have been an Italian sausage—collapsed in a tottering heap. The video image of it went around the world, and Simon paid a $432 fine for disorderly conduct. When he is playing, he has good bat speed. He can drive something deep, and as Duncan pointed out to Stephenson, he likes his meat up.

The first pitch is a curve low in the zone. Simon is way out in front of it, terribly fooled.

He fouls off the next pitch to make the count 0 and 2. Stephenson's in control now, and from the stands comes a rumbling murmur that yes, *yes!* he is going to squirm his way out of this thing with only two runs.

He throws a fastball outside, then a fastball inside. They're chase pitches, considerably off the plate but appropriate. Simon doesn't bite and the count is squared at 2 and 2.

Before the next pitch, La Russa sees Stephenson shaking off the sign from Chris Widger. He knows what *that* means: Widger wants Stephenson to go with a breaking ball, particularly because Simon doesn't hit curve balls well. Stephenson, however, still wants his fastball, feels most comfortable with it. Widger sets up inside to at least get the right location.

The ball floats up and away. Simon hits the bejesus out of it. He smacks it hard to the opposite field in left. Stephenson turns and watches and thinks, or maybe just prays, that it's carrying foul. Pujols goes into the corner in left to see what kind of play he can make if it stays fair: get a good carom off the wall and *maybe* hold the runner at first from scoring. He's on the run, readying for the zigzag off the bumpers. But then he stops and simply gazes at the ball as it opts for early retirement.

Simon has just hit a three-run homer. The Cubs lead 5–0.

Duncan squints in the dugout. There's a look of bemused irony on his face, as if to say, *Now, Garrett, what did I tell you about getting the ball up to Simon? What did I tell you?* As for Stephenson, he's visibly upset. He isn't thinking at all now—to hell with the game plan. With Aramis Ramirez up, he throws another fastball—a particular kind of fastball that pitchers in this situation often throw—a fastball that La Russa recognizes as a *first-pitch pissed-off fastball,* a fastball that invariably causes regret. Ramirez hits a home run four rows beyond the Budweiser sign in left center: 6–0 Cubs.

As Duncan trots out to the mound, La Russa opens the little black box in the right corner of the dugout just inside the tunnel entrance. He pulls out the phone and speaks to Marty Mason, who in turn gets Sterling Hitchcock up and throwing in the bullpen. Over in the Cubs dugout, Dusty Baker takes a healthy guzzle from a green Gatorade cup, then chases it with a healthy spit as a little toast to the Cubs' crooked number. Prior, with a white towel around his pitching arm, sits on the bench as implacable as ever, his hair barely matted even in the heat, his sideburns so long and straight, you could land a plane on them.

Stephenson glumly listens to Duncan. His head is down, awkwardly cocked, the goatee around his chin thin and insubstantial. He's getting a terse baseball lecture here, the look on *his* face like a child who knows that trying to throw the eraser past the teacher's head was stupid once and inexcusable twice. He will be punished for this. There will be another demotion to the bullpen.

He manages to strike out Alex Gonzalez to end the inning, and even that's scary, as Gonzalez rips the first two pitches foul into left field, pulling them just a little bit too much. But the damage is done —nine batters, five hits, six runs, two home runs—to raise Stephenson's death toll to twenty-eight. He is through for the night after three. He relied on his fastball too much, and he couldn't control it. He paid the price, exactly what La Russa predicted would happen if he pitched this way. His matchups now seem prescient given the collective performance of those three ex-Pirates in all of three innings: Six at-bats. One double. Two home runs. Three runs scored. Five RBIs. And Stephenson's hastening into oblivion.

II

THE DUGOUT is quiet after the top of the third ends. La Russa hasn't given up yet. A 6–0 disadvantage this early in the game is not insurmountable. Things simply happen to the Cubs because of the handcuffs of their history, and they particularly happen in St. Louis. Since 2000, the Cubs have won only four of twenty-seven games at Busch. And in the back of their minds must be the time last year when the Cards overcame a 9–4 deficit in the ninth to win 10–9 on a three-run homer by Edgar Renteria. But Prior is pitching tonight, and although this is nowhere close to the best game he's pitched this season—his fastball doesn't have the location that it usually does—he still has the *it*. He has what Scott Rolen describes as "presence," an intangible confidence. It may be impossible to quantify, but as Rolen puts it, "The difference between a 3-and-1 fastball fouled back or lined to center is who has the most confidence."

He easily dispenses with the Cardinals in the third and fourth, the only hit a go-nowhere single by Edmonds. In the foxhole, La Russa has trouble purging the top of the third out of his mind. The home runs bother him less than the very first at-bat of the inning when Bako, who doesn't even hit *two and a quarter*, got that gift pack of three straight fastballs. But he still refuses to become dispirited, pushes himself to grind away even harder whatever the reality. The game in 2001 between Houston and Pittsburgh—when the Astros lost after being ahead 8–2 with the Pirates batting with two outs and nobody on in the bottom of the ninth—creases his mind. Anything can happen in baseball: the beauty or the brutality.

But by the end of the fifth, with the score now 7–0 Cubs, thoughts of a comeback are fading. Prior has given up only two hits. He's thrown first-pitch strikes to eleven of the eighteen batters he has faced. No Cardinals runner has gotten beyond second base. The St. Louis faithful recognize the plodding, futile rhythm of a rout. The air was sucked out of them in the third with Simon's swing. They've uttered little since, and as they scan the out-of-town scoreboard, they find more bad news:

	1	2	3	4	5	T
LOS ANGELES	3	0	0	0	0	3
HOUSTON	2	1	1	0	6	10

If the Astros keep it up and the Cardinals keep it up and the Cubs keep it up, the dogfight atop the Central will produce a complete flip-flop in the space of one game:

HOUSTON	69–62	.527
CHICAGO	68–62	.523
ST. LOUIS	68–63	.519

In the bottom of the sixth, the crowd emerges from its funk when Pujols appears at the plate for another war against Prior. He got just under one in the first, and then he walked in the fourth. But Prior has nothing to lose now. He has a 7–0 score on his side and *you know what, Albert, let's put down the switchblades and go straight to sabres. My best against your best. Deal?*

Deal. Prior comes with a fastball on the first pitch. It rides the radar gun at 93 mph.

Pujols counters. He flicks his bat toward the dugout as if it's too hot even for his own hands, follows the ball with his eyes as it cracks the ozone layer and heads for some telecommunications satellite. It reenters earth with an innocent plop on the grassy knoll behind center field, 414 feet from where it originated. It's a meaningless run in the flow of Game 1. The Cardinals will still end up losing 7–4 on a three-run ninth-inning rally that fizzles. But as Pujols encircles the implacable Prior on the mound in his pulled-up blue stirrup socks covering up calves so big that his nickname is Calfzilla, there is the comfort that at least one score has just been settled.

III

LA RUSSA FACES the media after the game, just outside the clubhouse. His hair is damp and his uniform sticky from the breezeless heat. The small, harsh lights on top of the television cameras glare into his eyes, like being inches away from a truck's headlights, making him even more uncomfortable-looking than he already is. He answers the obligatory questions with obligatory brevity.

Once the press conference is over, he retreats immediately to his office. In the locker area, Stephenson, showered and in street clothes, finds himself surrounded by a circle of reporters and offers no excuse for what happened. "When you leave the ball up, more bad things are gonna happen than good things. And it's my fault."

Afterward, several reporters go into La Russa's office. One of them, reiterating a question posed to him in the press conference, asks his opinion of Stephenson's pitch selection. La Russa cracks, unable to conceal his irritation, convinced that the intent of the question is to provoke him, get him to say something publicly negative in the heat of the moment. "I have no problem with the way he went about it. Did you hear me say that? So why would you ask that question? I have no problem with the way he went about it. He just didn't pitch well. Why would you ask that?"

He won't show up a player publicly. But privately, he's deeply frustrated with Stephenson's ill-fated dependence on the fastball. He checks with the Secret Weapon to get an accurate tally of how many off-speed pitches Stephenson threw during his three innings: only twelve out of sixty-five, an unhealthy ratio. "The way he gets guys, he's got to be somewhere around even with his curve ball and his changeup," says La Russa as he unpeels his uniform. "But he kept going fastball, fastball, fastball . . ."

By the time he changes into his street clothes, the clubhouse will be empty. He will eat in silence at J Bucks restaurant several miles from the stadium. He will have a book with him, *Flags of Our Fathers,* by James Bradley, about the battle of Iwo Jima. He will climb into his Cardinals-red Cadillac Escalade. He will return to where he lives in St. Louis, a residential suite in a hotel in the city's west end. And he will follow the routine that he has followed since he first went into the foxhole. He will pull out the little lineup cards that he uses to keep score during the games. They help him keep track and stay ahead when he manages, and now he's reviewing certain situations the players faced—the count, an RBI situation or a steal situation or a hit-and-run situation—and whether he reacted appropriately. He uses the cards to learn something about his team that may be of help in the future, just as he uses them to learn something about his opponent that may be of help in the future: little glints of their personalities that came out in pivotal plays. The cards may also reveal something about baseball he has never noticed before, a slice of insight in a game that, after 3,767 of them, still has the capacity to humble him.

As he manages, he also makes tiny little lists of opportunities lost and not lost, moments when maybe he could have stolen a run or prevented one: how, for example, the Expos' Jose Vidro likes to punch it in the hole between first and second with a runner on first, so you shade the second baseman to take away the hole, even if it makes a normal double play more difficult, or that Expos pitcher Tomo Ohka is one of those inverse righties who pitches better against lefties, so you better stock your lineup accordingly. He learned to keep a list from Dick Williams, the manager of the A's when they won world championships in 1972 and 1973. Williams told him that if you don't make notes about a game as it's occurring and review them afterward, you will forget what happened, because of the daily grind of the season. But there aren't many notes here because, let's face it, the game was over by the floodgates of the third when Simon hit the three-run dinger into left.

He will project ahead to Game 2, when Kerry Wood is slated to go for the Cubs. His matchup numbers against the Cardinals are similar to Prior's, cause enough for brooding. But the style with which Wood pitches creates an anxiety for La Russa more terrible than anything else he faces as a manager. He will ponder the lineup. There's not much he can do about the neophytes Bo Hart and Kerry Robinson at the top except stick with them, but he hopes he'll be able to restore Renteria to shortstop. He will pore over every detail.

"I've been able to devote more concentration than most to it," he acknowledges. "My life revolves around the score." And then he admits, "I've had an incredible advantage at a terrific price."

IV

FOR EIGHT MONTHS a year, La Russa lives by himself. During spring training, he stays at a condominium near the Cardinals' complex in Jupiter. When the team moves north for the regular season, he stays in the residential hotel suite while his wife, Elaine, and their two daughters remain 2,000 miles away in Alamo near San Francisco. The support of La Russa's family has enabled him to focus his life 100 percent on baseball during the season. But the number of times he sees them during the season can be counted on two hands—a couple of series against the Giants and the occasional off day when he steals a plane to Oakland for a twenty-four-hour reunion. A plaque on a wall in the La Russas' home sums up their relationship: "We interrupt this marriage to bring you the baseball season."

Their first daughter, Bianca, was born in September 1979, a month after her father had started managing the White Sox. Their second daughter, Devon, was born in August 1982. Their births came when La Russa was most vulnerable, or felt he was most vulnerable — still cutting his teeth as the White Sox' manager. Living in Des Moines, where La Russa had the Triple-A job with the White Sox, Elaine begged her husband not to make the move to the parent club in Chicago. She was eight months pregnant and the timing was beyond bad. Since their marriage on New Year's Eve in 1973, they had moved nearly forty times, shuttling between spring training and the baseball season and Tony's law school studies in the off-season. Most of their possessions were in storage, bed sheets often served as drapes, plants inevitably froze in the car on the way to some strange and faceless apartment filled with the sour odors of transience. The thought of moving again, when Elaine was about to give birth, filled her with dread. *A child, Tony. We're having a child.* But they moved anyway.

Elaine played the baseball wife at first, quietly nursing Bianca in the stands soon after she was born. She loved the game — at least at first she loved it — and she loved even more to keep score. After the games, White Sox owner Bill Veeck held court at a bar called the Bard's Room in the upper reaches of Comiskey Park. Her husband's attendance was mandatory, so Elaine dutifully followed with Bianca, even though they weren't allowed in the actual bar itself, because women simply were not allowed: an unwanted governor on the bawdy, off-color atmosphere with which baseball defined itself back then. Instead, they sat in an adjacent room, falling asleep arm-in-arm until two or three or four in the morning, whenever Veeck, basically an insomniac, had had enough baseball talk for the night.

Elaine also took her husband's intense temperament in stride, even when his body language, after a loss, said *get the hell away from me.* All coaches take losses hard. But Jim Leyland, who coached under La Russa and then went on himself to manage fourteen years for the Pirates and Florida and Colorado, believes that La Russa magnified the impact. "Losing hurts all of us, but it probably hurt Tony too much," said Leyland. And it hurt others as well.

"I was paranoid about not doing the job right," said La Russa of those early years, paranoid about not being prepared, paranoid about missing some millimeter edge there for the taking if he could only find it. He found himself consumed by the philosophy of Paul Richards, who had managed in the big leagues for twelve years, was considered a master innovator, and was the director of the farm system for the Chicago White Sox when La Russa took over: *It's your ass. It's your team. It's your responsibility. There's a strategy for every situation. So start making some decisions.*

Early in the 1983 season, Elaine was taking care of their daughters in Sarasota. The White Sox had just broken spring training there, and she planned to bring the children north to Chicago in late May or early June so the family could be together. One night, she called from Florida: She had just been diagnosed with pneumonia and required hospitalization. La Russa responded to the news with a fateful decision, one that would cement his status as a baseball man but would also define him in another way.

Based on a strong finish in 1982, the expectations were high for the White Sox in 1983. But the season got off to a wretched start, mired at 16 and 24. Floyd Bannister was having trouble winning anything. La Marr Hoyt had a record of 2 and 6 and Carlton Fisk was a mess at the plate. In the middle of May, the team lost eight of nine games. Toronto swept them; then Baltimore swept them. La Russa found himself fighting for his life, or what he mistook for his life. He had a team that was supposed to win, that had spent money on free agents and had good pitching and still wasn't winning. The only reason he was still around was because of the vision of White Sox owner Reinsdorf, who continued to stand by him. So he did what he thought he had to do: He called his sister in Tampa and asked whether she would take care of the kids so he could take care of baseball.

Only with the benefit of hindsight, twenty years of it, did he realize that the right decision was the one he hadn't made. "How was I stupid enough? I should have left the team and taken care of my wife and kids. I've never forgiven myself for that and they've never forgotten."

Looking back on it, Elaine remembers feeling "terribly hurt" when her husband failed to come to Florida. But she also thinks that he was so overwhelmed by the myriad responsibilities of managing—so scared by it on the one hand and so determined on the other to succeed at it—that he lost all sight that there was more to life than his professional life. "I think at that time he was basically clueless," she said. She also believes she enabled his pursuit by taking care of everything that was family-related, so he never had to assume any responsibility. "Don't worry about me," she said to him over the phone when he elected to stay with the team. "Do what you have to do, because I know it's tough for you." She wanted to be supportive, but she believes now that she made a mistake in not demanding more of him personally: insisting upon it. "I know it helped him become what he is and where is he now," she said. "But on a personal level, I should have been more of a Scarlett O'Hara. In retrospect, if I hadn't been so efficient, it would have forced him to become more of an equal partner. He knew that everything would be taken care of. I think it just fed into the monster."

When La Russa moved to the Oakland A's in 1986 after getting fired by the White Sox, the dugout became a further entrapment. He joined the A's in the middle of the season—again carrying the weight of his enormous expectations—and the team responded to him. There came a game in August against the Yankees, one of those no-justice, manage-your-ass-off games in which the A's scratched back from a 6–5 deficit and brought an 8–6 lead into the top of the ninth, when all sorts of weird hell broke loose, the Yankees scoring three times on three singles and two walks and a sacrifice fly.

His wife and daughters were at the game that night. He made them wait an hour and a half before he came out of the clubhouse. He drove home from the stadium silent and stone-faced. He started to give the girls a bath, but he lost his temper and his voice rose and Elaine finished bathing them.

The A's played a night game the next day. It ended relatively early, and after it was over, he called Elaine and asked how long the girls were going to be up. Occasionally, if there was a night game followed by a day game, La Russa had slept in the clubhouse rather than get home late and head back to the park the next morning at 7:30. Elaine told him that the girls wanted to know how the A's had done: If they'd lost, she told her husband, the girls would prefer that their father spend the night at the clubhouse.

When the A's later played the Detroit Tigers, La Russa told Tigers manager Sparky Anderson, whom he also admired deeply, what had happened. Anderson dressed him down and told him that he had to keep his priorities straight. La Russa knew that Anderson was right, but by his own admission, "I still didn't fix it enough. I just got better at hiding it. I still got to the park too early. I still stayed too late."

Gradually, Elaine stopped taking the girls to the games; she didn't want them to become captive to the team's fortunes and their father's moods. "As I got more and more into it, more caught up, dumber and dumber," said La Russa, "she realized that the girls were not going to have a life."

Elaine still loved baseball, but she felt she had to step away from it. She began to feel that baseball ruined families, not simply in terms of the eight months it kept a man from his family, but also in terms of its antifamily rituals. "Baseball is wonderful for separating families," she said. "They are real good at that. Back in Sarasota [during spring training with the White Sox], they still had a stag night. Families were not allowed." She became increasingly independent in the raising of her children: schooling them at home, encouraging their love of dance through the Oakland Ballet. She also saw that even when her husband was at home in body during the season, he was never there in spirit, so consumed by achieving success in Oakland that he went into a place all his own. There could be no balancing work life with home life, particularly because a manager's obligations, unlike a player's, were ceaseless. She had first met Tony in 1972 in Richmond, Virginia, when he was a minor-league player, and his focus then was simple: He wanted to hit .300. But when he became a manager, it was like a tidal wave hit:

strategic responsibilities, off-the-field responsibilities, responsibility for players as needy and mercurial as they were so blessedly talented. When Tony had been a player, he and Elaine had shared everything, talked about everything. But as a manager, the last thing he wanted to talk about when he came home was his job after twelve nonstop hours of it each day, every day, from February to October.

In 1996, when La Russa went to the Cardinals, Elaine elected to stay behind with the children to lead their own lives while he led his. It wasn't for want of love, because the love in the family was intense, but because it was best for everyone involved, a division of labor that made sense in terms of what was important to each of them: Elaine in charge of parenting Bianca and Devon on the West Coast, her husband in the Midwest with nothing between him and baseball. From her origins as a dutiful baseball wife, Elaine realized how crucial it had become for both her and her children to have an identity beyond what her husband and their father did for a living, that he was the only one with his name spread across his shoulders. Back in the days when she had gone to the games, she had always noticed the other baseball wives huddled around in their enclave in the stands. Without being dismissive, she came to the conclusion that they were little more than fans with better seats and greater entitlement. *Where do you go beyond that?* she wondered. *What do you do? What is your life about?* She also noticed something else: how many marriages fell apart once the baseball stopped. It wasn't something she wanted, just as she also knew that if she and the kids simply followed Tony to St. Louis, they would have only ended up resenting him for the disruption he had caused, for the fact that he still would be the man who wasn't there.

"I know to somebody on the outside looking in, it must be strange and different and weird," she said of their separation for two-thirds of every year, "but it's what you have to do to make it work." And it had worked. It had kept their lives intact and made their marriage whole; the separation eased by phone calls to each other every night after every game. But it wasn't perfect, since few things ever are. "It's not the ideal. If I had written about my life and what I expected it to be, even in baseball, it would not be any way like it has been."

As for La Russa himself, there is the hindsight of what didn't have to be, the excess of obsession and the toll it must take. "I have huge regrets about it because I could have done just as well in my job with less significant time spent apart," said La Russa. But what's been done can't be undone. The truth of that particularly struck him one weekend during spring training in the 2001 season, when he saw Mike Matheny and Matheny's wife, Kristin, walking hand in hand.

When Matheny is disappointed with the way he plays, he gets a certain look in his eye, what La Russa knows too well as the "lost look" of someone thrashing himself for something he felt he should have done. When he glimpsed Matheny away from the game simply holding hands with his wife, it so affected him that he did something he almost never does as a manager—he gave unsolicited advice that had nothing to do with baseball.

"Look, you're not asking for this advice but I'm giving it to you. Ignore it. Tell me to shut up," La Russa said. "But it moved my heart to see you holding your wife's hand. Just before you held hands, you had that lost look because of something you did on the field—getting too hard on yourself. I made enormous mistakes with my wife and kids; now I have terrific regrets and it's too late to do much about it."

He admired Matheny's willingness to take responsibility in an era when fewer and fewer athletes ever take responsibility. He didn't want Matheny to lose his capacity for self-critique, but he also urged him not to let those thoughts spill over into his family. "The more you think about it, it only gets worse," he told him. "And when you're with your family, there's nothing you can do about it until you get to the park tomorrow."

He hoped that Matheny would listen to what he had to say, even though he knew it was something he was not remotely capable of himself. Which is why, as the clubhouse quickly empties out after Game 1 and the players attend to their lives beyond baseball—because there is life beyond baseball—La Russa is still there.

GAME
TWO

7

GONZALEZ MUST PAY

I

● ● ● BY ELEVEN on Wednesday morning, when he arrives at the clubhouse, La Russa has sublimated the sour memories of Game 1. Although he had hoped for the best before the game yesterday, he'd prepared for the worst. There's no use dwelling on it, although the simple reality is that the Cards have to win the next two to take the three-game series.

During batting practice in the watery afternoon light, La Russa walks the field with a red fungo bat in hand. The tapestry of batting practice is elaborately stitched, an ingenious workmanship behind the strategically placed cages and nets that rim the basepaths. Inside the empty stadium, its rhythm has deceptive leisure; it's the only time ever in baseball when all the puzzle pieces are simultaneously engaged: hitting, running, fielding, throwing. La Russa takes it all in, roaming here, roaming there, seeking omens.

He watches Edgar Renteria scuttling along the sandy apron of the infield, tucking the ball into his glove and then making the throw to first. Will his ailing back keep him out of another game at shortstop? La Russa needs Renteria tonight because he is a superb hitter, and he needs him because of his golden glove, his footwork as light and fluid as a ballet dancer's, able to reach deep into the canyon crevice between second and third.

There's also Renteria's attitude, the combination of competition and puckish joy that spills onto the other players. Team chemistry is its own odyssey, and different players contribute different catalysts. Rolen leads largely on the basis of his grinding performance; outside the field he's as careful with his words as he is with his emotions, no air leaking out of the tires. Albert Pujols leads because he is the great Pujols. Woody Williams leads because beneath his Texas twang is a pitcher who simply guts it out.

Renteria leads with *joie de vivre,* developing handshakes for each player on the team, customized to his own idiosyncrasies, ending hitters' meetings with his Latin hip-hop chirp of *Let's go play, dawg!!* He is the favorite of his fellow teammates, but his sense of the game makes him more than just another clubhouse cutup. He doesn't wilt when the heat is on. At the age of twenty-two in the eleventh inning of Game 7 of the 1997 World Series, he delivered the game-winning single for the Marlins off a breaking ball from the Indians' Charles Nagy. It was a feat for anyone that young, but behind it was an untold story of baseball intelligence: Jim Leyland, the Marlins' manager at the time, is convinced that Renteria set up Nagy with a deception worthy of a fifteen-year veteran, jumping out of the way of a first-pitch Nagy breaking ball to suggest that he was mystified by it, when he only wanted Nagy to *think* he was fooled so he would get another breaking ball on the next pitch.

Renteria gathers up a few more grounders; then he takes his turn hitting in the cage, fifteen at-bats. He turns to La Russa afterward and gives a thumbs-up. Renteria doesn't look 100 percent to La Russa, but he appreciates the determination Renteria's gesture implies. He's managed players who, given any reason to take a free pass because of the threats posed by tonight's opposing pitcher, would ride the entire bus system with it. So Renteria's decision has meaning to him, gives him a lift.

A few minutes later, La Russa's mood is yanked back to half-mast when he hears that Dusty Baker has juggled the Cubs' pitching rotation in anticipation of another series against the Cards starting Monday. The timing of it—on the heels of Prior's effortless victory last night even without his usual sharpness—only taunts him.

"Prior's starting on Monday," a reporter informs La Russa.

"Says who?"

"Dusty."

"The *Tribune* had him starting Sunday."

"Dusty said it today."

"I hope they get their *ass* beat on Sunday," he snaps like a door slamming shut.

Back at his desk, La Russa feels even more tense than he usually feels before a game. As he mulls the matchups, he knows that the Cards cannot lose tonight if they want to remain in the division race. There is still ample baseball left to be played: thirty-one games. But Game 2 is a rarity: It emits psychological reverberations capable of dictating the rest of the season. Beating the Cards tonight will guarantee the Cubs a series win at Busch Stadium, imbuing them with more confidence than ever that their time has finally come.

At least tonight's matchups offer the hope of a more even contest than in Game 1. The Cards' starter, Williams, has the better record—14 and 6—and earned his first stint as an All-Star this season. Kerry Wood, on the hill for Chicago, has struck out 208 batters in 168 innings. Tonight's game also promises to be one of memorable and beautiful contradiction because the starters' styles are so different: Dada versus minimalist, surfer versus swimmer, punk rocker versus song stylist. Williams was drafted in the twenty-eighth round as a shortstop out of college. Wood was picked fourth in the first round, already a bit of a legend because of his smoke artistry at Grand Prairie High School in Texas, with the inevitable comparisons to those other Lone Star legends: Ryan and Clemens. Williams knocked around the minors for five years and hardly became a household word when he finally made it to the majors. Wood stayed in the minors for only two seasons and in 1998, as a rookie, struck out twenty Astros to tie a major-league record. Williams is methodical on the mound, plugging away. Wood, five inches taller, with a small, punched-in face and a sneer across the lips, looks like the kind of guy who cuts you off on the Interstate and then gives you the finger. Williams wins with command and location. Wood wins by letting it rip.

One of three different Woods will take the mound tonight.

There's Wild Wood, who has no idea where any of his pitches is going and walks too many batters to be effective. There is Controlled Wood, who consciously tries to keep the ball around the strike zone and not walk batters. Then there's Effectively Wild Wood, with enough pitches in and around the strike zone to make him consistent but a few every now and then where he's simply not sure where they're going to go.

Williams has no similar dramatic aspirations. Like a lot of major-league pitchers, he's plain-looking, really, with a trim beard and no outward hint of the physique that can harness a ball on the mound. The stuff he throws is low-octane, but it leaves a trail of baffled hitters. This is a guy they *should hit,* should just *get to.* But they don't, because Williams has learned how to pitch; he's a textbook example of how finesse can trump velocity.

When asked to describe Williams, Dave Duncan uses one word —"pitchmaker"—and, as is his style, doesn't elucidate further. He goes back to his computer in his Spartan office, as if maybe he's already said too much. But coming from Duncan, it speaks volumes, the ultimate compliment from teacher to pupil. Williams throws three kinds of fastballs: the straight four-seamer, the cutter, and the sinker. The four-seamer is about speed; the cutter and the sinker, about movement and location. With the cutter going one way and the sinker the other, his fastball works both sides of the plate, creating particular havoc for right-handed and left-handed hitters. They don't know whether it'll run in on them or away from them, which makes them off-balance. They lose their senses in a fog of uncertainty. When he strikes out hitters, they retreat to the dugout, bitching about how in hell could they just have struck out against a guy who throws so slow—*90! Are you kidding me, I haven't seen 90 since Little League.* It addles them beyond a particular at-bat. Next time up, they arrive at the plate frustrated, and Williams's style only breeds more frustration: *The son-of-a-bitch just did it to me again.* Compounding the frustration are his three quality off-speed pitches—a curve, a slider, and a changeup—all of which he can locate with precision.

Williams is also the ultimate survivor, proof that heart still counts for something, that behind the dizzying array of statistical predictors and indicators is the exquisite mystery of flesh and blood. With San Diego in 2000, he opened the season with a 3-2 record. He was off to a good start, the only hindrance an odd numbness in the fingers of his pitching hand. He let it go—simply the price of doing business, he figured—and it hardly hampered him when he went eight and a third innings against Florida in early May. But the numbness persisted. A series of medical tests found an aneurysm near his right armpit. Had it gone untreated, it could have meant the amputation of his pitching hand. He underwent successful surgery in early June and was back in the Padres' rotation by July.

The essence of Williams—why La Russa and Duncan coveted him—could be seen in how he performed on his return. He pitched four complete games and recorded the best ERA of his career as a starter. As a Cardinal, he's become another of Duncan's prodigies, an ex-.500 pitcher whose winning percentage has increased by nearly a hundred points. In the days before he starts, Williams spends hours watching tape of past performances, feeding a video addiction almost as intense as Mike Matheny exhibits as catcher. He watches what he did with the hitters, how he got to them, and he compares his outings with the Cardinals to what he did in San Diego to make sure he doesn't fall into any bad habits. When he meets with Duncan before Game 2 to go over the Cubs hitters, he already has formulated a strategy to use against them. It relieves Duncan of the need to plot out the game plan entirely on his own, as he had to do with Garrett Stephenson. This meeting is much more productive than yesterday's—all the fat trimmed. Williams leaves with a pinpoint sense of what needs to be executed, how Ramon Martinez in the two-hole is susceptible to the slider, how Alex Gonzalez at the seven-spot likes sitting on curve balls late in the game, particularly if he has seen a lot of them, how Damian Miller at the eight-spot can't resist high heat, even if it's over his head.

Williams also won't be daunted by Stephenson's three nemeses. Kenny Lofton and Aramis Ramirez are a combined 9 for 40 against him, with only one dinger. Randall Simon's numbers are so lackluster that he isn't even starting tonight. In fact, the matchups throughout the Cubs' lineup benefit Williams nicely:

LOFTON	5-20-0
MARTINEZ	2-10-0
SOSA	2-14-1
ALOU	6-26-1
KARROS	8-29-1
RAMIREZ	4-20-1
GONZALEZ	3-14-0
MILLER	7-14-0

When La Russa looks at them, he doesn't smile, but he also doesn't grimace. The biggest threat comes from Miller in the eight-spot, which, if you're the opposing manager, would appear to be just the spot where you want a batter who has a bead on your pitcher. But La Russa perceives a potential danger there, obscure to the baseball layman but ominous to La Russa. He obviously fears Miller's coming up with men on base and maybe driving them home. But what also worries him is Miller's coming up with *two outs* and the *bases empty,* which seems like the very scenario a manager would want: Even if Miller does get on base, Wood comes up next in the pitcher's spot. But La Russa doesn't want to end the inning with Wood, because that might give the Cubs an insidious advantage when they start the next frame with the top of their order. So it's not only that Miller gets hits off Williams; Miller may get a hit tonight that imperceptibly tilts the game—as delicate a system of pulleys and levers as has ever been created—toward the Cubs.

La Russa frets over that behind his desk. But another sheet of stats reminds him of how meticulously ruthless Williams can be against the Cubs, the ball zigzagging all over the plate, like a pesky fly. The last time he faced them, about seven weeks ago, Williams went seven and two-thirds innings in a 4–1 Cardinals win to run his record to 11 and 3.

Of course, Wood's matchups against the Cardinals hitters also benefit him nicely:

ROBINSON	4-16-0
HART	1-2-0
PUJOLS	7-23-3
EDMONDS	8-27-2
ROLEN	3-16-1
MARTINEZ	3-17-2
RENTERIA	5-27-0
MATHENY	1-13-0

There are homers to be had, but with the exception of Pujols and Edmonds, nobody is hitting above .250 against Wood. Once you get past the cleanup spot, nobody is hitting above .200 against him.

If the two pitchers are on tonight, Williams pitching like Williams and Wood pitching like Effectively Wild Wood, the game will be taut and low scoring, an edge-of-the-seat nail biter from the top of the first to wherever it ends. But there's something else gnawing away at La Russa. Wood's past performance hints that tonight, the Cardinals' manager may have to make what he calls the "most gut-wrenching decision of all" in twenty-five years of making them, an agony affecting him even worse than losing.

II

WHAT WILL HE DO if he thinks that Wood is intentionally throwing at one of his hitters? Wood has already plunked fourteen batters this season. He not only leads the league but also is on a pace to hit more batters than any National League pitcher since 1907. There's certainly no love lost between him and Pujols after he brushed him back with a pitch on July 4 at Wrigley Field. His blazing high-and-tight fastball, which keeps hitters uneasy, may well be his most effective weapon. Which is why La Russa is feeling so on edge.

"There are so many conflicting emotions," he says, when your batter gets hit. Because how do you sort it out? How do you know for sure that the pitcher acted intentionally? Pitchers themselves, even his own, were generally mum about it, their own version of

Omerta. Throughout baseball in general, the whole subject was taboo, never honestly discussed, never acknowledged, although it is deeply embedded in the game.

Some managers ignored it. They expected the players to take care of it themselves. But La Russa knew that such inaction bred enormous ill will down the length of the dugout, the possibility of a silent but corrosive insurrection against a weak manager who wouldn't defend his own guys. A player took it personally when he got hit. The results could be lethal, not only physically but also mentally, in the form of a persistent fear that accompanied him on every trip he made to the plate. So at the very least, hitters expected their pitchers to protect them against that arrogant son-of-a-bitch on the mound who had just used them for target practice because his stuff wasn't good enough on its own. And if they thought they couldn't rely on their pitchers to defend them, they would sit in the dugout and become more angry and upset than they were already. But if a pitcher did respond on his own, he might pick the wrong victim or a strategically inopportune moment.

La Russa was managing Double-A in Knoxville in 1978 when Harold Baines, a beautiful hitter and the first pick of the 1977 draft, arrived there on his way up the White Sox farm system. From his own years of managing, Paul Richards, then the farm system director for the White Sox, knew only too well what pitchers might do when confronted with young hitters capable of launching a moon shot. So he gave La Russa some instructions on how to manage: "You must make sure Harold Baines doesn't get abused."

If a pitcher hit Baines, Richards told La Russa, don't let it fester. Don't let it spread beyond your control. Don't let the players determine how to retaliate. If Baines did get plunked, Richards added, it mightn't be such a bad policy to pick the best hitter on the opposing team and make sure your pitcher plunked him. A batter for a batter in the Hammurabi Code of baseball, a deterrent against future attacks.

La Russa took Richards's advice to heart. Over the years, he made it clear to his players that the Hammurabi Code was in his hands, not theirs. He told his teams: "If you think you should be protected, and there's no retaliation, you don't go to your pitcher. You come to me." La Russa would determine whether the plunk had been intentional and how to respond.

In determining whether a pitcher had behaved with malice aforethought, La Russa always checked with Duncan. As a pitching coach, he could be more dispassionate, could better tell the difference between a pitch that had simply wandered off course and one that had found its target.

Duncan's input helped, but the feelings that swirled through him were still agonizing, still worse than losing—the most difficult feelings he ever had to face in baseball. In virtually every case of a batter getting hit by a pitch, La Russa and most other managers went through a traumatic struggle to determine real intent. Much of the uncertainty had to do with teams needing to pitch inside to be successful. In ratcheting down an opponent's offense, the advantages of pitching inside were too numerous to avoid: the very reason Duncan had tried to pound the philosophy into Garrett Stephenson the night before. It was undeniable that by making a hitter "inside conscious," the plate then widened for a pitcher to make a pitch away. It was also undeniable that hitters, in combating pitches inside so they wouldn't get jammed, tended to start their swing early, which in turn made them susceptible to slower off-speed pitches. In today's style of baseball, where more and more hitters are able to reach the outside of the plate and get the thick head of the barrel on the ball, the only way to move them off that territory is to pitch inside.

Because pitchers do pitch inside, batters inevitably are going to get hit, and therein lay La Russa's dilemma. Was it simply a pitch that had gotten away? Was the pitcher trying to intimidate by going inside? Or was the pitcher taking a cheap shot and deliberately plunking someone? Other variables had to be considered as well: the pitcher's own reputation as a cheap-shot artist, and the club he was pitching for (some teams hit batters often enough to suggest that they'd made a policy of it). La Russa was also aware of his own innate bias, the same bias that all managers have: It was *intentional* if one of his batters got hit, *accidental* if one of his pitchers hit a batter. If sparks flew during a game, it was often this built-in bias that caused them. It's also why, when La Russa's batters were on the receiving end, he went to Duncan for help.

But once you were convinced of malicious intent, deciding how to respond got only more fraught. Because this wasn't about playing a hit-and-run. This wasn't about putting on a bunt. This wasn't about pushing for a run or saving one. This was about *hitting* someone. "If you put yourself in the manager's shoes, the responsibilities and the consequences are huge," La Russa points out. "You're telling someone on your club to hit someone on the other side." Thrown baseballs had ended careers; one had killed a major-league player. In meetings with pitchers during spring training, he issued clear guidelines: Any kind of message had to be aimed at the ribs or below, and nothing above the shoulder would be tolerated.

III

LA RUSSA KNEW that over the years, he had gained a reputation for being vengeful when perhaps vengeance wasn't necessary. He was also known as something of a headhunter himself, but La Russa says that he has never told a pitcher to throw at a hitter simply because he was too dangerous at the plate and needed to be quieted down. "If a guy is hitting good against us, I have never told a pitcher to go out and drill him. I have said, 'Pitch the guy tough, pitch the guy different.' If a pitcher does something on his own, I will take him out. I will not hesitate. You can pitch a hitter inside. You can try to open up the plate on him, get him to speed up the bat. But you do not drill him."

In July 1995, the A's played the Blue Jays at the Coliseum in Oakland. In the second inning, Mark McGwire, batting for the A's, got to a tough slider away and blasted a home run. The next day, David Cone, pitching for the Blue Jays, hit McGwire in the head, and McGwire had to go to the hospital with a possible concussion. Cone pitched into the eighth inning without giving up a walk, bringing La Russa to what he considered an obvious conclusion —other than beaning McGwire, Cone had exhibited no control problems whatsoever. He was furious, convinced that McGwire had been hit, *in the head,* as retribution for his home run the night before.

Taking the Hammurabi Code into his own hands, La Russa ordered Mike Harkey to hit the Blue Jays' Joe Carter. Harkey did so, literally bending over backward to obey the rule laid down in spring training. He hit Carter in the buttocks, an act of fleshy mercy compared to what La Russa believed Cone had done. But Carter didn't like it. He pointed to La Russa glowering in the dugout and yelled at him.

"*You* caused all this!"

Which brought La Russa steaming out toward Carter.

"We have a guy in the hospital with a concussion, and you're whining about a *bee sting!*"

Will Clark was more matter-of-fact than Carter when *he* got hit in retaliation for a pitcher again drilling McGwire. Clark had once signed a bat for the animal rescue foundation La Russa had formed so it could be auctioned off to raise money, and he sent a message back afterward:

"Tell the manager, no more autographs."

In older days, verbal histrionics rarely intruded on the quiet cause-and-effect of a pitcher punishing a hitter for some perceived slight. Pitchers like Bob Gibson and Don Drysdale laid down a clear-cut rule: In the fight for the Gaza Strip of the plate, middle away belonged to them, and middle in belonged to the hitter. As long as you didn't venture over into the pitcher's territory, you were okay. But if you did, you were going to get banged, and you had no one but yourself to blame. Naiveté, rookie eagerness, ignorance of the rule—none of it could excuse you from your fate.

Umpires, on the directive of major-league baseball, have become far more vigilant about keeping the game from devolving into a dogfight. When a hitter gets drilled, umpires are more inclined to warn both teams that any retaliation will get the offending pitcher and his manager ejected. But no amount of vigilance can erase the Hammurabian compulsion toward justice.

Early this season in Colorado, the pitcher on the mound for the

Rockies, Dan Miceli, threw one at Edmonds's legs in the twelfth, forcing him to dance out of the way. La Russa wasn't quite sure how it was intended. Pitchers have to throw inside at Coors Field more than at any other major-league stadium because the ball carries so far in the mile-high air. If you don't, hitters simply whack it like a tee ball. Which is pretty much what Edmonds had been doing all night, 4 for 6 with a homer, two doubles, and five RBIs.

In the second game of the series, Nelson Cruz's first pitch to Edmonds was up and in; he went down to dodge it. The second pitch hit him in the shoulder. Now La Russa had an answer to the question he had been agonizing over the night before.

He waited for the right time and the right batter to make what he considered the right move, in this case, a message. In the third inning, Cards pitcher Brett Tomko threw behind Todd Helton, the Rockies' best hitter—a shot across his bow that responded to Cruz's assault, while keeping Tomko in the game. Home plate umpire Mike DiMuro promptly put the warning into both benches. But La Russa wasn't so sure it was over.

"This guy Cruz thinks he's John Wayne," he told DiMuro. "He's gonna take another shot." And in the top of the seventh, he hit Tino Martinez. Cruz and Clint Hurdle, the Rockies' manager, were immediately ejected. But their ouster did little to soothe La Russa, still furious over what he saw as the original gutlessness of hitting Edmonds in the first inning because his bat had been so hot the night before.

The Rockies' bench coach was Jamie Quirk. In the early 1990s, Quirk had played for La Russa. He later went into coaching, and La Russa had recommended him as a manager. He considered Quirk a friend. But he also felt that Quirk had crossed a line, that he had played a role in what had happened, or at least could have done more to prevent Edmonds from getting drilled in the first place. He had Quirk's cell phone number and he left a message after the game. "You don't take cheap shots," he told him. "Just because Edmonds is swinging good, you just don't go out and drill him."

After the next-day's game, La Russa was heading to the team bus when he saw Quirk in the hallway that leads to the Coors Field parking lot. By now, La Russa had had twenty-four hours to ponder what had happened. He'd learned the hard way not to confront someone too soon after he had done something during a game that upset La Russa. One night in 1996, after the Cardinals had dropped a close game to the Braves, he zeroed in on John Mabry as a symbol of the loss because he played first and had been laughing at something with Fred McGriff after McGriff had gotten on base. Immediately after the game, La Russa went off on Mabry, accused him of not caring enough—too busy chatting with McGriff—to give the game the competitive focus it demanded. As soon as the words left his mouth, he knew he had made a mistake—looking for someone to kick after a tough loss and finding the wrong target in Mabry, who was a competitor. La Russa apologized the next day, but their relationship had been affected. Mabry began to mistrust his manager; his performance suffered. He ended up going elsewhere, and La Russa believes that his impromptu outburst caused Mabry's decline with the Cardinals.* As a result, La Russa began to enforce a twenty-four-hour gag order on himself: He would keep his mouth shut for a full day to assess how much of his anger might be legitimate and how much might be caused by the fresh pain of losing. If he still felt agitated, the twenty-four-hour rule also gave him time to figure out something constructive to say.

With a full day of distance from the current skirmish, La Russa could do something like that with Quirk here. They were friends. He had recommended *Quirk* for jobs. *Quirk* had played for him. Seeing Quirk in the hallway, he had the opportunity to chalk up what had happened to the passion that sometimes overtakes the game. Instead, still disappointed, he looked right through him as if he weren't there.

Less than two weeks later, the Cards were playing the Diamondbacks at Busch. It was a pitcher's duel between Tomko and Miguel Batista, scoreless into the fifth when Arizona scratched out a run on doubles by Craig Counsell and David Dellucci. In the bot-

---

* Mabry subsequently returned to the Cardinals for the 2004 season. He hit .296, an indication that he accepted La Russa's apology.

tom of the fifth, Tino Martinez led off for the Cardinals. Batista threw him a ball. Then he hit him in the right shoulder blade, and then he stared at him after he hit him, rubbing it in: Take that, you *son-of-a-bitch*.

Before the game, La Russa had felt the fluttering in his stomach over the prospect of facing Batista and what could occur. He was in that category of pitcher who had gained a reputation for plunking batters. But La Russa didn't anticipate it happening, not with the score 1–0. Now that it had, a shot near Martinez's head, the fluttering rose into the dread of how to respond. It was the stare-down that led La Russa to believe that he had acted on his own, that there might have been bad blood between Martinez and Batista left over from the 2001 World Series between the Diamondbacks and the Yankees. So now the gut-wrenching question arose again: *What do you do about it?* La Russa took up his inner Godot dialogue:

We've gotten hit a lot.

It's not coincidental that we lead the league in hitting and getting hit by pitches.

We don't see Arizona again until the end of the year.

Tino has been hit four times this season, and the first three times, I didn't do squat.

We have to send the right message.

La Russa scanned the Diamondback lineup and immediately found the appropriate subject for retaliation against, given the situation. It was Luis Gonzalez, who had hit fifty-seven home runs two seasons earlier in 2001 and had so nobly gutted it out against Mariano Rivera's rapier cutter in the ninth inning of the seventh game with one out, blooping it into center like a falling Easter egg to win the World Series for the Diamondbacks. On the basis of talent alone, Gonzalez was the obvious candidate. But the choice was complicated by personal entanglements.

Gonzalez, Martinez, and La Russa were all from Tampa. They had all gone to the *same* high school, Jefferson High, in Tampa. And Gonzalez was one of the classiest guys in the league, doing frequent charity work in the off-season because it meant something to him and not because some agent told him that he should do it for his image. One of those charity events had been a special appearance of behalf of La Russa's foundation.

There were strategic complications too. Once La Russa decided that he had to do something and that Gonzalez was the guy he had to do something to, the score was 1–0 Arizona in the eighth. Given where Gonzalez fell in the order, he might not get another at-bat, and justice might be denied.

So when the Diamondbacks' Junior Spivey singled and stole second with two outs, it was, oddly, a blessing for La Russa, the opening he needed. The count had run to 1 and 2 on the batter at the plate, Chad Moeller, when Spivey stole. Suddenly, La Russa gave the sign to intentionally walk Moeller. With first base open, it appeared as if he had simply decided to pitch around Moeller. But that was just the cover: Moeller's free ride to first had nothing to do with thinking that the next batter would be an easier out.

He didn't want Moeller to end the eighth inning with an out, because that might put Gonzalez out of reach in the ninth, as he would be batting fourth. So he put Moeller on even though the count had run to 1 and 2. He took a chance on runners on first and second in a 1–0 nail biter, just to make sure that Gonzalez would definitely come up in the ninth.

The score was still 1–0 going into the top of the ninth when La Russa brought in Jeff Fassero. He told the reliever that he hoped he could get the first two batters out. And then he told him to do what is standard in a situation such as this—throw a breaking ball away so it looks like he's having a little control problem, then hit Gonzalez in the ribs with the next pitch. Fassero executed it perfectly. Gonzalez got hit. Fassero and La Russa were both ejected, and the Cards ended up losing 1–0.

La Russa knew that he had possibly affected the game's outcome for the sake of retaliation. He also realized that his friendship with Gonzalez might suffer. That bothered him immensely because Gonzalez, in a game so littered with go-through-the-motion fakes, was the real thing both professionally and personally. After the game, he left him a message on his cell phone, just like he had done with Quirk, trying to explain his reasoning:

"You can think what you want, but you check with anybody who has played with me. We don't hit someone just because they're hitting good against us."

He still didn't like what he had done. He sifted through the layers of his decision deep into the night and through the off day on Monday before the team chartered out to Atlanta. He knew that if he didn't protect his players, didn't stand up for them, the respect they gave him—a porous bond to begin with in the distracted world of the modern athlete—would crumble away. Richards had once told him that sometimes, you have to be willing to lose a game to win more later. And this, La Russa concluded, had been one of those times.

La Russa isn't sure that Wood intentionally pitches up into the danger zone as much as he doesn't quite know where the ball will land when he throws inside. Wood himself insists that his victims have been plunked by innocent curve balls that simply got away from him. But Wood's role models are Ryan and Clemens, pitchers without qualms about drilling batters. La Russa also believes that Wood is susceptible to the media frenzy that occurs over the prospect of beanball wars, stories that only encourage young power pitchers to take the bait and feel compelled to strut their machismo. Because Wood is normally so aggressive—trying to reach the mid- and upper nineties with his fastball—he tends to hurry and fall out of his delivery, which causes the ball to sail even more than usual into uncharted territory. But to La Russa, that's not much of an excuse when the result is a batter getting hit. It's still a dangerous headball, which is why La Russa is also so adamant that the baseball commissioner's office give out automatic suspensions in all but obviously accidental circumstances. If major-league baseball is not proactive, he is convinced, more and more players will get seriously injured. "The key," he explains, "is whether or not a club is trying to pitch inside just for effect. That's okay if they have command. But if they're pitching without command and guys keep getting hit, then at some point, they should quit doing it. We're not gonna be targets."

8

LIGHT MY FIRE

I

● ● ● IT QUICKLY becomes clear that Kerry Wood and Woody Williams are waging the pitchers' duel La Russa anticipated tonight. Each stays within the sphere of his respective strengths and style: Wood flailing about like a restless child; Williams so economical he's almost invisible.

In the top of the first, Williams dispatches the Cubs with fourteen pitches, unfazed by a double that Ramon Martinez, batting in the two-hole, strokes into the right-field gap. Wood follows with a style whose only constants are unpredictability and success. His fastballs fly so high that the Cubs' catcher, Damian Miller, reaches for them as though he's scurrying up a stepladder. His breaking balls fall off the plate because he finishes his delivery in such haste. Then he uncorks a rat-a-tat of nasty stuff in and around the zone, striking out Bo Hart and Scott Rolen. He seems all confusion on the mound: *Hey, it's not my fault the ball won't tell me where it's going.* But it's misleading. La Russa can already tell that they're facing Effectively Wild Wood tonight — hitters at the mercy of his orchestrated whimsy.

Through three innings, Williams is achieving the same end by the opposite means. He's thrown only thirty-nine pitches, including a five-pitch second inning. By the bottom of the third, when Kerry Robinson comes to bat for the Cardinals with one out and nobody on, Wood's flailing has already produced four strikeouts. Robinson's in the lineup by default because of the injury to J.D. Drew, and it looks like that way when Wood sends him a nasty slider, and he responds by weakly swinging through it. Wood comes next with a fastball outside and away on the black. The pitch is more difficult to handle than the first one, that lethal combination of high-heat velocity and location you see sometimes on the Autobahn. But Robinson stays with it and slaps a single past third base, going the opposite way with it. In the dugout, La Russa has a lovely thought about Robinson: *That was a great piece of hitting.*

It proves to him what Robinson can do if he sets aside his sulkiness about not playing every day and accepts his place in the puzzle, not some tiny piece, but of ample size because of what a strong bench can do for a team beyond trying to capitalize on occasional playing time. It is a difficult role, and La Russa readily concedes the difficulty. But the spirit of bench players is as essential to the chemistry of a team as the spirit of a star player. You have a star player who treats his colleagues like inferiors; that's an essential edge your team has lost. You have a bench player who sulks; that's a valuable edge lost as well. Which is why La Russa wishes that Robinson would follow the lead of Eddie Perez and Miguel Cairo, bench players who not only do the obvious—make the most of their playing opportunities—but also act as assistant coaches for the very reason that they can soak up the game. They can often figure out an opposing pitcher's pitch beforehand because of the way he holds the ball in the glove. They can offer subtle advice to infielders who are getting into the habit of laying back on the ball instead of charging, or sweetly scold fellow hitters who are getting pull-happy and flying open at the plate.

Certainly Robinson's approach to the game has improved since an episode several weeks ago against the Phillies when he was pinch-hitting and took a pitch pretty much down the pipe for a strike instead of swinging, then ultimately struck out. La Russa likes his hitters to be aggressive on the first good strike they get in an RBI situation. Especially pinch hitters, because they often get only *one* good strike in the entire at-bat. La Russa and his coaches inculcate this philosophy into players from the earliest stages of spring training, and Robinson's failure to apply it irked the manager. After the game, he summoned Robinson into the visiting manager's office in the penal colony of Veterans Stadium to discuss why he wasn't following such a basic precept.

"As a general run-producing philosophy," he reminded Robinson, "you have to be aggressive and ready to swing at the first good strike. It's true for most hitters. Especially true for pinch hitters."

"No, no. I don't challenge that philosophy," said Robinson.

"Well, that's good because it's been developed by watching too many guys produce."

Case closed. Meeting over. Since then, Robinson seems to have given the basics more of the respect they deserve.

To Robinson, this hit against Wood is further proof that he should be playing *every day,* that with a little faith, he can be another Juan Pierre. He knows he's no slugger, but he has speed; he can steal and stretch doubles into triples. And he believes that he can handle the bat better when he plays every day, because he admits that it's difficult for him to get into any kind of rhythm coming off the bench, a cold can of soup barely heated up. On a visceral level, coming off the bench profoundly contradicts his self-image. "This is my third year in the big leagues, and I don't want to just be labeled as a bench guy without even having an opportunity to start at the big-league level," he says.

He has impressive local lineage, a heralded three-sport St. Louis high school athlete who set school records in 1991 for the highest batting average (.557) and for the most goals scored in hockey (twenty-nine). His first year with the Cardinals in 2001 was the first time he had ever been on the bench in his athletic life. During the following season and this one as well, he has made a deliberate attempt not to think about baseball except when he has to —when he's taking batting practice or loosening up in the cage in the fourth or fifth because he may go in at some point or on those rare occasions when he's in the game from the beginning. Otherwise, he would only dwell on not starting. "If I go there and think about it all the time, I'll drive myself crazy," he confesses. And now that he is getting a chance to play regularly, he does wonder whether his moment has arrived. "Maybe this is my time now, for all I know," he muses.

La Russa would like nothing better than for now to be Robinson's time, although one sweet hit is still a single. It's not stealing home in the bottom of the ninth. It's not a bases-clearing double. It's pretty much what you should expect from Robinson under the circumstances that he is not an everyday player.

Because it should be Drew in there, the pivotal series in the pivotal point in the season with first place at stake and the possibility of one of those momentum surges that pushes you through September and into the shadowy, sublime October light when playoff games are waged. It is the reason to play baseball—getting to that moment where, as Dusty Baker put it just before tonight's game, the "leaves turn to brown and somebody wears the crown."

History is here. Finely aged rivalry is here. Tension is here. Competition is here. Everything you want in baseball is here, everything you can still hope for in this era of narrowing expectations. Except for Drew, the parable of the modern-day athlete.

II

DREW ROCKS FIREBALLERS like Prior and Wood. He rocks anybody who thinks he can throw fire by him. Like he did earlier this season when he hit a 514-foot dinger, the longest home run ever recorded at Busch by a left-handed hitter, blocked in its flight by the scoreboard or it would have gone even farther. He's pressure-proof, like the home run he hit in the eighth inning off Curt Schilling's forkball in the deciding fifth game of the 2001 playoffs to tie the game at 1–1. It's why the Cardinals spent $7 million on Drew as a first-round pick in the 1998 draft. It's why, when they got their first look at him in the uniform—saw the speed, the fluid left-handed stroke, the way the ball just launched off the bat—they thought *Mickey Mantle,* as dangerous, maybe, as thinking *Sandy Koufax* when they saw Rick Ankiel.

But his talent was that big, and La Russa wonders whether perhaps it still is that big, submerged within that remote exterior like other great players have been remote, wearing a Cardinals uniform but never really a part of the team, alone in the clubhouse most of the time, shunning membership in any of the cliques, saying little in his southern accent as thick as an Irish brogue, shuffling to the cage during batting practice like a tired old man, taking his cuts in silence and then shuffling away in silence. And then he does something prodigious and spectacular and beautiful because his swing is so beautiful, tight and compact and as effortless as walking. But La Russa has resigned himself to wondering whether he'll ever get to *it,* whatever that *it* is at this point. And as much as he believes that there is nothing he can do—that he can't create fire—part of him knows that his very job as a manager is to create fire, whatever its temperament. And it pulls at him that his best wasn't good enough.

Like others, La Russa's early hopes for him were maybe too heady; there's no surer doom for anyone than great expectations. In the history of intercollegiate baseball, it was difficult to find someone with more of a can't-miss pedigree. In his junior year at Florida State in 1997, Drew recorded the first 30-30 season in NCAA Division One history, with thirty-one homers and thirty-two steals, but that was just a small part of the almost supernatural epic told by his statistics:

G	AB	R	H	2B	3B	HR	RBI	BB	SO	SB	AVG	OBP	SLG.
67	233	110	106	15	3	31	100	84	37	32	.455	.599	.961

The irresistible comparisons came out—that here, after all those years and all that sifting in the dust of some diamond for gold— was a true find, a natural stroke as pure as Musial and Mantle and Aaron and Mays. The references put him under a cloud from the very beginning, the notion that he was bound for the Hall of Fame before he'd had a single big-league at-bat.

As such, he was the *unsuperstar.* Other players talked about him, much of it disparaging, much of it along the lines of *Who the hell does this kid think he is?* and *Who cares how many homers he hit at Florida State?* He won few admirers when the Phillies made him the first-draft pick and he scoffed at their record-setting offer: $2.6 million signing bonus and $6 million overall for a five-year contract. Through his agent, he said that he was thinking more in terms of a $5 million signing bonus and $11 million overall. Drew ultimately refused to sign with the Phillies, an act that drew headlines and condemnation around the country. Fairly or unfairly, he was portrayed over and over as selfish, the personification of everything wrong with the modern young athlete. He played for the St. Paul Saints in the Independent League and re-entered the draft in 1998. The Cardinals made him the fifth pick overall and signed him to a four-year deal worth $7 million guaranteed and as much as $9 million, including various bonuses and incentives. The signing was announced with much fanfare and ballyhoo, particularly because the Cardinals had done what the Phillies could not. In the euphoria of it, only one question remained: How good was he?

He came up to the Cardinals in September 1998 after a mere forty-five games in the minors at Arkansas and Memphis. In his first eight games, he batted .350, with three homers, seven RBIs, and a .900 slugging percentage. La Russa said that he hadn't seen a better first week in the majors since 1985, when Jose Canseco had played against his White Sox. "Let's take it easy," La Russa also cautioned at the time. "He doesn't need more notoriety. He needs less." Even that first week, as good as it was, contained the tiny hint of something to watch for when he was scratched from the lineup in one game because of back stiffness. It became a leitmotif of his career, the rhythm of his performance continually broken by injury.

His first full season in the majors, 1999, was not the stuff of immortality but the stuff of a mortal player still trying to get a handle on the potential humiliations of a big-league curve. He hit .242, with thirteen home runs and nineteen steals. He played in only 104 games, spending six weeks on the sidelines because of an injury to his quadriceps.

The next two seasons—2000 and 2001—were improvements. He hit .295 in 2000, with eighteen home runs. In 2001, he rose to .323, with twenty-seven home runs. But he still made frequent trips to the disabled list. His average number of at-bats in both those seasons was less than four hundred, and in 2002 he slipped badly:

G	AB	R	H	2B	3B	HR	RBI	BB	SO	SB	AVG	OBP	SLG.
135	424	61	107	19	1	18	56	57	104	8	.252	.349	.429

There were also more injuries, this time a tendon in his knee. He had surgery in the off-season to repair it, meaning that he would start this current season on the disabled list. Injuries are part of baseball; there's no way to avoid them. But something else about Drew began to concern La Russa, something trickier and more elusive than a damaged knee or a strained quadriceps.

Increasingly, La Russa wondered whether Drew's underlying ailment, like it was for so many young players coming into sudden millions, was an absence of sustained passion that had no medical remedy. Did he simply lack the will to play in a way that would fulfill all those auguries? La Russa urged him to not be satisfied with what he had done, that there was so much more he could do if he committed himself to doing it. La Russa knew that Drew was making $3.6 million this season and told him that he could probably pull in double that in future seasons if he put some added heat into his game, went into it with the same kind of relentlessness that Albert Pujols did on every at-bat. He even offered to put Drew into the same batting practice grouping as Pujols from the very first day of spring training in the further hope that the great Pujols would rub off on him. He told Drew that he could make the kind of money in baseball that could guarantee a lifetime of security. But as he spoke, it dawned on him that for a small-town boy from Georgia who still lived where he had grown up, $3.6 million a year was already ample bounty. He told Drew that it was a waste for him to simply go along like this when he could be so much more. They'd had these talks more than once, but La Russa knew that he had never gotten through to him, except when he threatened to bench him if he didn't choke up with two strikes to better defend himself against striking out.

During spring training this year, when Drew couldn't play because of his knee rehabilitation, he left the dugout in the middle of a contest against the Expos to head back to the clubhouse. La Russa had no problem with the regulars doing that once they were done playing for the day. It was a little bit of the special treatment that a regular got, the extra care and stroking. But Drew wasn't a regular at this point. It upset La Russa, because if Drew couldn't play, the least he could do was watch, see what a pitcher was up to, put it in the back pocket somewhere for the regular season. Williams was in the dugout even though he wasn't pitching. So was Matt Morris. And even when Drew had been physically there, his whole body language suggested to La Russa, *Why am I here?* His head lolled back and he seemed to be looking at everything he could except for the game on the field. La Russa's feeling was, *You're in the big leagues. Watch and learn.*

The next morning, La Russa called Drew into his office in the Jupiter compound. "If you come, you stay the full nine, that's the deal," he scolded, and then he fined him $250. Drew left the office, looking like most players do when they leave the manager's office, the look of a pained little boy suddenly unsure how much he really likes his mother because of all these rules she makes you follow. But because the fine came out of his meal money check, it didn't even dent his $3.6 million salary. And even if it had, it would amount to approximately .00015 percent of his compensation. To La Russa, the issue wasn't money. It was the message he was sending, maybe an ultimatum, about what he expected of Drew and what Drew should expect of himself.

Drew returned to the lineup toward the end of April. He struggled, as any player will struggle coming back from knee surgery. Against the Expos in early May, with first place on the line and the score 3–1 Cards in the bottom of the eighth, La Russa tried a delayed double steal with Drew on third, Jim Edmonds on first, and Rolen at the plate. It was a daring play—on the surface, managerial aggressiveness *without* common sense—but the Expos' third baseman, Fernando Tatis, was playing so deep, almost on the outfield grass, that La Russa saw an opening and went for it. With Tatis too far off the bag to pick him off, Drew could take an unusually long lead off third. He should have broken for home with fury once it became apparent that the catcher's throw was going straight to second, where Edmonds was heading, instead of being cut off by the pitcher. But Drew took a short lead off third, despite Jose

Oquendo's urgings, and then got a lousy jump off the throw. He was caught in a rundown, and instead of scrambling for his life to avoid it, he simply surrendered.

God damn, J.D.! The words coursed through La Russa in the dugout, but he said nothing to Drew as he sheepishly returned with his head ducked down. The play was as blown and ugly as it gets, and now La Russa would have to explain to Rolen why he'd put more faith in a misplaced fielder than in Rolen's dependable bat.

Later that night, La Russa had dinner at Dominic's in suburban St. Louis with one of the Cardinals owners. Despite winning the game 3–1, he was brooding about Drew, wondering once more whether there was some way to get to him, let that talent pour out in terrific torrents. He pulled out an index card and began to write down possible things to say to him, all of which he realized he had said already. He put the card back in his breast pocket after several minutes. The conversation turned to how many players La Russa had managed who have had that rare combination of talent and fiery heart, refused to settle for good as long as there was the horizon of greatness. La Russa approached it methodically, combing carefully through each of the three teams he had managed. He deliberated carefully because it was an interesting question that required an interesting answer. It was easy to think of players who had one or the other. *Most* players who had hit the big leagues had one or the other. But *both* was rare, very rare. As he gave out a name, it got written down on a list.

Seventeen. That's what it came out to when he was finished. He looked at the names to make sure he hadn't missed anyone. Seventeen. In twenty-four years of managing, seventeen players who had willed themselves to put it all together. It was a small number—depressing, really—reflective of how many ballplayers are content to coast along on the basis of the talent they have when they could do so much more. As La Russa looked at the makeshift list, he wondered how many more there could have been had he done a better job of managing, had he figured out a way to punch through. The conversation circled back to Drew, and the nagging question arose in La Russa's mind once again: Was it J.D.'s fault that he wasn't playing to his level, or was it the fault of the manager he played for?

In the weeks since, Drew has shown glimmers of the magic that set apart those seventeen. He continued to play according to his own mercurial rhythm, such flashes of brilliance you still knew that it was all going to pour out one day; other moments when he was slowed down or stopped completely by injury. Which meant that four months down the road in the three-game series against the Cubs, he would not play at all, replaced by a player who would never match fire with fire on a fastball but who was consumed by the burning desperation to play each and every day.

III

WITH ROBINSON on first after that slapped single into left, Hart comes up to bat, and one of baseball's most controversial plays becomes a possibility: *hit-and-run.* Some managers loath it because the swing that puts the ball in play usually costs a precious out and the dividend—moving the man on first to second—often doesn't materialize. Other managers embrace the *hit-and-run* because they believe that it's worth giving up an out to put a runner in scoring position and stay out of the double play. Plus, if it's executed properly and the ball finds a hole, the play has created a run-scoring opportunity, maybe even a crooked number because of the *hit-and-run's* unique momentum.

When La Russa was a novice manager with the White Sox, he spent a great deal of time at the Bard's Room. It was the kind of place that doesn't exist in baseball anymore, a seedy, stinky hole in the wall, where baseball men congregated to drink and smoke and debate the game's intricacies into the small hours. La Russa showed up just about every night, finding the back-and-forth dialogue tantamount to "getting your Ph.D. in baseball." So did luminaries from the White Sox front office, such as general manager Rollie Hemond and Paul Richards. So did Billy Martin and Sparky Anderson, skippers who would attend when their teams were in town, as well as some of the game's greatest scouts. Presiding over all of it was the one-in-a-millennium Bill Veeck, with a beer in one hand and a cigarette in the other.

Veeck made it a point of his life to never view himself, or anyone else, with too much pomp and circumstance. He titled his memoir *Veeck as in Wreck,* and he brought a similar mindset to baseball, which he saw above all as entertainment. In gauging his life in baseball, inevitable disputes arise as to which of his promotions was the most inspired. It may have been the one in 1951, when, as owner of the St. Louis Browns, he sent 3'7" Eddie Gaedel to the plate for his only major-league appearance. His uniform bore the number ⅛ and he drew a walk, even though the catcher, trying to frame the proper strike zone, dropped to his knees. Or it could have been the one later that season when he sat the Browns' manager in a rocking chair next to the dugout and invited the fans to manage by consensus. Browns' coaches showed placards suggesting various options—bunt, hit-and-run, pinch-hit—and the spectators delivered their verdict by holding up cards showing either yes or no. Or maybe the one in which he had six midgets race from the outfield to home plate in Cleveland, with Bob Hope as the emcee. Less successful, however, was the infamous Disco Demolition Night right before La Russa's arrival.

But not all of Veeck's stunts were designed to work laughs. He hated the stuffy sanctimony of the game, but he also revered the game. It was Veeck who planted the ivy on the outfield wall of Wrigley. It was Veeck who first put the names of players on the back of their uniforms. It was Veeck who invented the exploding scoreboard, and it was also Veeck who in 1947, half a century before it would become reality, first suggested interleague play.

The White Sox were his last hurrah, the hiring of La Russa one of his final acts. The sheer surprise of it was typical of him, for La Russa was far too young—only thirty-four—and unproven by anyone's standards except Veeck's. But bringing him in was no stunt; Veeck could see that La Russa more than loved the game— he thirsted for it, studied it voraciously, couldn't get enough of it. Veeck also liked the fact that La Russa was studying law in the off-season. Before hiring him, Veeck made him promise that he would pass the bar and get his license.

An important part of La Russa's baseball indoctrination was the Bard's Room, where Veeck purposely pitted him against dyed-in-the-wool baseball men to see how he handled himself, how he struck the balance between deference to the elders and defending his convictions. He loved to see arguing, and one of the best ways to achieve that was simply to mention the phrase *hit-and-run*. Before you knew it, Richards and La Russa would be debating with each other, La Russa thinking it worthy in certain circumstances, his mentor thinking it worthless in all circumstances. Richards saw it in much the same way that Woody Hayes at Ohio State viewed the forward pass: Three things could happen, and two of them were bad. In the middle would be Veeck, adding saucy comments just to keep the debate going—*it's smart, it's stupid, it can work, it can't work*—his only break from stoking the fire when he flicked his cigarette ash into a little hole he had built into his wooden leg.

In this particular moment in Game 2, with a runner on first and one out in the bottom of the third, La Russa is weighing the matchup between Hart and Wood as a reason to consider the *hit-and-run*. It's not a great matchup for Hart, given Wood's nasty curve. So if he can *hit-and-run* Robinson to second, it will give Pujols a better opportunity to drive in the run, which, in La Russa's mind, makes it worth any potential sacrifice.

Because La Russa believes in the *hit-and-run*, he has his players work on it exhaustively during spring training and throughout the season during batting practice. The goal he sets for them is simple: to hit the ball on the ground as hard as you can. He does not advocate guiding the ball toward a certain location, because trying to do that only takes away from how hard a hitter can sting it. If the ball is middle in on the plate, you try to pull it. If the ball is middle away, you take it to the opposite field. La Russa also believes that by practicing the *hit-and-run*, you can dramatically increase the number of hits you get out of it: from five out of fifty to possibly fifteen.

It is a winning play if the result is a hit. But even at 15 out of 50, it's still not a great percentage. The other problem is that the more successful you are with it, the more opposing managers look for it and try to defend against it, the Darwinian evolution of baseball working much like it did when steals were getting out of hand.

Opposing managers will pay obsessive attention to the kind of lead a runner is taking off first base, trying to glean whether it's a true base-stealing lead or the slightly less precocious *hit-and-run* lead. In a base-stealing lead, the runner must explode toward second at some point in the pitcher's delivery, commit himself to swiping the bag, which is why most managers, faced with the choice between a runner's getting picked off first or getting thrown out at second, will take the pick-off because at a minimum, it implies aggressiveness. In a *hit-and-run* lead, the runner must not risk the possibility of a pick-off, so there is no similar explosion: Once he takes his lead, he's just a little bit more stable.

Opposing managers will also scrutinize the divinations coming from the third-base coach and see whether their own code breakers on the bench can decrypt them. If they think they have sniffed right on the *hit-and-run,* they may call for a pitch out, which for the offense can result in a hitter's swinging through a lousy pitch *and* the runner's getting thrown out at second, a terrible result and yet not even the worst one, precisely why Richards hated it so much.

A manager contemplating the *hit-and-run* continually struggles to evade detection. So many eyes are watching him all the time, his only recourse is to bury himself in the corner of the dugout as deeply as possible. For La Russa, one of the subtle benefits of day games is the opportunity they give him to wear sunglasses, and La Russa likes wearing sunglasses because they make it impossible for an opposing manager to read his eyes. But most games are played at night.* And in some dugouts—Wrigley, for example—it's impossible to hide effectively, because the layout ensures that a manager remains in view. So managers often resort to other measures. The highly respected Tom Kelly, when he was managing the Twins in the early 1990s, purposely picked lousy *hit-and-run* counts—0-1, for example, when the batter was already at a deficit—to work the play and preserve the element of surprise. The gamble worked for a while, until other managers got wise to Kelly's *hit-and-run* pattern and began to pitch out. La Russa himself will put a *hit-and-*

---

* In 2004, La Russa switched from regular glasses at night games to tinted ones. The reason for the switch was to shield his eyes from code breaking.

run on from the bench without even telling all the parties involved. The way it works, the number two batter due up in the inning is told before the inning starts that he is going to *hit-and-run* on the first pitch if the hitter ahead of him gets to first. But the initial batter isn't told anything unless he makes it to first. Then the first-base coach tips him off in the kind of casual chitchat that occurs throughout the game, and the spontaneity of the information prevents him from making his lead too obvious. In these situations, of course, there are no signs, because the last thing you want to do is alert an opposing manager with signs, particularly if it's a runner you don't normally *hit-and-run* with.

Such a strategy has worked effectively, as it did against the Pirates earlier in the season. But the overriding problem with the *hit-and-run* is that it can blow up beyond all belief by making a complete fool out of the normally reliable line drive. Earlier this month, when the Cardinals were playing Atlanta, La Russa put on a *hit-and-run* with runners on first and second, no outs, and pitcher Woody Williams hitting. The likely play here was a bunt to advance the runners with the score tied 1–1 in the fifth. Williams did indeed show bunt on the first two pitches. But he is also a superb hitting pitcher, one of the best in the game, and with the count 1 and 1, La Russa pulled the trigger.

Williams swung away with the runners going. He hit a line drive to the left of the second-base bag. Shortstop Rafael Furcal leaped to catch it. First out. Second baseman Marcus Giles yelled to Furcal to give him the ball so he could step on the bag and double up Matheny at second. But Furcal had a certain moist look in his eye. He told Giles he could handle it all by himself. He stepped on the bag to double up the catcher Matheny. Second out. He tagged out Orlando Palmeiro as he vainly tried to get back to first. Third out. An unassisted triple play. Only the twelfth in major-league history. Thanks, *hit-and-run*. Go screw yourself.

It was the second triple play the Cardinals had hit into during the season on the basis of La Russa's *hit-and-run* fetish, the first against Colorado. It said something about La Russa's love of the play. It also showed how little he had moved from what coach

Charley Lau—impressed by La Russa's balls if not necessarily his brains—had said about him twenty-five years earlier when La Russa had first begun to manage.

The memories make using the *hit-and-run* here fraught with implications. As soon as Hart settles in at the plate, La Russa starts flashing signs to the third-base coach, Oquendo. He knows that Baker and the other Cubs coaches are vivisecting Oquendo, asking themselves what's up with all those scratches and sweeps and ear squeezes. La Russa wants Baker to ask what's up, just as Baker wants La Russa to think that maybe he's thinking, *C'mon, Tony, I wasn't born in a barn. I know your style, so I know all you're trying to do is fool me into thinking that something is up,* a diagonal back and forth from one dugout to the other, tracer bullets of dekes and feints and sucker punches.

Hart swings through a slider. Nothing's on: 0 and 1, a tough *hit-and-run* count. If Baker wants to go with a pitchout, 0 and 1 is a good time to do it, as there is little harm done even if he guesses wrong, the count moved only to 1 and 1. The 0-and-1 count also favors Wood. He can afford something nasty here off the plate that will be difficult to hit, which in turn only makes a successful *hit-and-run* that much more difficult to achieve.

Hart takes an up fastball. Nothing's on. The count goes to 1 and 1 as La Russa continues to flash signs to Oquendo. Simultaneously, Robinson takes an antsy lead off first base, not enough to show flat-out steal, but enough to suggest the flirtation of something. It's back to Baker, because maybe he should pitch out here. Or maybe that's exactly what La Russa wants him to do—*think* something is on so he does pitch out and drives the count back toward the hitter's favor to 2 and 1.

Baker does nothing. La Russa makes his move.

Robinson goes on the pitch. Wood throws a fastball that sails high, very high. It's a difficult pitch to hit: It defies all natural order to even touch it. Hart takes a kind of punchy tomahawk swing at it, a wondrous reflex action, and he gets it into the hole between first and second for a single. Robinson easily advances to third; this time, the *hit-and-run* has paid off handsomely. Suddenly, in the bottom of the third, it's gotten interesting, the ersatz top of the lineup working singles off Wood on two great pieces of hitting, with the heart of the order due up.

Pujols walks on four straight pitches, La Russa wincing only slightly when he takes an up curve ball on 1-0, because it's a hittable pitch and one that maybe he should have swung at. But now the bases are loaded and Edmonds is up, still with only one out.

No one can carry a team like Edmonds can when he's on his stroke. Since coming over to the Cardinals from Anaheim in 2000, he's averaged more than thirty home runs and a hundred RBIs a season. But he has been bothered by shoulder soreness lately, and possibly no hitter gets pounded inside as much as Edmonds, causing him to flinch and bail out even when pitches come nowhere close to the inside.

La Russa is familiar with the theory, promoted to gospel by *Moneyball,* that the most important hitting statistic today is on-base percentage. He doesn't dispute the value of players who can work walks in any situation and have a diamond merchant's eye for the strike zone. But he also sees it as akin to the latest fashion fad —oversaturated, everybody doing it, everybody wearing it, until you find out the hard way that stretch Banlon isn't quite as cool as originally perceived. And he tries to teach his players that the better decision is to play the scoreboard.

If you're leading off an inning, it makes sense to push the count into your favor, to be "really fine" in searching out that good strike. You might take a ball right over the plate, even if you think you can hit it hard, in the hope of drawing a walk. But if you're coming up with the bases loaded and one out, as Edmonds is now, the table obviously is *set.* You don't want patience here. You want aggression, which is what he pounded into Robinson after that game against the Phillies. You need to expand the zone in which you're willing to swing. Don't wait around like some haute couture stylist to get something perfect—be ready to go on that first good strike.

Edmonds has a nice advantage here. With three Cardinals aboard, Wood can't be too fine about what he brings. Which means that in the continual back and forth between hitter and pitcher, Edmonds now has the power. Wood throws a slider middle down on the plate. It's there for Edmonds, right in his "happy zone," as La Russa later puts it.

Edmonds takes it, looking for 0 and 1, clear that he was hoping for something else and had no intention of swinging. Wood comes in with a slider on the outside corner. Edmonds takes it, looking again for 0 and 2.

Now the power returns to Wood; he can pick Edmonds to death with nothing more than temptation. Forget a good strike in the zone, because Wood has no use for them. He threw one, the first one, and one is enough, and he finishes Edmonds off a pitch later with a chest-high fastball. It brings up Rolen, with two outs and the bases, of course, still loaded.

Wood comes in with a slider low, almost at Rolen's ankles. He swings and misses and La Russa can almost hear the chorus of critics asking themselves why he chased at a pitch like that. But La Russa prefers his aggressiveness here, would rather see it than not, convinced that this aggression will produce more runs over the course of the season. The only problem is that Rolen strikes out four pitches later to end the inning. The Cards have just squandered one of the stronger scoring opportunities baseball ever offers.

La Russa knows that they should have put a run on the board here, maybe even a crooked number with the bases juiced and one out and your four and five hitters up. He mourns the wasted chance, and he worries about the emotional momentum that has just swung over to Wood's favor. Escaping a jam like that will give him a dangerous spillover of confidence, make him fall more deeply in love than ever with the quality of his stuff, think he can do anything and maybe actually do it. If the Cardinals had gotten a couple of runs here, Wood's emotions might have gotten to him. He might have gotten pissed off, overthrowing so much that he'd morph from Effectively Wild Wood to plain old Wild Wood. Instead, he just tucked the killer knot of the order into bed in the bottom of the third without a peep of protest.

9

WHODUNIT

I

● ● ● SAMMY SOSA leads off the top of the fourth by grounding out to second on a breaking ball from Williams. Moises Alou strikes out on a breaking ball from Williams. Eric Karros flies out to center on a breaking ball from Williams. It's a fourteen-pitch inning. He is moving deeper and deeper into that zone of pure performance, each inning better than the previous. Unlike many pitchers, his stuff gets, as La Russa says, "more oiled" as he progresses further into a game. Because he is a pitchmaker rather than a thrower, he has to feel out his pitches, make sure that the cutter has bite and that the curve isn't too fat. So he often does in the first inning what Darryl Kile did: checks out his equipment like an auto racer to see what is working and what may need a little bit more fine-tuning. After the first two or three innings, the location and command of his pitches only improve, and he tends to sail ever more smoothly on to the seventh or eighth.

It's beautiful to watch a pitcher who can work a ball like this, somehow make the plate seem spacious and roomy and easy to target when it measures less than 20 inches across. In his foxhole, behind the camouflage of his get-away-from-me grimace, La Russa entertains an effusive thought: *He's nailing it.* And against Kerry Wood, he has to nail it if the Cardinals are to hang on long enough to force Dusty Baker to resort to his bullpen. There is no margin for carelessness or frustration or mental lapse.

Williams has done yeoman work in speeding up right-handed hitters' bats with the fastball inside so that they're way out in front when he comes in with his curve. His best side of the plate is the first-base side, the away side for righties, but tonight he's also been effective pitching inside to them. Which means that he's working both sides of the plate, so vital to the success of any pitcher. He's showing the kind of stuff that took him to a 12-and-3 record before the All-Star break.

He fell into a rut after the break and lost some confidence; tonight marks his sixth straight attempt to push his win total to fifteen for the season. La Russa and Duncan noticed that after the All-Star break, Williams had changed his style, trying to pitch everybody as if they were Babe Ruth. Instead of going after hitters to get strike 1, he tried to be too fine with his pitches, even with nobody on when a get-me-over fastball or curve would have the least consequences. The culprit, they suspected, was fatigue. Because of the crisis in the bullpen the first half of the season, Williams went deep into virtually every game he pitched. La Russa and Duncan needed him, and he responded beautifully, but the use wore on him. His arm inevitably got tired, which led to a lack of confidence in the sheer quality of his stuff, which then led to a greater urge than usual to pinpoint the ball in the perfect location. Which ironically only created even more fatigue because he might throw as many as twenty pitches in an inning in which he got a zero. Aware of the cycle, La Russa and Duncan have made a deliberate effort in Williams's recent starts to not overuse him. They have let him regain his strength, and it's showing tonight in the style that made him an All-Star, the proper symbiotic balance of aggression and pitch mixture.

Wood's parry to Williams in the bottom of the fourth confirms La Russa's premonition that getting out of the bases-loaded jam the inning before, neutering Jim Edmonds and Scott Rolen with strikeouts, has only added to his hubris. On the mound, he stares down batters with eyes that seem almost dead, no spark or sparkle at all: flat, cold executioner's eyes. Tino Martinez takes a curve ball looking for a strikeout. Edgar Renteria strikes out on a high fastball.

Mike Matheny strikes out on a slider that follows a 97-mph fastball. He threw first-pitch strikes to all three hitters, not to mention that he now has five strikeouts in a row. After four innings, the line score of Game 2, slotted into the center of the dark green scoreboard of Busch with its barebones essentials, reads like chapters in an unfolding thriller:

	1	2	3	4	R	H	E
CUBS	0	0	0	0	0	2	0
CARDINALS	0	0	0	0	0	3	0

The continuing contrast in style between Wood and Williams only accentuates the drama. Wood with that big kick and follow-through. Wood with those dead-fish eyes. Wood with that scraggle-haired Fu Manchu. Wood stepping off the mound after a strikeout and encircling it in a little warrior stomp. Wood picking up the rosin bag and heaving it down like it's a black barbell at a weight-lifting competition. Williams with a demure kick. Williams with the trim beard. Williams taking the ball after a strikeout and going right back to work. Williams picking up the rosin bag and putting it down like it is, after all, a rosin bag.

Williams builds a quick 0-2 count on Aramis Ramirez with a fastball and a sinker to begin the top of the fifth. He throws three straight balls, trying to get him to chase something high. But he comes back with a fastball low and away on the full count to strike him out. Alex Gonzalez grounds out to Williams in a three-pitch at-bat. Up comes Damian Miller in the eight-hole with two outs—Miller, who is 7 for 14 against Williams before tonight and has had more success against him than any other Cub.

It's the precise scenario that La Russa fretted over at his desk before the game, the possibility of Miller's getting on with two outs, failing to score before the third out is made but affecting the lineup so that the Cubs start off the following inning at the top. If Williams gets Miller out here, the pitcher, Wood, leads off the following inning, a major difference in terms of momentum.

Williams goes to 1 and 1 on Miller with two sinkers. Then he comes with a slider. From the foxhole, La Russa can see that the location is perfect, just perfect. It's down and away to the right-handed Miller, a sweet chase pitch. You can't throw a better slider in that situation. It's not humanly possible. Miller takes an embarrassed half-swing and manages to flare it into the outfield for a yappy little double: further proof that baseball *is* the cruelest game, that the best execution can still produce an unfair outcome.

Batting in the ninth spot, Wood pushes Williams to 2 and 2 before he grounds out to short to end the inning. It means a zero for the top of the fifth, a relatively easy zero, but that little fear La Russa nurtured has come to pass. The Cubs will start off the sixth with Kenny Lofton, the top of their order. But with Williams pitching the way he is, La Russa's fear might border on paranoia. Lofton has a meaningless hit tonight. So does Martinez in the two-hole. After them, the three-, four-, and five-hole hitters are a combined 0 for 6 against Williams, with two strikeouts. Sosa and Alou haven't even gotten it out of the infield. And Williams is getting better as the game continues, his impassivity belying the competitiveness that ticks inside him like an old-fashioned alarm clock; nothing can muzzle its insistent beat. On the dark green scoreboard, another chapter has been slotted into the whodunit:

	1	2	3	4	5	R	H	E
CUBS	0	0	0	0	0	0	3	0
CARDINALS	0	0	0	0		0	3	0

Leading off the bottom of the fifth, Williams burnishes his reputation as a great hitting pitcher by singling on a 1-and-1 curve that hangs a little high. It brings up Kerry Robinson, the Cards' lead-off man pro tem, and now La Russa has another crucial decision to make. But it won't sneak up on him, the very panic of indecision because a decision is demanded. In keeping with his mantra that the only way to keep up with the game is to stay ahead of it, he started playing out different what-ifs before the Cardinals came to bat in the fifth, the same as he does before every offensive inning. Leaving the foxhole and retreating to the back bench in the left corner of the dugout, pulling out his cheat sheets to make sure no nugget of prior information is missed, he considers the possibility of having Robinson bunt if Williams gets on base. By examining the scenarios this way, La Russa will be ready for the moment whatever moment arises—putting out his signs quickly to the players involved so there is no confusion or hesitation. The variable here, because in baseball there is always a variable, boils down to this in the bottom of the fifth: how hard to push in a 0–0 game that shows no signs of yielding runs without a fight.

First, La Russa considers Wood's pitch count. It stands at seventy-nine, which hardly suggests that the Cardinals are about to get rid of him, particularly as Baker is infamous for taking his starting pitchers deep into games. No one in the major leagues did it more last season; nineteen times he kept his starters in for more than 120 pitches. But once Wood's pitch count creeps over 100, even Baker has to think about calling the bullpen. The Cubs' bullpen is their soft spot; their setup men are greeted with relief by opposing hitters, vulnerable fill-ins after starters as good as Prior and Wood and Zambrano, their closer, Joe Borowski, getting through on grit without classic closer material. So, from La Russa's perspective, the most exploitable aspect of Wood's performance tonight is his pitch count. The best way to win against any top-shelf pitcher is not always trying to rack up runs against him, because however much you try, you may not rack up any. Instead, the most effective path is to work the count, resist the itch to chase after junk food off the plate, realize that a foul ball sometimes has more value than a fair one because it lengthens your at-bat.

If Wood's count were a little bit higher—if La Russa could look over at Baker in the visitor's dugout and know that he was thinking *bullpen*—pushing for a run now might not matter much. With Wood gone, a run would be easier to come by. But he'll be around for a while.

So pushing is important to La Russa, but *how important?* Because doing so entails some likely sacrifice. A successful bunt by Robinson moves Williams to second, with Hart and Pujols up next to try to drive him in. With Williams standing on first now, La Russa's internal debate takes up the antibunt argument in full drive:

Robinson got a base hit last time.

It's only the fifth, and you want to do a little something more than get the runner over.

There's something else unsettling him: who's on first. If Robinson bunts, Williams will have to dig for second. He's fully capable of doing that, but La Russa doesn't want him to run hard and chance an injury when he's pitching so well. (For the same reason, La Russa is also leaning away from putting on a *hit-and-run* here.) He juggles all these variables in a couple of seconds. No amount of pre-inning planning could buy him any time here; baseball follows its timepiece, not his, and he has to pull the trigger.

He places his faith in Robinson's bat: His fine piece of hitting last time up takes precedence. Wood throws a fastball high to make the count 1 and 0. He does the exact same thing on the next pitch to make the count 2 and 0. It's a hitter's count, and if Robinson gets a pitch to hit, he's going to get it now. Wood no longer has the luxury of trying something nasty off the plate. He's going to go with his strength, which is his fastball.

It's a 95-mph fastball. But lacking movement or location, the fastest fastball has all the subtlety of a streaker—little to it beyond the gainly flab of the buttocks. This fastball is down the pipe, just like that pitch the Phillies threw at him was down the pipe, about belt-high. It is *the* pitch to hit.

Robinson doesn't lift his bat. Everything that favored him suddenly dissolves. Wood, knowing that he got away with something and feeling good about it, hits the outside corner for a strike to make it 2 and 2. That gives him a little breathing room to expand the zone, which he does by throwing a 12-to-6 curve for strike 3.

Hart bounces up to the plate and hits a little nubber down the first-base line, slow enough so that the only play is to first for the second out. That summons Pujols, with Williams on second. La Russa draws a breath, wondering whether this is the moment of headball he's been dreading, particularly with first base open. Wood throws a fastball a little bit up in the zone, and Pujols swings through it.

It gives Wood the crucial first-pitch strike, but against Pujols, it has the effect only of making things a little more balanced for the pitcher. Wood knows this, as this is the twenty-fourth time he has faced Pujols, with the outcome seven hits and three homers. The other Cubs know this. The fans know this. And so does La Russa. Alhough he has managed Harold Baines and Carlton Fisk and Jose Canseco and Rickey Henderson and Mark McGwire, and although he is not prone to gratuity, La Russa calls Pujols the best player he has ever managed. He is loathe to ever single a player out, but he is also convinced that Baines and Henderson and all the rest—given the opportunity to play with Pujols season after season—would also conclude that he is the best. Pujols has the consummate qualities that every manager looks for in a player: good hands, a strong and accurate arm, instinctive hitting reflexes. But it's more than just the skill: In the best of times and the worst of times of baseball, the constant thundercloud of money overhanging the game, Pujols tries to exploit his skills *every* day through *every* at-bat.

He has achieved the status of superstar. His statistics are too irrepressible for him to be treated otherwise. But because he plays in a small media market, he is a superstar of unknown portfolio, rarely mentioned in the same breath as Alex Rodriguez or Barry Bonds, although the numbers he has put up his first two seasons are the best that any player in the history of the game has ever put up:*

AB	R	H	2B	3B	HR	RBI	BB	SO	AVG.	OBP.	SLG.
590	112	194	47	4	37	130	69	93	.329	.403	.610
590	118	185	40	2	34	127	72	69	.314	.394	.561

This season his numbers are even better, on a pace once again to hit thirty or more homers, drive in a hundred or more runs, score a hundred or more runs, and hit well over .300.

Wood follows his fastball with a curve up and away. Pujols doesn't chase, and the count goes to 1 and 1. It's typical of Pujols to

---

* Rodriguez hit 59 home runs, scored 241 runs, drove in 207 runs, and averaged .329 his first two seasons. Bonds hit 49 home runs, scored 196 runs, drove in 117 runs, and averaged .272. Pujols hit 71 home runs, scored 230 runs, drove in 257 runs, and averaged .321 his first two seasons.

lay off the pitch, his whole approach a remarkable combination of preparation, concentration, adjustment, and self-discipline. It is a combination that La Russa has seen before but never quite like this, the thick mix of all these different portions. It also explodes the supposition that hitting is fundamentally some inexplicable natural talent that cannot be substantially refined or perfected, something either you have or don't have. For Pujols, talent is where he begins.

II

HE SLIPPED IN out of nowhere. He wasn't a big-time bonus baby. He wasn't a first-round pick or even a tenth-round pick. At the outset, he seemed like nothing beyond a guy with a pretty good bat and an interesting glove who could tell people in twenty years around the grill that he once had a shot.

He was born with the real first name of Jose in Santo Domingo in the Dominican Republic. His family came to New York, where he was raised by his grandmother. After he saw a man get shot outside a grocery store as a teenager, she moved the kids to Missouri. He went to Fort Osage High School in Independence, then to Maple Woods Community College. A highly respected college coach who watched him play in a summer league over in Hays never thought that Pujols would make it, and he wasn't singing a solo. Pujols's body was soft. He was considered slow, never better than 4.6 or 4.7 seconds to first. His bat was slow as well, and he rarely pulled the ball. In a world buzzing with scouts and the coming of the next new thing—in which promising players are tracked from the age of twelve by the publication *Baseball America*—Pujols was the antithesis of the prodigal player. Before he was drafted, he was mentioned only once in the *St. Louis Post-Dispatch*, in 1997, as a "player to watch" in the Class 4A Missouri high school baseball tournament, alongside such unfamiliar names as Chris Francka and Eric O'Connor.

The Cardinals made him a thirteenth-round pick in the 1999 draft, the 402nd player taken overall, signing him for around

$30,000. In the annual "Down on the Farm" story in the *Post-Dis-patch* in April 2000, he was listed as a future possibility for the Cardinals at third base, although the story made it clear that Chris Haas was considered to have the rosier prospects. He was still obscure, another player in the minor-league shuffle of Johnson City and Peoria and Potomac and New Haven and Memphis. But then he took off, first in Peoria, then in Potomac, ending up the season in Triple-A Memphis, where he clinched the Pacific Coast League playoffs over Salt Lake City with a homer in the thirteenth inning. He went to the Arizona Fall League afterward, and although he hit well, there was continued concern about his weight. The Cardinals set him up with a nutritionist and a strength coach. He came to spring training in 2001 with a body toned and svelte. On a Wednesday afternoon during a throw-away intrasquad game at Roger Dean Stadium, he hit a pitch that went over the left-field wall and smashed into the adjacent offices of the Montreal Expos—perhaps the most exciting thing that had happened to the Expos in their history—and La Russa wondered just what kind of prospect he had on his hands.

Younger players, particularly those who had spent most of the previous season at Class A ball, viewed spring training as a vacation because they figured they had no shot to make it. They floated through the bunt drills and the cut-off drills and the soft-toss drills in the mesh of the neatly laid-out batting cages with sweet smiles on their faces, just happy to be there and waiting for the next roster cutdown when they would be returned to the hinterland for further tenderizing. A manager, at least a manager with a clue, went out of his way to give a prospect a positive spring by keeping him out of difficult situations, to nurture his head a little bit. But Pujols was different, so different that La Russa did the exact opposite, had him bat cleanup, put him in day in and day out against the best pitchers, because he had to see what was really there. "He has a serious, mature approach," La Russa told reporters at the time. "He's almost too good to be true."

But he still felt compelled to test Pujols, unwilling to give him a spot on the club if there wasn't ample opportunity for playing time. Shortly before spring training ended, the Cardinals played Atlanta at the Braves' complex in Disneyworld in Orlando. La Russa didn't have Pujols in the lineup that day, instead making sure that the regulars got in some final at-bats before the regular season began. Mark McGwire started at first, took his three cuts, then headed for the shower and stood behind La Russa in the dugout runway in his street clothes. The game was tied in the ninth when La Russa called on Pujols to pinch-hit against Matt Whiteside. Amid all the curiosity about his immediate future, Pujols didn't just hit the ball, he hit it over the scoreboard in center field. From behind, La Russa suddenly felt McGwire's huge hand smacking him across the back, a little bit like being hit with the wing of a 747. "Dude, I told you, he's on the club!" McGwire said to his manager. While La Russa knew at that moment that McGwire was right, he still subjected himself to second-guessing when the Cards ended up losing that game. His father was there that day, and afterward, when he saw his son, his comment was succinct and to the point: "You should have played Pujols the whole game."

Since then, he has only gotten better, his determination unwavering despite the fact that every day, he gets more and more attention—his performance this season at the All-Star Home Run derby in Chicago, where he hit fourteen home runs in the semifinals, a kind of coming-out party for him—a nation discovering what only a few truly knew before.

Just like pitching well, hitting well is a mental act masquerading as a physical one. A lot of hitters become afraid to consistently do well because it creates expectation and extra pressure—the curse of responsibility to perform. So they disengage their higher faculties and simply guess what a pitcher might throw. They don't go through the admittedly laborious study of video beforehand to try to pick up patterns, which is why some of them keep the bat on their shoulders when they should swing and swing when they should keep the bat on their shoulders. They also feel the creep of self-satisfaction, willing, if they get two hits in the first two or three at-bats, to let it go at that, 2 for 4 a perfectly nice day's work in the big leagues, the tired truism that if a hitter went 2 for 4 every day, he would be the greatest hitter ever.

But Pujols *was* different from the beginning and stayed that way.

"He has this relentless ability about not throwing at-bats away," says La Russa. "A lot of players throw an at-bat or two away every couple of games. They don't concentrate the same way."

Like other players who routinely hit over .300, Pujols is equipped with what La Russa calls "high batting average mentality." Going into each at-bat, he has a specific war room strategy for countering the pitcher's likely line of attack. He also works continually on what La Russa calls a "very productive high average stroke." After developing a relationship with Alex Rodriguez through a mutual friend, he traveled to Rodriguez's home in Miami one winter, and together they worked on about fifteen different drills off a batting tee that Rodriguez had developed, further advancing a hitting style to all parts of the field that isn't just pull-happy. He's perfected a stroke in the mold of the revolutionary batting instructor Charley Lau, passed down from generation to generation of great hitters from George Brett to Hal McRae to Fisk to Wade Boggs to McGwire and now to Rodriguez and Pujols.

Lau was the batting instructor for the White Sox when La Russa managed there after having already left his trademark on the Yankees and the Kansas City Royals. Lau died tragically of cancer in 1984, but he left a profound legacy. La Russa believes that Lau single-handedly influenced the game of baseball more than any other individual in the past quarter century, because of the way he used video when nobody really knew what video was. He broke down the swing frame by frame, saw that great hitters have certain absolutes. He studied the swing, examined it, instead of simply assuming the mechanics of it, and he figured out a new approach for it, saw the similarities between hitting and a golf swing but also made sure that the absolutes of the great hitters were never shed. Head on the ball at all times. Weight shift from back to front. An inside path to the ball that, if you're a righty, aims for center and right center. Top to bottom swing with no uppercut. And great extension, which is why the top hand comes off the bat of some hitters as they finish to give them the right arc through the ball. Pujols inherited the Lau style without ever meeting him, of course. So have hundreds of other hitters.

Before every game, Pujols keeps to himself in the clubhouse. He is not a talker. He makes himself available to his teammates, but he views reporters with sulky perspective, as if he is suddenly being encircled by a large cluster of dermatologic oddities that don't spread infection but do cause copious itching if they hover around too long. His face seems hung with a "do not disturb" sign. He has no time for the obvious answers to the obvious questions from the radio and television boys looking for their soundbites. He is busy in these moments, intensely busy, shuffling back and forth between the clubhouse and the blessed off-limits-to-reporters sanctuary of the darkened little video room where the Secret Weapon is screening tape of today's opposing starter. It is difficult to characterize Pujols's expression as he watches one of the monitors. It isn't rapaciousness or blood lust or any kind of particularly strong emotion. In baseball, less on the outside is usually more on the inside. But there is the glimmer of desire, almost a kind of dreaminess, the eyes narrowing ever so slightly as he watches, a big cat who, when the time is right, will consume the mouse who needs a mound to stand tall.

He showed that look four days earlier in preparation for Kevin Millwood, the Phillies' starting pitcher. He watched Millwood pitch against the Brewers, reacquainting himself over and over with the cutter away that Millwood deploys against righties. He showed that look when he watched footage of his own two homers in one recent game against Cincinnati, the first on a sinker that seemed impossible to hit, much less tattoo, almost surfing the dirt. He replayed the first homer in slow motion, silently following the trajectory of the pitch followed by the trajectory of his bat with that high-finish stroke, the reaffirming of mechanics and muscle memory. He showed that look when he hit a home run against Prior earlier in the season in the bottom of the eighth to tie the game at 1–1.

As good as his swing is, Pujols still treats it as a work to be meticulously refined, studied, examined, pulled apart, mercilessly critiqued. He adjusts it continually, bearing in mind the natural human tendency toward entropy and the fact that no two pitchers are any more perfectly alike than any two snowflakes or two fingerprints are alike. He has sustained periods of Zen, such as the thirty-game hitting streak that ended only the week before. But on certain days, in quiet conversation with Chad Blair, he assesses the complex components of his swing that have failed a little bit: too down on his legs, moving around too much, too *busy* at the plate.

Pujols's obsession over video isn't relegated simply to the small hours before a game. He has also retreated to the clubhouse for a fix during games, disappearing from the dugout to confer with the Secret Weapon about what has gone wrong with the at-bat he has just taken. In early May against the Expos, Claudio Vargas was pitching and beforehand was talking it up a little bit, telling a mutual friend of Pujols's that he was coming to town to strike him out. And in fact Vargas had done just that on the first at-bat in the minimum three pitches. "He got me that time, but I got three more at-bats," he said to Blair, meticulously charting the game pitch by pitch with the perfect vantage point of that camera in center field. Pujols watched what Vargas had done to him, how he had gotten him out. He studied his hands, his stride in reaction to Vargas and made the adjustments he thought necessary. But actually he had it all wrong: He didn't need three more at-bats to right the equation. He needed only one more, when he hit a 452-foot shot to center field.

As a manager, La Russa couldn't help but luxuriate in Pujols's search-and-destroy approach to hitting. During his career, he has felt lucky and blessed to have been placed in situations that provided him with the tools necessary to win. On each of the three teams that he has managed, he has had supportive owners—Bill Veeck and Jerry Reinsdorf in Chicago, Walter Haas in Oakland, and Bill DeWitt in St. Louis—unafraid to spend when spending was needed. He has had strong front offices. The result has been the one ingredient a manager must have for success regardless of how clever and crafty he is: players.

But still, there was nothing quite like Pujols. Players like that don't come along once in a lifetime; they never come along. Yet Pujols had another quality that La Russa treasured even more, maybe because he himself had come of age in the game during the 1960s. It was selflessness in this ultimate age of selfishness, a joy in others' accomplishments that exceeded whatever joy Pujols took in his own accomplishments. He liked baseball, all of baseball, didn't condescend to it. He was the first one to leap to the dugout's top step to celebrate someone else's hit. He took a walk when he needed to take a walk. He liked the challenge and surprise of bunting with men on. It made Pujols a new old-fashioned superstar, in the mold of other Cardinals greats such as Red Schoendienst and Stan Musial and Lou Brock. "The numbers and the money take care of themselves," said La Russa of him. "He's just out there playing to win. That's why I admire him."

III

WITH THE COUNT evened at 1 and 1, Wood comes in with a fastball. It's slightly up and inside. It hits Pujols, nicking his shirt. As he heads to first, he mutters something to Wood in Spanish, his first language. Wood, who doesn't speak Spanish, doesn't know what he said and doesn't particularly care. "Imagine that," he will remark later. "It stinks to get hit."

From the corner of the dugout, La Russa glares at Wood, as that sickening feeling he has felt so many times already this season comes over him again, the agony of what to do worse than losing. He isn't convinced that Wood meant to hit Pujols. Trying to be dispassionate about it, he acknowledges that the ball wasn't too high and tight and was considerably below head level. But Wood's intent matters less than the fact of yet another hit batsman. It's a problem that all managers share, and it means that a message must be sent. He sifts through possible candidates, although the choice is clear. An eye for an eye. A Sosa for a Pujols. But this game isn't against Arizona in April, when La Russa could risk losing in return for winning the hearts and minds of his players. This is late August against the Cubs in a division firefight. The cost of a message is still potentially huge, because of what the home plate umpire may do. The best antidote would be the Cardinals scoring a run here. But Edmonds flies out to left on a fastball to strand runners at first and second, and another chapter is published:

	1	2	3	4	5	R	H	E
CUBS	0	0	0	0	0	0	3	0
CARDINALS	0	0	0	0	0	0	4	0

Williams works Kenny Lofton with cutters and straight four-seam fastballs to begin the top of the sixth. The ball moves around the plate like jazz music: up, down, in, out, arrhythmic, no opportunity for Lofton to anticipate the next note. There is no youthful swagger here between Williams and Lofton, just two pros in their midthirties with a collective thirty-two years of professional experience trying to outfox, outthink, outmaneuver the other.

With the count 1 and 1, Williams comes in with a cutter so high and inside that Matheny can barely get to it. But it's a little piece of catnip, the next pitch a fastball to the other side of the plate that Lofton slaps at and fouls. Williams goes the other way on his next pitch, back inside. Lofton slaps it again and fouls it off again because it's down to gut-level survival now, trying to outlast Williams and maybe get something reasonably hittable. With the count 2 and 2, Williams throws a slider down and in. It's a jam pitch in on Lofton's hands, right where he doesn't like the ball. It's the spot Williams wants to get to, the spot Duncan pinpointed for him during the pregame meeting, *in on the hands because Lofton doesn't like it there.*

Lofton swings. It's one of those defensive just-trying-to-make-contact swings. He gets a little piece without any particular inspiration. The ball meanders in the air, a halfhearted ennui, the kind of existentialist hit that would keep Camus or Sartre in the money if they had played baseball, before it simply runs out of energy and plops into right field well ahead of Robinson. The ball is bored, so tired of itself, it doesn't even roll once it plops. Lofton stretches the weary little thing into a double when Robinson, again building a bigger, better doghouse for himself, fails to get to it quickly.

It brings up Ramon Martinez. Williams's first pitch to him is a curve that sails above Matheny to the backstop. Lofton advances to third with no outs, and now La Russa faces the issue of what to do with the infield. His split-second deliberations begin with the basic question: *How much will this run hurt us?*

Then he resumes the internal dialogue. He weighs the inning: *top of the sixth*. He weighs who is pitching: *Wood*. He weighs how he's pitching: *lights out*. He decides that this run could hurt quite a bit. So it does mean playing the infield in. It sounds easy enough once the strategy is decided on, just wave the boys in and wish them luck, but given all the variables, it isn't simple at all.

Option A puts all the infielders in on the grass. It affords an infielder the best opportunity of stopping a runner on third from scoring if he can get to the ball, but his range is obviously limited because he has less time to get to any ball that's out of his immediate reach. Option B would be to place the infielders halfway in. It would make it slightly more difficult for some punky grounder to get through, and it would give the infielders more room to roam than the naked exposure of option A. It's effective against slow runners, but Lofton isn't slow, so option B is unlikely. Option C plays mind games a little bit by starting the infielders back and then having them charge as the pitch is thrown. The advantage of option C is that it can confuse the third-base coach, who is responsible for sending the runner and may not be prepared for a suddenly charging infield. Another advantage is that all the sudden movement can distract the hitter just enough so that he doesn't make good contact if he hits it. The disadvantage is that it doesn't allow the infielders any time to get set. There's also option D, which is a variation of option C. It's basically a half-charge; within option D are two suboptions: option D-1 in which only the second baseman charges, and option D-2, in which only the shortstop charges. If the hitter is right-handed, you charge only with the second baseman. Because of the natural line of sight of a right-handed hitter, a charging second baseman offers the maximum in terms of distraction, and he still has a chance to make a play since balls to the opposite field are not hit as sharply. Vice versa if it's a left-handed hitter; you send the shortstop.

The complexities are dizzying, the effort to prevent something perhaps encouraging the very thing you want to prevent, the system of pulleys and levers vengeful and sadistic, damned if you do and, given the normal shelf life of a major-league manager—about four years—damned if you do anyway. They are small choices, tiny ripples in the game, but they can also save a win. After examining them, La Russa decides to go with the most comprehensive version, option A, in which *all* the infielders are playing in. With no outs, it's a strategy that has to succeed twice to keep Lofton from scoring, and the odds of such success aren't very good. But La Russa can find no alternatives. He doesn't want that run to score. There is major risk involved: If playing the infield in backfires, the Cubs are set up for a crooked number to put the game out of reach. But he simply doesn't want it. Not with Wood pitching the way he is tonight: ninety-four pitches after five innings. If his ceiling is around 120, he could easily last into the eighth, precisely what La Russa didn't want to happen.

Williams comes in with a curve on the 1 and 0. Martinez hits it hard toward second base. Hart dives for it on the infield grass, getting to the ball quickly and getting it out of his glove fast enough to throw out the runner and hold Lofton at third. The infield-in strategy pays off, and now it has to pay off again with Sosa up.

Sosa approaches the plate in his usual style, more decked out than an overeager groom, tight blue batting gloves stretched tight, a guard to protect his right shin, plus the strangest-looking bat in history, even minus the cork that popped out earlier in the season. From the bottom of it hangs an oversized knob that, as one Chicago sportswriter put it, looks like an ever-expanding goiter. He also has something working in his mouth, gum or tobacco, that seems to grow exponentially the closer he gets to the batter's box— a complement to that goiterish knob. But all his trappings can't distract anyone from his 529 home runs to date. He'll pound any pitch that ventures into his wheelhouse.

Williams works Sammy with four straight fastballs. But three of them go high: 3-1. It's a hitter's count, and Sammy makes his living off counts such as this, seizing on vulnerability. The expectation is fastball, something that can't afford to be too nasty, too in love with the edges. Walking Sammy would put runners on first and third with Alou up, and Alou wears out the Cardinals. As for plunking Sammy in retaliation for Wood's plunking Pujols, now's not a good time, for the same reason that it puts runners on the corners and moves the Cubs closer and closer to the possibility of a crooked number. So Williams has to give him something. But if he gives him too much of something . . .

He comes with a curve. It's a smart pitch on 3 and 1, unexpected. But it hangs a little bit, not quite where Williams wanted to put it. And Sammy gets a swing on it, a good swing.

He singles sharply into left. Pujols takes the ball and, still not taking any chances with his cranky elbow, shuttles it to Edmonds, like a screen pass, so he can make the throw in just in case Sammy has any ideas about going to second. Sammy stays put, but Lofton trots home: 1–0 Cubs.

Williams engages Alou with heart-pounding symmetry. Curve. Foul. Curve. Foul. Curve. Foul. Curve. Foul. Until a fifth curve in a row, the best one Williams has thrown in the at-bat, gets him on a dribbler back to the box. Williams gets out of the inning two batters later. He nicely puts down a first-and-second jam, turns a possible crooked number into a footnote. But because this is baseball—so much decided by who does what first—the fact of the damage is still undeniable: The Cubs have struck first.

10

BEING THERE

I

● ● ● WITH TWO OUTS in the bottom of the sixth and Mike Matheny at bat in the eighth spot with nobody on, La Russa opens the black box mounted on the wall beside him. He picks up the phone and tells Marty Mason to get Cal Eldred up in the bullpen.

Just because he's warming up doesn't mean that Eldred will see any action tonight. If Matheny gets on base, La Russa may decide to pinch-hit for Williams here, which would mean Eldred's entering in the top of the seventh. It's the right place for Eldred, who has generally been used as a middle-inning reliever. But Williams handles a bat as well as any pitcher can. Besides, he's still pitching exquisitely, so it's likelier that La Russa would bring in Eldred sometime later in the seventh, if Williams falters then. If he makes it through the seventh, Eldred may never get in the game, with other relievers in the Cardinals bullpen more suited to the down-to-the-short-hair moment of the eighth and ninth.

It's the fate of the modern-day reliever to live an unrequited life: get up, never mind, sit down, get up, never mind, sit down, just wait for my call, actually we just found someone we like better now. Eldred is inured to this, as is everyone in the Cardinals bullpen, because of La Russa's penchant for tossing relievers in or pulling then out at a moment's notice, guided by his matchups. The blunt truth is that Eldred shouldn't even be here tonight — he should be home in Iowa, in retirement, yet another of those pitchers who burned too brightly and then fell to earth. Which makes the sight of him reassuring, restorative. He is special to La Russa in the same way that Pujols is special to La Russa beyond the skills applied to the field. He represents something that La Russa takes comfort in and admires, a reminder of what still persists in this age of narcissism and personal stat building.

When you have spent so much of your life in baseball that it becomes your life—when you have managed thousands of games and thousands of players—you see the timeline and transformation of the game from a unique point of privilege. You see the changing strike zone and the current mania over pitch count that never existed when Koufax and Gibson and Ryan were going at it during your own formative years. You see the dawn of sweet little cookie-cutter parks where a guy can hit a home run into the short porch in left simply by flicking his wrists. You see the rise of the sinker as the preferred pitch and the neglect of the forkball like an old widow. You see hitters routinely milking the count, whereas when you came up, hitters came to the plate to swing because that was the very point. But what you see most of all is the changing attitudes.

La Russa saw the old attitude on the 1983 White Sox, whom he managed to a division championship, where veterans Jerry Koosman and Greg Luzinski embraced their roles as team leaders. They relished spending money on pizza and beer for team parties at which baseball talk would fill the interchangeable hotel rooms in Seattle and Milwaukee and Boston and Cleveland until sunrise. Carlton Fisk joined those same White Sox as a free agent after all his fame with the Red Sox and jettisoned his pride in favor of work ethic. Under the eye of Charley Lau, Fisk reconstructed his swing and contributed with the freshness of a rookie yearning to prove something to the game instead of the game proving something to him. Like Fisk, Tom Seaver came to the White Sox after a career that had already guaranteed him a plaque in Cooperstown. He was past his sublimity with the Mets, that seven-year stretch from 1969 to 1976 when he won twenty or more four times. But he could still handle a game from the mound in a way that La Russa still talks about with the starry eyes of seeing magic. In 1984 against Toronto, Lloyd Moseby came up in the late innings, with the White Sox clinging to a one-run lead and runners on second and third with two outs. Still in the habit of inquiring over the inevitable, La Russa came out to the mound to ask Seaver how he felt. But Seaver refused to sugarcoat it:

"I don't have much else left."

And then he proceeded to tell La Russa precisely how he was going to pitch to Moseby: purposely run the count on him to 3-1 to lull him into a false sense of superiority, give him a hitter's count, then get him out with a changeup.

"Don't worry about it," he told La Russa.

La Russa trotted back to the dugout, trying not to worry about it. He watched as Seaver threw a fastball in and off the plate to run the count to 3-1. Then he watched as Seaver threw Moseby a changeup that was down and away but still fat enough to desire. Moseby swung, his timing upset by the fastball Seaver had just thrown. He popped the ball up behind third base to end the inning.

La Russa and Seaver ultimately parted, La Russa to the A's and Seaver to the end of his career with the Red Sox. But La Russa's respect for Seaver never diminished, only became stronger when he learned that Seaver turned down an extra year he was entitled to by contract because he didn't have it anymore and didn't want to take something he no longer felt he deserved.

The old attitude showed itself after the hideously painful loss in Game 4 of the 1992 American League Championship series to the Toronto Blue Jays, when A's pitcher Dave Stewart stood in the silent and crestfallen clubhouse and told his teammates to have their bags packed for a return to Toronto, because there was no way he was going to lose Game 5 to let the Blue Jays walk away with the ALCS. You just knew he'd keep his promise, because of that angry take-it-personal fire in his eyes, and he did, pitching a complete game in a 6–2 win. The old attitude could also show itself in defeat, as when Eckersley refused to flinch from the fury of reporters' questions in the clubhouse after he gave up The Home Run to Kirk Gibson in the 1988 World Series against the Dodgers on that fateful back-door slider that went through the front door instead.

There are occasional splendid throwbacks, such as Pujols, and La Russa has had more than his fair share because of the situations in which he has managed. But he also believes that no aspect of the game has changed more profoundly in the last twenty-five years than the values of the players — what turns them on and turns them off and whether some of them can be turned on at all.

He spends more time than ever now schooling players on the value of competition. He explains to them in spring training the challenge and magnificence of getting a World Series ring, because "it won't happen accidentally. You gotta tell 'em to want it." He sees how quickly clubhouses empty out regardless of how sweet the win or how tough the loss, suburbanites hoping to catch the 5:05 home, all-night talk of baseball replaced by simply wanting to get to wherever they're going. He wishes there were more team parties, but when so many players are glancing impatiently at their Rolexes because it's almost ten o'clock, no party could generate much esprit de corps.

In recent years, La Russa has noticed that many players' careers run on either of two settings. Most seasons, players do what they have to do and plug along because when you have talent, you can plug along. During the *free-agency* year, their intensity picks up, and they're like hungry rookies again, eager to prove themselves and to avoid injury. Certain players display increased selfishness, free-swinging on the first pitch because they're 0 for 2 and frantic to get a hit when they really should be working the pitcher for a walk. The only scoreboard they're watching is the one in their head, tracking their stats that may mean nothing during a game but could be worth millions at arbitration. In La Russa's playing days, and during his first years in the foxhole, a manager's tactical ability was the greatest determinant of his shelf life. The psychiatric component of the game — urging players along with pleas and prods and love and tough love — getting them to play hard all the time and focus on competition, was only an occasional duty. The biggest problem that players had in the 1960s and 1970s was, according to Duncan, insecurity: the knowledge that if they didn't perform, they would be up and out. It was a merciless environment for players. But now the problem is overconfidence, the job security they have earned over the years breeding, as he puts it, "a different monster." La Russa calculates that for today's players, winning is "third or fourth on their list behind making money and having security and all that other BS."

Over two and a half decades, La Russa's job description has drastically changed. The strategy is still crucial, but the ability to coax players now is just as important, if not more so.

He was aware of Jose Canseco, the most talented player he has ever managed, sitting with teammates around a hotel pool in Texas in 1990, complaining about the rigors of the baseball season. The A's had been to the World Series the last two years and had clinched the division the night before, but Canseco admitted to a certain ambivalence. "Why is it always us that has to go to the play-offs?" he asked without irony. The A's realized his fears by getting all the way to the World Series against the Reds. But Canseco clearly wanted to be somewhere else—weary of the red, white, and blue bunting and all that other hype. He was still a prodigious hitter when he wanted to be, but what was the point of making a man play in the World Series who didn't want to play in the World Series? He dogged a play in the outfield in Game 2 that cost the A's a victory, so La Russa benched him in Game 4. He tried to cover for Canseco by claiming that he had an injury, and Canseco did in fact have an injury, the crippling baseball disease of disinterest that comes with too much security and too much money and too much attention. Of all the players La Russa ever managed, no one ever had a more virulent case of it.

After the great season of 1988, in which he set the baseball world on fire, Canseco had become a portrait only of distraction. In the middle of the 1990 season, he signed a multiyear, multimillion-dollar contract, but it didn't result in better play. It resulted in the opposite—flailing at pitches nowhere close to the plate, playing the oufield with all the vigor of waiting for a bus—so La Russa called him into his office.

"What the hell are you doing? You're not playing the game. This is not how we play."

"Tony, people would rather watch me take three big swings and try to hit the ball into the upper deck and strike out than shorten up with two strikes and try to play the game."

"You're kidding me?"

"No, I'm serious."

"You're serious but you're wrong. You're a baseball player."

"I'm a performer."

Canseco was also dogged throughout his career by rumors that his prodigious feats on the field were enhanced by taking steroids off the field. During the 1988 American League Championship series against the Red Sox, Boston fans chanted "Ster-oids! Ster-oids!" as Canseco took his spot in right field. Rather than ignore the taunts, he turned, pulled up his sleeve, and flexed his biceps, perhaps just a taunt of his own, given that he hit three home runs in the A's four-game sweep of the Sox. On the eve of the 1988 World Series, Tom Boswell of the *Washington Post* accused Canseco of being on the juice. La Russa had established his own criterion to determine whether a player was taking steroids—a dramatic, bloatlike increase in size and strength in the off-season, without any previous dedication to strength training. But Canseco did not fit the criterion in 1988. Instead, La Russa saw him working out nearly every day in the clubhouse gym under the tutelage of first-base coach Dave McKay, who as a player had been one of the first to discover the fruits of weight training and aerobics. Canseco was stronger than he had been when La Russa came to the A's in 1986, but his tall physique was still relatively lean.

But by 1992, before the A's traded Canseco to Texas, his body was notably different. He had the bloated look—as if he could be popped by a pin—and he wasn't the only player who looked that way during the early 1990s. "That's when it became clear to baseball people that we have something developing here that's not right or normal," said La Russa. But word was out that steroids did make a competitive difference, whatever the medical risks or the illegality (the federal government had classified them as controlled substances). La Russa suspected several players on his teams were juiced, although he also believes that steroid use on his clubs was "not excessive" when compared to other teams.

By the late 1990s, La Russa saw something even more troubling: a widespread pattern of steroid use in the minor league. "Minor leaguers became convinced that to compete they had to do some form of steroids because they were looking at other guys in the minors going from .270 to .300 and fifteen homers to twenty-five." La Russa approached various minor-league players in hopes of discouraging their steroid use: Most were still in their teens, which made the health risks even more acute. They were also spending money they didn't have on juice. But their responses to his warnings only further defined the horror of the situation that organized baseball had created by not testing players for steroids. "How am I gonna make it if I don't?" they asked him. "I'm gonna be released. I got to do it to have a chance. Guys are going right by me."

Of course, steroids were only the latest in a line of enhancers that players had taken over the years to improve performance. In the 1960s, there was "red juice," a liquid stimulant that players of that era favored. Then came "greenies," culminating in a criminal trial in which a doctor admitted he had supplied amphetamines to various members of the Phillies in the early 1980s. After greenies disappeared, it was inevitable that ballplayers would find something else rather than, in the parlance of the game, "play naked."

If it was evident by the late 1990s that taking steroids improved performance, it was also evident that the one entity that could curtail it most effectively—the Major League Baseball Players Association—would not do so. "In each case where any of us would approach a player, what ended up happening was that the union made it clear that you're not going anywhere with this one," said La Russa. So he and other managers and coaches were left to deal with the problem on their own. During spring training, La Russa talked to the team generally about steroid use, pointing out the health risks as well as the consequences of getting caught, because it was a federal crime to use them. He instructed his training staff and coaches never to suggest a player use them. But he didn't make a stump speech about the issue, aware of how little his harangues could achieve in the absence of league testing.

Baseball's owners could have exerted their clout on the players' union to agree to testing, but every time the issue was raised, the union said it was a violation of players' privacy and sealed off further discussion. The owners may have had their own motivations to let the problem continue to escalate. In the late 1990s, the owners—desperate to reclaim the game's fan base after the strike of 1994 that had cancelled the World Series—latched on to the home run as a marketing tool. Fans liked it, and if steroids helped fuel the home-run frenzy, so be it. The tacit sanctioning of steroids upset La Russa and other managers and coaches, and their unease wasn't simply altruistic. Throughout the 1990s, several innovations had gradually shifted the game in the hitters' favor: a lowered mound, added expansion teams (which enlarged and diluted the pool of pitching talent), new teacup-sized ballparks, a tighter strike zone. Add steroids to the list, because they gave strength to drive balls farther, and it was like "piling on," as La Russa put it; crooked numbers became almost effortless in certain parks.

Home-run hysteria peaked in 1998 when the Cards' Mark McGwire and the Cubs' Sammy Sosa battled to break perhaps the most sacred record in all of baseball, Roger Maris's sixty-one home runs in a single season. Both players didn't just break it; they shattered it: McGwire hitting seventy home runs and Sosa sixty-six. La Russa managed McGwire when he broke the record, and McGwire admitted that during the season he had taken a steroid precursor known as "Andro," short for androstendione. Andro was available over the counter at the time, although the NFL and the Olympics had banned it. McGwire made no attempt to hide his use of it. He kept a bottle on the shelf of his locker in plain view, and La Russa does not believe that McGwire ever used anything other than Andro (he also stopped taking it in 1999 and still hit sixty-five home runs). He was big when he came into the league in 1986 and over time became dedicated to working out as often as six days a week in order to prevent further injuries. In the early 1990s, he actually lost weight to take pressure off a chronically sore heel; weight loss runs counter to the bloated look of someone on steroids. But the same could not be said of Canseco. Despite a body that ultimately metamorphosed into an almost cartoonish shape—Brutus meets Popeye—he denied throughout his career that he ever had taken steroids, until his playing days ended in 2002. Two weeks later, ever the performer, he admitted with much ballyhoo that he had indeed been on the juice.

Rickey Henderson was another high-profile player who moved to his own brooding rhythms. In all of La Russa's years of managing, no player in baseball has ever been more dangerous than Henderson with his combination of on-base percentage and base-stealing skills and power. Impervious to pressure unlike any player La Russa had ever seen before, he became a marked man around the league because he could beat you in so many ways, and he still starred for almost the entire decade of the 1980s. Henderson was a popular teammate, friendly and respectful. But he could be difficult.

In 1991, he started turning to La Russa before games and saying that he could not play because of hard-to-pinpoint injuries. La Russa appreciated Henderson's talent and knew that his own job was to tap into the pool of it. He understood that Henderson always believed that he was being taken advantage of, screwed with. It had driven him nuts in 1990 when the A's, after saying that they could not pay any single player more than $3 million a year, signed Canseco to a $5-million-a-year contract. Henderson was pissed and rightly so, La Russa felt, given that he was having an MVP year.

Henderson became convinced that Canseco was getting preferential treatment and watched obsessively for evidence. By 1992, Henderson made sure that Canseco got nothing over him, including the disabled list. When Canseco went, Henderson went. If Canseco said he couldn't play for a couple of days, Henderson said he couldn't play for a couple of days. As the manager, La Russa could insist that Henderson play if there was no apparent injury. But what good would that do? When Henderson said he couldn't go and La Russa put him in anyway, he'd simply stand in the outfield "like a cigar store Indian. Balls would bounce here, bounce there, all around him."

La Russa established a rule: When Henderson felt he couldn't play, he had to tell him directly instead of relaying it through the trainer, as players usually did. That way, at least, La Russa and Henderson could discuss why he couldn't play. This system worked well; Henderson opted out only a few times, until one game against Baltimore around the All-Star break in 1993. The A's were trying to stay in the divisional race, and there were rumors that Henderson might be traded for a pitcher.

"I can't go today," he told La Russa.

"What do you mean you can't go?"

"I'm telling you, Tony. If I tell you I can't go, I can't go."

"Rickey . . ."

"Rickey's head's not right."

"What do you mean your head's not right?"

"I hear I'm being traded. So my head's not right. I can't go."

In the decade since then, La Russa has had dozens of such conversations, conversations that can steal his faith.

And then there's Eldred, warming up in the bottom of the sixth of Game 2. And La Russa's faith returns.

II

HE WAS a phenom once — a first-round pick of the Brewers in the June 1989 draft. He had the label in the late 1980s as he rolled through Beloit and Stockton and El Paso and Denver. His face — sweetly round and soft — contained a corn-fed quality that people liked to associate with a big, strapping 6'4" kid from Cedar Rapids who could bring it. He had a four-seam let-it-rip fastball, and he liked letting it go. The notes from the Cardinals media guide about Eldred, one of those elliptical athlete's biographies, testified to its power:

1989 — . . . named the No. 2 College Prospect in the country by *Collegiate Baseball.*

1990 — Struck out a season high 15 batters on 5/10 vs. San Jose . . . opened the season at Stockton with a one-hit, 14-strikeout performance.

1991 — . . . led Class AAA pitchers in strikeouts, IP and games started . . . was named the Brewers' Minor League Player of

the Year . . . made his ML debut on 9/24 vs. NYY, becoming
the first Brewers rookie since Rickey Keaton (1980) to win
his starting pitching debut.

1992 — Was named AL Rookie Pitcher of the Year by *The Sporting News* . . . posted an 11-2 record with a 1.79 ERA . . . set
club record with a .846 winning percentage surpassing Moose
Haas (.813 in 1983) . . . tied club record with 10 straight wins
from 8/8 to 9/29 . . . limited opponents to a .207 BA, best
among AL starting pitchers . . . was named AL Pitcher of the
Month for September after going 5-0 with a 1.17 ERA and
two complete games.

Following that sublime rookie season in 1992, Eldred established himself as the Brewers' workhorse. In his first full season
in 1993, at the age of twenty-five, he led the American League in
innings pitched, with 258. He finished third in the same category
in 1994. After all, he was a big kid from Iowa, and that's what
big kids from Iowa are supposed to do, work on the mound just
like they're working back on the farm. Myth became reality and
reality became myth. Had they not been keeping him so busy
pitching, the Brewers might have put Eldred in a milking contest
during the seventh-inning stretch against some western Wisconsin
magic-fingers udder expert. During both years, he tied for the
league lead in games started. And then the media guide begins to
read differently:

1995 — . . . was placed on the disabled list on 5/19 and missed the
remainder of the season after having Tommy John surgery
on 6/23.

1996 — . . . began the season on the 60-day disabled list . . .

1998 — . . . was placed on the 15-day disabled list on 7/27 with a
small fracture in his right elbow and missed the rest of the
season . . .

1999 — . . . began the season on the 15-day disabled list recovering from a small fracture in his right elbow . . .

2000 — Injuries to his right elbow cut short one of his best major-
league seasons . . . did not pitch from 7/15–9/26 . . . left his first
start of the second half on 7/14 vs. STL in the fifth inning after
experiencing discomfort in his right elbow . . . injury was later

diagnosed as ulnar neuritis . . . was placed on 15-day disabled list on 7/17 . . . allowed four runs in 2.0 IP in his second rehab start on 9/3 before experiencing pain (diagnosed as a stress fracture below his right elbow) . . . had a five-inch screw surgically inserted near his elbow on 9/7 by White Sox senior team physician Dr. James Boscardin . . .

2001 — Made two starts, both against Cleveland, before missing the rest of the season with an injury to his right elbow . . . was placed on the 15-day DL on 4/12 and did not pitch again . . .

2002 — Sat out the entire season as he continued to rehab his injured right elbow.

From 1995 to 2002, there was only one season in which Eldred had not been sidelined by injuries involving his right elbow. He was on the disabled list six times. He missed large chunks of the 1995, 1998, 2000, and 2001 seasons. He went through Tommy John surgery. He suffered a small fracture in his right elbow and then a stress fracture below his right elbow, requiring the insertion of the 5-inch screw to somehow patch it back together. It isn't unusual for a pitcher to miss an entire season because of arm troubles and then come back. Arm troubles are to pitchers what girl troubles are to country singers. But Eldred didn't miss one season; he basically missed *two,* his last game on April 11, 2001, when he was with the White Sox and pitched two innings against Cleveland before knowing the elbow still wasn't right. In 1992, he'd been named AL Rookie of the Year. Nine years later, his arm was useless; he couldn't pick up one of his children, much less pitch. Hindsight suggested that the Brewers had done him no favors by working him so hard early in his career.

He went back home to Cedar Rapids. His wife was pregnant with their fourth child, and Eldred realized that there were certain things about baseball he didn't miss at all, such as the travel or the time away from his family. In August 2001, he had the *fourth* surgery on his right elbow, to remove the screw that had been inserted. When the next baseball season rolled around, Eldred was still in Iowa. And then he felt something, or more precisely the absence of something, and he thought it was worth telling his wife:

"My arm doesn't hurt."

For the first time in what seemed like forever, he could do household chores without pain. And then came the usually catastrophic thought that comes to every former pro athlete—*Do I have something left?* This too was worth telling the wife:

"I think I'm gonna try to pitch again."

Eldred missed the competition. He missed being part of a team. Those are the things that you expect an athlete to mention when you ask what he misses. But there was something else. He knew that his wife might have a difficult time truly understanding it, as would anybody who hasn't done it. It was the feeling of what it felt like to grip a baseball, know the grip felt right in the fingers because you were coming with a full-heat hothouse four-seamer, throw that four-seamer to the very spot you intended, then watch it *pop* into the back of the catcher's glove as the hitter swings through it. It wasn't a macho feeling to Eldred. It was simply one worth trying to have again.

His wife, slightly more detached about it all and therefore less sanguine, advised him:

"If it hurts again, stop."

Eldred mentioned his intention to a trainer he was friendly with, Mitch Doyle, at nearby Coe College. Doyle was surprised, maybe a little dubious about the ability of a pitcher to come back from *four* elbow surgeries. But if that's what Eldred wanted, Doyle was willing to help.

They started by playing catch around the Coe College campus. Bit by bit, Eldred's tosses became a little stronger. He threw with a little more authority, although the worst thing to do was to overdo it, so he didn't. In September, he went to a clinic in Tempe to further rehab his arm. At the end of September, just before he returned to Iowa, he got up on the mound for the first time in nearly two years. He was nervous and excited and also practical. *Well, if it works, it works.*

He wasn't throwing anything close to fire—his old fire was long gone, and he knew it would not come back. But he was exquisitely pain free, the most beautiful term there is to a pitcher who has felt pain, the roots of something still there. About a month later, he went back to Arizona to throw again, this time in front of about twenty scouts. One of them was Marty Keough of the Cardinals, dispatched by Walt Jocketty, the general manager. Keough was interested in Eldred's control, as the lack of it would indicate a physical problem that forced him to push the ball instead of throwing naturally. Eldred's control was excellent.

The Cardinals signed him as a minor-league free agent. He came to spring training as a nonroster invitee, a thirty-five-year-old rising from the dead. He threw off the mound in the spring training complex, lined up in a row beside kids who had been thirteen when he had won his first major-league game. When Dennis Eckersley visited the Jupiter complex and heard that Eldred was in camp, he told La Russa:

"Hope he doesn't break down."

La Russa and Duncan watched Eldred carefully, refusing at first to let him throw a curve because of the arm stress it could cause. They watched him in his first appearance of the spring against the Marlins, the first game he had pitched in 690 days. He went two innings and struck out three and gave up one run on three hits. They watched him five days later, again facing the Marlins, when he gave up no hits in four innings and struck out four. And they watched him again five days later when he threw four scoreless innings for the second time in a row to lower his ERA to .90. His next two outings were wobbly, more than wobbly, nine runs and sixteen hits in eight innings.

He was on the cusp. As the Cardinals began to trim their payroll to somewhere around $83 million, they questioned the efficacy of keeping Joey Hamilton and Al Levine, who had been signed in the off-season as relievers. In the best of all possible worlds, they would have kept them, but baseball is not the best of all possible worlds except for the Yankees, and by dumping them in the spring, they could save on their salaries. The Cards let them go, and the space they vacated allowed Eldred a spot on the opening-day roster as a right-handed setup reliever.

La Russa admired his guts. He admired his professionalism. He admired the way he went about his business, one of those guys you never had to sit down with to remind him why he was playing. But La Russa also knew that he had made it by omission. Had there been no need to pare payroll, he might well have been back in Iowa. The team's right-handed relief pitching, particularly with the closer Jason Isringhausen on the shelf until June, scared the hell out of La Russa and Duncan. And although there had been moments of shine in Eldred's performance so far, La Russa had been through enough springs to know one thing:

"Never fall in or out of love too early in the spring."

In the ninth inning of the opening game of the season, with the Cardinals nursing an 11–7 lead against the Brewers, La Russa put in Eldred to get him reacclimated, give him a margin of error if there was error. The results did not inspire confidence:

IP	H	R	ER	BB	SO	HR	ERA
0	3	2	2	0	0	1	Infinity

He put Eldred in three days later, in the last game of the four-game series against the Brewers:

IP	H	R	ER	BB	SO	HR	ERA
⅓	3	3	3	0	0	1	135.00

Not much confidence there either. But Duncan worked with Eldred. He encouraged him to develop a two-seam sinker as a complement to his four-seamer. He helped him to modify his breaking ball so it had more of a side-to-side movement across the strike zone. In keeping with his belief in the value of the first-pitch strike, he urged him not to cut it too sharp on the first pitch, just throw something get-me-over and then nibble. Five days after his outing against the Brewers, Eldred came in to relieve in the twelfth in the pitcher's punishment of Coors Field in Denver:

IP	H	R	ER	BB	SO	HR	ERA
2	0	0	0	0	2	0	19.29

It was his first win in the major leagues in 1,014 days.

His ERA started to resemble an Internet stock bubble, plummeting from that high of infinity and confirming the wisdom of the investment: scoreless inning against the Rockies on April 10—13.50. Two scoreless innings against the Astros on April 13—8.44. Three scoreless innings against the Marlins on April 27—5.06. Scoreless inning against the Mets on May 1—4.63. Scoreless inning against the Cubs on May 16—3.94. Scoreless inning against the Red Sox on June 10—3.46.

He was prone to the ill-timed dinger. Sometimes the cutter slipped a little bit, landing over the plate when he wanted it more inside. Sometimes when Matheny wanted to go back away, Eldred shook him off and went inside, with the result a double pulled down the line. But he had appeared in fifty games during the season up until this moment in the bottom of the sixth. He had thrown fifty-one innings and struck out an equal number. He led the Cardinals relievers in wins with seven. And sometimes, when he threw the four-seamer and it went to the spot he intended and it exploded with a pop in the back of the catcher's glove as the hitter swung through it, he knew exactly why he was here: not for money, not for glory, not to build up his own statistical package, but because it was still where he belonged.

III

WHILE ELDRED gets loose, Matheny continues to gut it out against Kerry Wood. He fends off two fastballs foul before he flies out to left on a tough curve low and outside. It puts down the Cardinals in the bottom of the sixth, still behind 1–0, and it brings out Woody Williams for the seventh, as he didn't come up to bat in the previous inning. Eldred remains in his holding pattern, La Russa delaying any decision until he sees how Williams fares.

He has an eleven-pitch inning, retiring the Cubs in order, even his nemesis Damian Miller. He's shown remarkable economy so far through seven: 104 pitches, 74 strikes, and 30 balls. He's thrown 13 first-pitch strikes to the twenty-seven batters he's faced and his line score up to now is about as good as it gets, all you could possibly want from him:

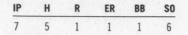

IP	H	R	ER	BB	SO
7	5	1	1	1	6

Which is probably why he slams down a bat in frustration in the back of the dugout when he learns that he is being lifted for a pinch hitter in the bottom of the seventh. He's pitching well, more than well, but the decision is easy for La Russa, given a fresh bullpen that should be able to hold the Cubs at bay for the eighth and ninth. Conversely, there are only nine outs left offensively, and when he pinch-hits for Williams, his thinking is clear: *We need to start the rally.*

He picks the right-handed So Taguchi. Actually, he's already picked him; while Williams was still pitching the seventh, La Russa moved down the dugout and whispered into Taguchi's ear to get ready.

Taguchi is from Japan. He starred for the Orix Blue Wave in the Japanese Pacific League after a distinguished career at Nishino-myia Kita High School and Kansai Gakuin University in Osaka. He won five Gold Gloves for his defensive play, generally ranked around the top fifteen in batting average, was a teammate of Ichiro, and signed as a free agent for a million dollars. He is still a star in Japan, and when he's up with the Cardinals—he's been back and forth between St. Louis and Triple-A Memphis—a little knot of Japanese reporters follows his every move, seeking ways to extol his contributions even when all he does is pinch-run. He speaks little English, is polite to a fault, smiles to those he sees while offering a little self-effacing nod, and spends most of the time in the clubhouse, studying video. He first started playing baseball when he was three and it shows; his fundamentals are beautiful, a purer foundation of the game than with most American players. There is only one major flaw to him—he's had trouble hitting major-league pitching with consistency. It's why he has spent much of the season at Triple-A.

Like every move that La Russa makes, this is not some seat-of-the-pants calculation, which isn't to say that it also won't fizzle: At the very least, he has some prior logic for it. Before each game, La Russa prioritizes his bench players, subject to the matchups they have against an opponent's pitching, and the crucial explanations of performance those numbers reveal. The choice of Taguchi here means not choosing Miguel Cairo or Eddie Perez or Orlando Palmeiro, pinch hitters La Russa feels he must save for the eighth or ninth innings, given that nobody is on base right now and the game is still close. That may make the decision easier, but it becomes complicated again since Taguchi has never faced Wood before, which means there are no matchup numbers to provide a glimmer of the future.

In evaluating Taguchi, however, La Russa has discovered several key attributes about him. One is that he has never been in awe of the major-league baseball scene ever since coming over from Japan, which means that he won't be a deer in the headlights against Wood. Whatever his abilities—and they are not limitless—they will not disappear late in the game: take a leave of absence in the face of Pinch Hitter Madness, a hitter who by mandate is cold—thrust against a pitcher who has had seven innings to get hot and stay hot. La Russa has also seen Taguchi make a greater effort as of late not simply to stay inside the ball and hit the opposite way, but also to use the pull side of the plate. It means he's starting to cover both sides of the plate, crucial against a pitcher such as Wood, given that he is throwing to both areas tonight.

Just like Williams, Wood has gotten sharper as the game has progressed. He's given up one hit since the third inning, and he's already struck out ten. He comes with a fastball low and on the outside, and Taguchi fouls it off for 0 and 1. Wood throws a slider that nibbles low and outside, and Taguchi hits another foul for 0 and 2. Wood throws a waste pitch nowhere close to make the count 1 and 2, but then he gets serious again. Taguchi's helplessness is palpable.

Wood comes with a slider on the outside black, and Taguchi fouls it off. Wood comes with a curve that bites low, and Taguchi has no choice but to protect himself because of the count, and he *fouls* that off too, his fifth in six pitches. He's hanging in there in a decided pitcher's count, the reason La Russa went to him. Finally, on the seventh pitch, a fastball on the inside of the plate, Wood puts Taguchi away with a fly out to right.

It goes down in the record books as a failure, of course, an 0 for

1. But to La Russa, it is a beautiful at-bat, a testament to Taguchi's deceptive grit and his obsessive scrutiny of video. Even though he's a bench player who's never faced Wood before, Taguchi is familiar enough with his pitches that he could at least battle them off. He won the at-bat without ever leaving the plate. It's also the most important at-bat the Cardinals have had thus far, because it took Wood to seven pitches at a time when each pitch he throws is a precious commodity, one more drop from a drying well.

His count is up to 116 after Taguchi worked him for all those fouls. Kerry Robinson follows with a grounder to second, but he doesn't go down gently either, pushing Wood for six more pitches. Bo Hart doesn't do as well. He strikes out in three pitches to end the inning.

Another agonizing chapter is slotted into the scoreboard with few pages left to figure out the whodunit:

	1	2	3	4	5	6	7	R	H	E
CUBS	0	0	0	0	1	0	0	1	5	0
CARDINALS	0	0	0	0	0	0	0	0	4	0

But Wood's count stands at 125. Even though he retired the side in order, and even though he's pitching a finer gem than Williams, Baker must now ask the very question that La Russa has been waiting for: *Will Wood pitch the eighth?*

11

UNDER PRESSURE

I

● ● ● *Wood's at 125.*

La Russa doesn't envy Dusty Baker here, facing one of those decisions that, if it doesn't pan out, will have half the sports talk of Chicago saying he blew it because *Whaddya crazy, how can you take Wood out of the game when he's pitching like he is, and look, don't get me wrong, Dusty's been really nice for the Cubs, but let's face it: He handles pitching about as well as he handled his little kid when he was the batboy for the Giants and almost got run over in the World Series* and the other half saying, *Whaddya crazy, it'd blow out Wood's arm, and look, don't get me wrong, Dusty's been really nice for the Cubs, but let's face it: He handles pitching about as well as he handled his little kid when he was the batboy for the Giants and almost got run over in the World Series.*

No decision has more public glare for a manager than when— or whether—he should remove the starting pitcher in a close game. In other sports, starters and substitutes routinely slip in and slip out. A coach makes a mistake and gets a chance to rectify it. It's a momentary lapse at worst. But in baseball, when you're out, you're out.

Last inning, it was the scoreboard that pushed La Russa to hook Woody Williams, down 1–0 with only nine outs left. He knew he had to make a move, the only question was what move to make. As usual, he began with the matchup numbers of the Cardinals relievers against the top of the Cubs' lineup coming to bat in the eighth, then excavated behind them. It came down to a choice between Cal Eldred and Mike DeJean, the new arrival from Milwaukee. La Russa elected to go with DeJean, based on the fact that his out pitches—a running fastball to the third side of the plate and a forkball—would be more effective here than Eldred's out pitch, a cutter to the first-base side. Eldred has been working on a two-seamer to the third-base side, but he has yet to develop full confidence in it, which is another vote for DeJean. It all sounds smart and wise, but baseball doesn't care right now. DeJean gets Lofton on a fly ball to left for the first out. Then he gives up a single to Martinez, followed by a double by Sosa.

Sosa's hit burns even more, since this was supposed to be the moment when DeJean sent a little message to Sosa in return for Wood's nicking Pujols's shirt, suitable retaliation for La Russa under the circumstances that Wood's act was probably inadvertent. At least make him dance a little bit, feel the heat. But the message got mixed up. His first pitch was a fastball way outside, off the plate. Then he left his second pitch, which was meant to be inside, on the center of the plate. Sosa killed it into the gap and Martinez easily scored for the added cushion of a 2–0 lead.

That doesn't help with Baker's pitching choice, though; because it rotates around the noose of the pitch count, the extra run gives Wood and the bullpen equal room to maneuver. The bullpen is fresh; Wood is not. So that's a vote for the bullpen. But Wood only looks stronger, not weaker, and the Cubs bullpen, even when it gets the desired result, is best watched with both eyes closed. So that's a vote for Wood. Baker can use his bullpen to match up the Cardinals hitters to death, a pursuit he relishes almost as much as La Russa does. But Wood is overpowering tonight. But . . .

Wood's at 125.

Pitch counts are another part of the Darwinian evolution of the game, ignored for the first one hundred years, creeping into the consciousness over the next twenty, and now a sacred commandment. In the late 1950s and early 1960s, pitchers threw somewhere around 155 pitches a game. But one manager, Paul Richards, was beginning to consider the wear and tear on a pitcher's arm. When he was running the Orioles, he put Milt Pappas on a seventy-pitch count to nurture his arm, with the net result a seventeen-year career for Pappas and 209 wins despite the nickname of "Gimpy." It made sense to Richards, just as it made sense to him when, tired of watching Gus Triandos failing repeatedly to catch Hoyt Wilhelm's evil knuckleball, he invented an odd-looking catcher's mitt—as oversized as a clown bowtie—because there was nothing in the rules saying you couldn't. Close to twenty years later, Richards introduced La Russa to the concept of pitch count when he told him as a minor-league manager to place a strict hundred-pitch threshold on the arms of White Sox up-and-comers Steve Trout, Richard Dotson, and Britt Burns.

Today, that threshold is the golden rule, the moment when managers instinctively start to make appointments with the bullpen. But Richards, when he first started keeping track, was an anomaly. In the 1970s, when pitch counts were not recorded with the religiosity that they are today, Nolan Ryan once threw 235 pitches in thirteen innings against the Red Sox.* In addition, the relief game, of which La Russa may well be the key cultural anthropologist, had yet to evolve. The ninth-inning closer was not yet born, never mind the legions of setup specialists, each of whom might be called in just to get one out. Situational matchups between hitter and pitcher in the late innings, which La Russa probably relies on more than any manager ever has, weren't remotely contemplated. Counts eventually did begin to drop, among increasing suspicion that starters, particularly young guys, would inevitably blow out their arms if subjected to the rigors of the past.

Like other aspects of baseball, a significant evolution was also taking place in the use of the bullpen. In the early 1970s, when La

---

* Ryan struck out nineteen Red Sox hitters in the game, on June 14, 1974. Chief among them was Cecil Cooper, who struck out six times in a row. He also walked ten batters before being lifted, achieving a rare baseball double-double. The Angels won in the fifteenth 4–3.

Russa was playing at Triple-A in Des Moines and Wichita, he noticed a manager in the league named Vern Rapp, in Indianapolis. Rapp's team maintained a stoked bullpen far beyond the traditional setup guy and closer—he had his own little legion of relievers—which set off La Russa's curiosity. Rapp said that it had become obvious to him that hitters, faced with the choice between seeing an effective starter in the late innings or a fresh reliever of good but hardly lights-out vintage, would still opt for the starter. Familiarity didn't breed contempt for a starter as much as it did comfort, Rapp noticed; a hitter, even if he were 0 for 3 against a starter with three strikeouts, would still rather face him because of the considerable value of having seen his full repertoire of pitches. Also, unlike a starter, a reliever could rely almost exclusively on his best pitch, and air it pitch after pitch because he knew he would be in on only a limited basis. Unlike a starter, he never had to worry about fatigue and pacing himself.

If it made life even more miserable than usual for a hitter, it also made life easier for a reliever, particularly one who knew the rigors of starting. Eckersley, for example, after a career of starting, chafed at being sent to the bullpen by Oakland in 1987 after his trade there. He considered it banishment, purgatory for lesser pitchers, an absolute affront to his machismo. Until he realized the joy of being able to come into a game and throw whatever you wanted as hard as you wanted, just let it rip and not fret too terribly much over pitch selection. Along with his imperviousness to pressure, it's what made Eckersley a Hall of Fame reliever, the luxury of concentrating his stuff into ten or twelve pitches.

Beginning in the 1990s, the role of the bullpen was refined even further so that hitters weren't routinely facing a reliever or two in the late innings but virtual swarms of them, each with a speciality pitch, each one able to simply let it go because they knew they would not be hanging around for very long, maybe only one batter. Managers, if they were holding a lead into the small hours of the game, also began to break down the last third into *individual* outs, nine opportunities to make life as miserable as possible for every hitter coming to the plate. Hence greater use of relievers than ever for only one at-bat.

The change in bullpen use had an obvious effect on pitch counts. By 1989, the average pitch count for a starter had fallen to ninety-four, according to the *Cultural Encyclopedia of Baseball.* By 1991, it was down to eighty-two. In 1987, 106 pitchers had games in which they threw 140 pitches or more. The number had dwindled to thirty-six by 1995. Even nearer extinction was the complete game, plummeting from 40 percent in 1950 to 4 percent in 2001.*

Some former managers—Jim Leyland, for example—believe that the one-hundred-pitch threshold too often becomes a crutch. He's worth listening to, perhaps, as La Russa credits him with having a better instinct for when to take a pitcher out than any other manager he has ever played against. "Just because a pitcher has thrown extra pitches doesn't mean he's done," says Leyland. "One of the areas where a manager falls into a trap is when he worries about who he will have to answer to after the game."

He believes that pitch count is as much a function of greed as it is keeping young arms safe and strong. "You got agents involved. You got big money at stake. You got lawsuits. Trainers are scared to death." For him, the irony of reduced pitch counts is that today's pitchers are much better conditioned than the men who routinely threw 150 a game back in the 1960s and 1970s. "These guys are in better shape and they run more and half of them have home gymnasiums and strength trainers. I think managers baby them." Nor, Leyland believes, do they ever effectively learn their trade in the minor leagues. "They used to have to get out of their own jams. Now someone else there does it for them."

Baker, who doesn't think much of the one-hundred-pitch threshold, would no doubt be heartened by Leyland's comments. When he came up as a player in the 1970s, the pitch count that most managers went by was an occasional glance at the mound to make sure that the guy's arm was still connected to his shoulder. Despite withering criticism in the media and the sports talk shows that he

---

* The last major-league pitcher to throw thirty complete games was Catfish Hunter of the A's in 1975, and the last to throw twenty was Fernando Valenzuela of the Dodgers in 1986. In 2001, Curt Schilling was the National League leader with six, the lowest complete game total ever.

doesn't know how to preserve pitchers, Baker has had only two during his ten-year managing career who required arm surgery. But it still doesn't solve the immediate problem of what to do:

Wood's at 125.

Baker has managed against La Russa enough to know what La Russa would like him to do: pull Wood and let the Cardinals finally get a shot at the bullpen. He knows that Wood is pitching as well as he's pitched all year. He knows that Wood has thrown more than 125 pitches in a game already this season, going as high as 141 against the Cardinals in the hitter's Club Med of Wrigley. And all he needs is *six outs*. Granted, it is *six outs* against the meat of the Cardinals lineup, with Pujols followed by Jim Edmonds followed by Scott Rolen. But Wood has been *blowing them away*. They are an aggregate 1 for 6 against him today with three strikeouts.

But Wood is one of those young pitcher poster boys who developed arm trouble early in his career. He exceeded 118 pitches in twelve of his twenty-six starts as a rookie and once threw 175 pitches in a single game in high school, because if you think major-league managers are tough on arms, you should take a look at high school and college coaches. It's true that Edmonds is a lefty, and late in the game, that's a matchup you would probably rather avoid because Edmonds can go downtown with the pressure on. And all the bullpen needs is *six outs*. It's why you have those guys sitting around back there doing nothing for most of the game, and if you don't have a bullpen that can't get *six outs,* there's no point even pretending you're going to get anywhere near October.

Wood's done at 125.

He's been hooked. Antonio Alfonseca has come out of the bullpen to face Pujols to begin the bottom of the eighth. He's big, 6'5", and unlike other pitchers that tall, there is nothing string bean about him. His chest is large, very large; it barrels beyond his uniform. His physique makes you think of a small-town sheriff who likes his barbecue big and doesn't mind confrontation. He's also an anomaly, with six fingers on his pitching hand, which may help to explain why he has dominated Pujols more than virtually any other pitcher, getting him out five of the six times he has faced him.

He's in the classic role of specialty reliever, probably in only for this one at-bat, with a lefty due up next, so he can flaunt his out pitch with impunity because he doesn't have to worry about seeing the hitter again. His strength is hard and down to the third side of the plate, which for a hitter means "cheating" a little bit—getting the bat head out early—or keeping his hands inside the ball. Alfonseca has no need to save up strength and pace himself, think down the line. He comes in throwing hard and leaves throwing hard, and the whole time he's in, he exudes contempt and swagger. To La Russa, someone like Alfonseca is perhaps the most difficult pitcher in the game to do something against. The worst approach for a hitter to take here is the misguided heroism of going for the bomb.

With only six outs left for the Cardinals, with first place, maybe the division championship, at stake, the pressure is enormous. Sabermetricians—those numbers-crunchers who have come to dominate thinking about strategy over the past few years—believe that they have debunked clutch situations as statistically irrelevant. La Russa has read the various studies. Based on his own forty years plus of experience, he believes those studies to be bunk of their own. To say that players don't react differently to the tension of a clutch situation is to deny the existence of human nature. He has seen thousands of players under pressure, and he knows that they have varying but distinct reactions to it: some so pumped up that you must remind them to breathe, some rendered tentative by it, a distressing number not wanting to deal with it at all. "Players can make a lot of money on their stats alone. They can play below their optimum and still make a very good living," says La Russa. "There are a lot of players that don't really want to dig deep enough to try to win."

Some coaches think that the best way to deal with pressure is to ignore it, treat every moment of a game the same so as not to heighten the tension even more. La Russa believes that players need to openly acknowledge pressure—literally embrace it as "your friend," in his words—because the more they embrace it, the less it can intimidate them. He teaches hitters that the best way to deal with pressure is to prepare for it, come into the at-bat with a keen sense of what the pitcher is likely to throw and how you should handle it. Most important, when you're up there, focus on the process and not the result; don't project into the future. Forget about the noble but irrational concept of going for broke. Put away the hero complex and simply try to get something started. But don't hesitate, either: In clutch moments, you're unlikely to get your perfect pitch, so don't wait around for it. Be aggressive.

Nobody lives these principles better than the great Pujols. Alfonseca serves him a sinker low and inside to start the inning. It's a good first pitch: difficult to drive, difficult to get into the gap. Pujols stays inside of it with his hands. He doesn't try to do too much with it; he simply makes contact, and the ball scoots up the middle, past the shipwreck hulk of Alfonseca. It's a single, an Oscar-worthy short-form documentary on focusing on the process and not the result.

Edmonds is due up next, but before he gets to the plate, Baker goes to the mound and makes a quick little jab signal to the bullpen, like a New Yorker hailing a cab. Alfonseca is hooked, replaced by the lefty Mark Guthrie. It's a good matchup for Baker, as Edmonds is a negligible 2 for 11 against him. Guthrie's stuff is not as good as it used to be; he has to stay away from the strike zone, or he'll get tattooed. Nowadays, he lives off chase pitches, and he's been pretty good at it. If he's not as strong as he once was, he's also smarter.

He comes with a curve low and away on the first pitch. Edmonds swings through it, and Guthrie has the coveted first-pitch strike. He throws a forkball high. Edmonds holds off, and the count evens to 1 and 1. He follows with a sweet curve on the outside black, and Edmonds is now 1 and 2 and not looking very good in the process, Guthrie tying him into knots with effective junk. He comes with a forkball, and this pitch is even better than the curve he just threw: sweeter, nastier. Edmonds holds up, but this is strike 3. In the foxhole, even La Russa concedes that it's strike 3. In fact, the only person who doesn't think it's strike 3 is the home plate umpire. He calls it a ball. Guthrie comes with a curve that sails outside to make the count 3 and 2. He follows with another curve, close enough to the strike zone that Edmonds can't afford to hold up on it. It's in on the hands a little bit so that Edmonds's only alternative, which isn't much of one, is to fight it off and see whether he can turn it over just enough into the outfield. It drops for a single to right.

Rolen is now due up, with runners on first and second and no outs. But before he gets to the plate, Baker goes to the mound again and hails another cab. Guthrie is hooked in favor of Kyle Farnsworth because righty-versus-righty would be a better matchup for the Cubs.

Pacing back and forth in the foxhole, La Russa privately debates about putting on a bunt. But it feels like too defensive a play right now, given that Rolen has the power to turn the game into a 3–2 lead with one swing. Looking ahead, he begins to consider the possibility of pinch hitters after Rolen. J.D. Drew's presence as a bench player would be enormous if Baker sticks with Farnsworth. Drew *kills* Farnsworth; La Russa has it written down on the little cheat sheets he keeps in his back pocket:

DREW   5-7-3

But Drew isn't here, and La Russa can't dwell on what he doesn't have.

The count runs to a quick 3 and 0 on Rolen. But Farnsworth fights back with two strikes, and the count is full. La Russa thinks about trying a double steal to break up the double play that might result if Rolen hits the ball on the ground. But he worries that the runner going from second to third might distract Rolen at the plate, upset his timing or maybe push him to swing at a bad pitch. Even though Rolen has swung and missed twice, they were two good swings, so he's not looking cold at the plate. La Russa also figures that even if he puts the ball on the ground, Rolen has just enough speed to possibly beat it out and hold the Cubs to a force-out. He keeps the runners where they are. Farnsworth throws his fifth straight fastball. It's high, and the bases are loaded with nobody out.

Tino Martinez is now due up. Because he's a lefty, La Russa waits for Baker to hail a cab. Surely he'll send in a lefty pitcher to face the lefty hitter. When he does, La Russa may counter with his own move to push the matchup back his own way. He may remove Martinez for a pinch hitter, but it's not an easy emotional decision for him. He knows that Martinez has four World Series rings from his days as a Yankee. He knows the way in which, all his career, he has accepted the responsibilities of being a key hitter in key situations. That's the Martinez the Cardinals signed for $21 million after the 2001 season. But La Russa also knows the struggling Martinez, and in clutch situations with runners in scoring position, Martinez has been struggling terribly. So the question for La Russa, the one he will have to make in a matter of moments, is to somehow try to glean which Martinez is going to come to the plate.

II

MARTINEZ'S RESPONSE to pressure has been like a 45-rpm record, a timeless hit on one side and the flip side maybe best forgotten. When La Russa needs an example of how to deal with tension, he points to the bottom of the ninth inning of Game 4 of the 2001 World Series between the Yankees and the Diamondbacks at the Stadium, fifty days after September 11. Martinez was up with two outs against Byung-Hyun Kim and the Yankees down by 3–1 with a runner on first. He remembers what anyone who has ever watched baseball will remember: that game-tying two-run homer into right field that didn't simply shake Yankee Stadium to new levels of hysteria but unleashed torrents of pride through a suffering city. La Russa was curious about what had gone through Martinez's mind in the ultimate clutch situation: whether he was thinking home run or at the very least trying to pull the ball. Tino said no; he knew that Kim was a fastball pitcher, so that's what he was looking for, a fastball that he could put his best swing on. To La Russa, it was the perfect answer: putting his best swing on the pitch—not his home-run swing, not his pull swing—just his best one. Focusing on the process and not the result.

The flip side could be seen once Martinez came to St. Louis after the 2001 season. He signed a fat three-year deal, which placed the noose of expectations on a player who many around the league thought was losing bat speed, nowhere close to hitting the forty-four home runs he'd hit for the Yankees in 1997. Martinez also had to fill the shoes of Mark McGwire at first base, an expectation no man could fulfill given McGwire's season-breaking seventy home runs in 1998. Martinez immediately became a fall guy for St. Louis fans who, by this season, had begun doing something they almost never did: booing a Cardinal when he came to the plate. Because Cards' fans are the most knowledgeable and loyal in all of baseball, they booed almost reluctantly, polite as booing goes, what would have passed for a standing ovation in Philly.

But in this moment in the bottom of the eighth with the bases loaded and no outs, Martinez is hitting .225 against left-handed pitching. Coupled with his performance the prior season, .262 with twenty-one home runs and seventy-five RBIs, it is clear that Martinez's pride is increasingly at odds with his output. He felt burned when La Russa pinch-hit for him against the lefty Dan Plesac in the Phillies series just prior to this one. He felt humiliated, and in the clubhouse, he had become privately snappish, telling others his problems at the plate were largely the fault of La Russa's incessant tinkering. He *should* feel burned, as any man animated by competitive spirit should. La Russa likes such qualities in a ballplayer, but he also knows that players are often unrealistic about their situations. Earlier this season, Martinez complained about hitting sixth or seventh in the Cardinals lineup; he said that when he played for the Yankees, Joe Torre never juggled him around but always batted him fourth. The comment rankled La Russa, so he pursued the substance of it and found that Torre did indeed have Martinez hit sixth or seventh in the Yankee lineup. It indicated to La Russa there were times that Martinez struggled as a Yankee and was dropped in the lineup, just as he is struggling now. Which is only further incentive for La Russa to lift him if Baker calls in for the lefty.

But Baker stays put. He doesn't head to the mound to hail a cab. Martinez won't be burned this time, unless it's by Farnsworth.

Martinez hasn't faced him much: two at-bats, no hits. Given his .203 average with runners in scoring position this season, this is not an optimum situation for him with the bases juiced. It only gets worse when Farnsworth gets a favorable call from the umpire for a first-pitch strike. Farnsworth follows with another fastball. It's clearly a ball if Martinez holds up on it, and all year long, even in troubled times, he has always maintained savvy plate discipline, more than willing to squeeze a walk here, not succumb to visions of immortality. But he doesn't.

La Russa would be content with a sacrifice fly to right, and so would Martinez. It would send Pujols home and put the next batter, Edgar Renteria, in the situation he thrives in — two runners on and only one out, a seventh-hole hitter with seventy-eight RBIs. But it's a grounder to the right side. It's going somewhere, but it's unclear *where,* in that uncertain zone between sharp and not sharp enough, just out for a little summer-night stroll. Cardinals fans don't know whether to cheer or groan. Cubs fans don't know whether to cheer or groan.

It could be a single. Or it could be a double play. Rolen, who has taken a healthy, smart lead off first, is off on contact to try to avoid the latter. As he's going, the ball skitters by and almost hits him. He dodges it somehow without breaking his momentum. The ball has opted for the path between first and second, with just enough force that the Cubs infielders on the right side can't quite get to it.

Pujols comes home: 2–1. Edmonds comes home: 2–2.

Martinez stands exultant at first, just the little trace of a smile, basking in the kind of adoration he has so rarely enjoyed in St. Louis. He has tied the game on a gritty piece of hitting, getting to a pitch up and out of the zone and simply staying with it. It is beauty under pressure. But even more beautiful to La Russa is Rolen's base running. It's a lost art because there's no money in it; no incentive clause rewards you for doing it well, so those who actually do it want something from the game other than money. They play it right because it was meant to be played right.

Rolen is a superb athlete, the ingredients still there of someone who was good enough back in Jasper High School to be offered basketball scholarships from the University of Georgia and Oklahoma State. He looks too big to play third base the way he does, an outside linebacker in a baseball uniform. Yet he's quick down the line with his backhand scoops, and nobody ever in baseball, at least nobody La Russa has ever seen, comes in better on the ball barehanded with that big right hand of his, followed by such a punishing throw it's a wonder that Martinez at first doesn't end up head over heels in the stands. The one thing he's not, however, is lightning fast. But a base runner's skill has to do only in part with speed, in La Russa's mind. The more essential ingredient is how well you maximize your opportunities relative to your speed, which is why Rickey Henderson was a great base stealer—where wheels matter —but not a great base runner. When he wasn't stealing a base, he tended to relax, as many great base stealers do: no joy in the mundane and certainly no Benjamins. La Russa could only watch helplessly as Henderson took a few halfhearted steps off first and kind of plopped there. Much slower players got from first to third more often than Henderson did, the ultimate example the bottom of the ninth in Game 6 of the 1993 World Series when Henderson, then playing for the Blue Jays, somehow failed to get from first to third on a dumpy single by Paul Molitor hit slow enough so that there was ample room to run. He made it only to second, and were it not for the epic three-run homer against the Phillies by Joe Carter—a batter later to win the World Series—Henderson's lackadaisical attitude could have well made him the goat.

But Rolen took a good primary lead off first. Then he extended it into a secondary lead, pushing out more and more, all the while zeroed in on what was happening at the plate, ready to explode off the bat. And he was agile enough to keep his stride even while evading the ground ball. Brains and focus propelled him to third.

With Renteria up, Baker continues to stick with Farnsworth. The pitcher responds to the vote of confidence by throwing a wild pitch that makes Rolen's base running more than simply an instructional video. Because he's on third, he easily trots home, the system of pulleys and levers rewarding him for his quiet savvy: 3–2 Cardinals.

Farnsworth is a wreck at this point. He walks Renteria to put runners on first and second, and suddenly, improbably, the Cardinals are in the land of the crooked number on the basis of three singles, two of which were of the seeing-eye-dog variety, two walks and a wild pitch. They are scoring because they are lucky, and they are lucky because they are scoring. There are still *no* outs. Now La Russa and Baker are going mad with moves, like men frantically emptying a suitcase, racing to find the one item that actually fits.

La Russa's move: He brings in Miguel Cairo to pinch-run for Martinez at second, having already decided that he's going to have the next batter, Mike Matheny, bunt here. So he wants a quicker runner at second, as it's slightly easier for a team on defense to make a force play to third on a bunt. For a split second, he toys with a *hit-and-run* but then rejects it, as the speed of Farnsworth's fastball, in the mid-nineties, would make it more difficult than usual to get something on the ground. So he sticks with the bunt, which Matheny successfully executes to move the runners to second and third.

Baker's move: With the pitcher due up and knowing that he isn't going to hit, Baker hails another cab. He hooks Farnsworth in favor of the lefty Mike Remlinger, the *fourth* pitcher he has used this inning.

La Russa's move: He anticipates Baker's move to bring in Remlinger. But he still counters with Orlando Palmeiro to pinch-hit, even though he's a lefty, because he knows from his cheat sheets that Remlinger is one of those inverse pitchers who gets out righties better than lefties. Because of this slight advantage, he thinks that it gives Palmeiro, a good contact hitter, a decent chance of getting something on the ground and moving another run home. Also, he figures that if he had gone to the righty Eddie Perez off the bench, Baker would have pitched around him, with first base open, to set up for a force at home or a double play. This way, Palmeiro at least has the chance of getting something to hit. But Remlinger is all over the place. He walks Palmeiro. The bases are once again loaded.

Baker's move: He hails yet another cab. He benches Remlinger and brings in Joe Borowski, his ninth-inning closer, even though it's the bottom of the eighth with one out. It's the *fifth* pitcher he has used in the half-inning, a National League record.

La Russa's move: He sends Perez to the plate to pinch-hit for Robinson at the top of the order as he's gritty in the clutch with nine home runs and thirty-three RBIs in only 219 at-bats. With the bases loaded, Baker doesn't have the luxury of pitching around him. Perez has a swing as free as his laugh, capable of driving one into the seats. It would be a marvelous result, but La Russa's decision to use Perez here, lifting the number one hitter in the lineup, even though he's a lefty and Borowski a righty, goes far beyond home-run hope. Perez may be a free swinger, but he's also a smart one, who spends requisite time before each game studying prospective relievers; he knows what Borowski likes to throw and can recognize his pitches off the delivery. Borowski's main pitch to a right-handed batter is his slider, and it's more of an out-and-over-the plate slider. It matches Perez's own hitting strength, making him in La Russa's evaluation more likely to have a productive at-bat than Robinson.

Perez hits a puny little ground ball. It should be an easy double play to get the Cubs out of the inning, down by only one run. But Martinez at second base bobbles it, the pressure of the moment tapping him on the shoulder just as he fields the ball to ask him whether everything is okay. He recovers the ball. He does that much as the volume at Busch tops 100 decibels, fans going delirious in the best chapter yet in this thriller. He manages to make the play to first. He does that much. But Cairo comes home. The Cards lead 4–2.

III

LA RUSSA still looks all steel from the foxhole in the top of the ninth, no change in the glare. But it's a front. His head throbs with what feels like a migraine. His throat is so dry, he can't swallow. His stomach is flipping so much, he feels he's going to vomit, only he knows he can't, because of the dryness in his throat. He is inevitably thinking to himself, *Why am I doing this for a living?* just as he also knows that if he somehow gets the third out here in the top of the ninth, he will inevitably think to himself, *What a great way to make a living!* He occasionally turns back to look at the lineup sheet posted on the wall. He's also dipping his head down after every batter to keep score in his little runic scribblings. But it's more force of habit than anything else, because the game has basically left his hands. It would be easier emotionally if the score were more crooked in the Cards' favor, but La Russa is still where he wants to be, the journey of his managing in Game 2 of three getting him to the right crescendo.

It's why his favorite player on any team is always the closer, if he's a real-deal closer and not some knock-off closer, the only player piece of the puzzle who can guarantee a win if he does what he is paid to do. He believes that he has the real deal in Jason Isringhausen. He was hurt at the beginning of the season, a situation that La Russa knew would make almost every game a psychological circus. The Cardinals hit the burrito out of the ball, but their record in one-run games was abysmal: 2 and 14 in one-run games through the end of May.

One of the few philosophical disagreements between him and Dave Duncan is the greater premium he places on the bullpen; Duncan believes that the starters matter more. In La Russa's opinion, Duncan can do enough things with a starter—get him to see the rewards of mixing speed and location, offer him up a new pitch to make hitters uncomfortable—to keep him going for six innings. You can elevate a starter. But it's his view that a reliever, whether he's setting up or closing, must have an effective out pitch. And that's difficult to teach—a rare instance in which preparation and hard work can't improve much on innate baseball talent.

Since Isringhausen's return in June, there is every indication that his stuff has returned with him, hard cutter—his out pitch—backed up by a good hook:

W	L	ERA	G	SV	IP	H	R	ER	HR	BB	SO	Opp. Avg.
0	0	2.36	26	14	26.2	20	10	7	1	10	26	.198

With the score 4–2 here, Izzy has some insulation. The Cubs are slotted to send up Ramirez and Gonzalez and Miller, and La Russa's cheat sheets show that the matchups are good, but not great, because of Gonzalez and that home run:

RAMIREZ	0-3-0
GONZALEZ	1-3-1
MILLER	0-1-0

Baker has carte blanche now. He can use his bench to drive the matchups however he wants, as La Russa isn't going to budge off Izzy. No situational relief here by countering a lefty hitter with a lefty pitcher. For eight innings, La Russa has slowed the game down by staying ahead of it, but now the game has caught up.

La Russa knows what Izzy has been thinking as he was warming up: *We've just gone eight innings in this hugely meaningful game, and we've had this great comeback, and it's all on me to get three outs.* He knows that not just anybody can do that, has that combination of guts and attitude and stuff. La Russa himself is thinking about the single thing that separates the highest-caliber closers from the next level: *Keep the ball out of the middle.*

It's also why he gave his little conspiratorial laugh in spring training when he heard of the Red Sox plan, based on analysis by statistical guru and team consultant Bill James, to have rotating closers instead of one designated pitcher. James, in part because of what he felt was the inflated statistic of the save (you get one even with a three-run lead), believed that it wasn't always necessary to bring in a classic closer to pitch the ninth. La Russa respected James, but based on managing nearly 4,000 games, was convinced James was wrong. La Russa was also right: the Red Sox ultimately dumped the idea when it became clear that closer-by-committee was no-closer-by-committee.

Of all the ways to lose in baseball, none is more painful to La Russa than failing to hold on to a close lead going into the ninth. If it happens enough, it creates a cycle of frustration and discouragement that can unravel a season. Hitters, aware that the only way to win is to score unrealistic bunches of runs to neuter the ninth, can't shoulder the burden after a while.

Izzy has the face for what he does: impish, suggesting good times, with a softness about the chin and cheekbones, a certain buoyancy to it without the weight of self-reflection and overanalysis. He also has the requisite balls. He loves working the ninth. It has become his domain when he is healthy, although staying in one piece has been an issue with Izzy since birth. Some of his ailments have been downright scary, well beyond the typical arm sufferings. But his medical history also implies a sure-fire way of identifying future relievers, based on a childhood propensity to almost get themselves killed in small towns. The lefty setup reliever Steve Kline also exhibited such pathology when his brothers, in the name of what passed for science in the central Pennsylvania town he grew up in, tried to electrocute him.

Izzy's wounds were more of the self-inflicted variety. As a child growing up in Brighton in southern Illinois, he enjoyed jumping off the roof of the family's two-story house to see what the chances were of flying (not good). On a long car ride to Virginia when he was twelve, he occupied himself with counting up his scars and got pretty close to 115. During his career in the big leagues, he has undergone surgeries on his elbow and shoulder. He was diagnosed with tuberculosis, and he once fell off a third-floor balcony in spring training, cracking his sternum and several toes.

He began his career as a starter and had nice success with it, a 9-2 season for the Mets in 1995. But recurring shoulder and elbow problems made him a natural candidate for the bullpen. Izzy remembers the first time he ever came in in the ninth. It was against the Yankees in 1999, when he was with Oakland; he had never pitched in the stadium before. He didn't feel fear. He felt *total fear,* as he put it, the way the façade, like one of those Tim Burton sets in *Batman,* just seemed to go straight up for miles and miles to the lip of the moon. He finished the game that night and notched a save. "I succeeded, and the first rush came about," he said, even better than jumping off the roof of his house and seeing whether he could fly; on this night, he really could fly. The next year, he took the mound in a similar situation, with a one-run lead in the bottom of the ninth, and gave up back-to-back homers to Bernie Williams and David Justice—just about the same as jumping off the roof and landing with a thud. It was then that Izzy learned the other crucial component of being a closer, besides keeping the ball out of the middle: "A short memory."

Izzy takes a little journey off the mound after his warm-ups. He removes his red cap to wipe the heat off his brow, draws in a breath. He gives a little whisper to Rolen and returns to the top of the mound. He's casually chewing gum as if to say, *It's no big deal coming into the game like this to either preserve it or destroy it, be a well-paid hero for very little work or a complete asshole.*

He comes in with a hard cutter against the lead-off batter, Ramirez. It's similar in style to the one that Mariano Rivera throws, bearing in on you with ninety-plus velocity so that the only thing you can do is use your bat as a weapon of meager defense. Ramirez hits it meekly foul, readjusts his blue batting gloves, and settles back in to the plate. Izzy counters next with a nice curve low and away. Ramirez hits it to the right side, one hop, two hops, three hops, four hops, each hop smaller and thinner than the previous. Hart at second has to come in for it, a nasty little nubber. He's almost on the infield grass when he gets to it, then has to make the throw in a fast and fluid motion across his body. It's hit softly enough for Ramirez to have a chance even though he's a lumberer. It all depends on the throw.

La Russa watches Hart from his corner. Baker watches from his corner, leaning forward slightly, peering through the green-padded bars on the top and bottom of the dugout. He has a slightly shocked look, unable to cleanse his mind of the surreal ugliness of the bottom of the eighth when a 2–0 lead became a 4–2 deficit on the basis of three puny singles rolling into the outfield like little winks, three walks, a wild pitch, and a bobbled grounder. Izzy no longer faces the plate, because he's watching Hart too.

Ramirez is out by several steps. One away.

Izzy steps off the mound to get a new ball from the home plate umpire. He works it in, rubbing his palms and fingers over it to add his own imprint. He takes off his glove to touch the peak of his cap. He flexes his shoulders. Then back to work with Gonzalez up.

La Russa has the right fielder, the so-called off outfielder because Gonzalez is right-handed, shade in two or three steps from his usual depth. With the tying run on deck, he's trying to take away what he thinks is the most probable hit, a line drive or bloop single the opposite way. Like the infield-in options, shading outfielders has a dizzying set of variables, so much so that La Russa often puts his outfielders in almost continuous motion in the late innings. If the hitter is right-handed and gains the count in his favor, La Russa will immediately shade the outfield to guard against the likely tendency of the hitter to pull the ball. If the count goes even or to the pitcher's advantage, La Russa will then immediately shade the outfield to straighten up within the same at-bat. He also takes into account the minute knowledge of hitters gained through scouting and video and Duncan's pitching charts, as there are some who, even in classic pull counts of 1-0 and 2-0, still simply try to cover the plate and put the ball in play.

Izzy knows that he has a great defense behind him with three Gold Glovers in Renteria and Rolen and Edmonds. So the thing he's fixated on, the only thing besides the muscle memory of throwing hard and hitting different halves of the plate, is not giving up a home run. He didn't do that once in sixty games last season, and he's given up only one this season. *Keep the ball out of the middle.*

He works Gonzalez over with cutters, none of them center-cut over the plate. Gonzalez swings through the first, resists the second because it's outside, then breaks his bat fouling off a hellacious one down to make the count 1 and 2. A piece of it splinters toward first base. He goes to get a new bat from the batboy, and La Russa is thinking *finishing curve ball here.* Izzy's stuff is too good not to try overpowering Gonzalez with it. He's got a big hook, so *throw the big hook.* But instead, he flips a *do-somebody-a-favor* curve.

Gonzalez loops a single to left center. The Cubbies are alive.

With a man on first and one out, Baker sends Troy O'Leary to pinch-hit in the eighth spot for Miller. La Russa switches to a no-doubles defense in which all three outfielders play deep. Izzy goes with his cutter against O'Leary on the first pitch. It's inside for 1 and 0.

It's never the best way to start, but beyond simply the count is another exposure. With the first baseman positioned deep to provide more range, Gonzalez isn't even being held. La Russa is obviously aware of that, just as he's aware that Izzy normally doesn't have a quick move to the plate and is easy to run on. Gonzalez could be running early as a result to take away the possibility of the double play; it's an almost sure steal. But Baker doesn't make the move, at least not now.

Izzy comes with a fastball on the next pitch to even the count. Gonzalez still stays put at first. Izzy throws a cutter inside. O'Leary has to dance out of the way a little bit, but Gonzalez *still* stays put. He throws another cutter. It comes in low. O'Leary chops at it.

It bounces in front of the plate, takes another bounce toward the left side. Izzy stabs at it, but it's simply a reflex action; the ball is way over his head. It comes in to Renteria several steps from second base. It's fitting justice, given the ball's well-established pleasure and penchant for perversity: In Game 1, it immediately sidled up to Cairo, playing in place of Renteria because of his ailing back, and Cairo threw wide for an error. Now in Game 2, it has fixated on Renteria in a potential game-ending double-play situation to see just how that ailing back is really feeling. He sidesteps toward the bag at second, the footwork smooth and gliding except for a little baby step at the end to make sure he touches the base. He keeps his motion going as he throws to first. *Double play.*

Izzy opens and closes his glove in a little jawlike snap, his own private victory salute. He steps off the mound and is immediately swarmed by acolytes. High-fives are tossed about like prom-night bouquets as Cardinals players blanket the infield. The Cubs walk the line of the dugout into the tunnel with the joy of prisoners being led back into the dim-bulb fortress after recreation. Their bench empties out quickly, except for Remlinger, who lingers there after everyone else has left. He's staring glassy-eyed at the field, no doubt wondering what everybody else on the Cubs is wondering, with no sensible answer except that it is, after all, the Cubs: *What just happened?*

GAME
THREE

12

D.K.

I

● ● ● THE LOWEST MOMENT of the season for La Russa came eleven days before the Cubs series started, in the androgyny of a Hertz rental car heading south on Broad Street in Philadelphia. He was on his way to the closest thing in baseball to a rat-infested sewer-spewing urine-stinking public-housing high-rise, when he got a call from Barry Weinberg, the trainer. It was bad enough going to the Vet, where the pipes routinely leaked and the clubhouse carpet was a deep purple momentarily popular during the tie-dye heyday of the 1960s, when LSD was considered a dietary supplement. But a call from Weinberg at eleven in the morning?

Weinberg was the ultimate grim reaper when it came to unexpected phone calls. He was Rasputin in red Banlon, the angel of death in a Polo shirt with little red birds on the front. Nothing was worse in a rental car on the way to the ballpark than a call from Weinberg. It meant that whatever Weinberg had to tell him couldn't wait for the clubhouse, just like the time Weinberg had called him to tell him in 2000 that Mike Matheny had cut his hand and wouldn't be able to catch in the playoffs.

"Morris turned his ankle. I'm taking him for an x-ray."

"How serious is it?"

"It's got a chance to be a problem."

La Russa hung up. He continued driving in his soundproof

silence. By the time he got to the visiting clubhouse of the Vet, his mood was even more foul, disappointment mixed with disbelief. Because there went the Thing of Beauty that he and Dave Duncan had worked so hard on just the night before. Forget the three-game series against the Cubs, with Matt Morris scheduled for the third game, the perfect coda. For that matter, forget the season if the ankle was as serious as Weinberg was indicating it might be by trying not to indicate anything.

Morris had come into this year as the deserved ace of the pitching staff. In the previous two years, he had put together numbers as good as anyone in baseball, not only wins and losses but also innings pitched, a two-hundred-plus inning workhorse:

W	L	Pct.	ERA	G	GS	CG	IP	H	R	ER	BB	SO
22	8	.733	3.16	34	34	2	216.1	218	86	76	54	185
17	9	.654	3.42	32	32	1	210.1	210	86	80	64	171

But this season had been star-crossed, almost freakish. It had started out brilliantly, peaking in two back-to-back complete-game shutouts in the middle of May: the first against the Cubs, and the next against Pittsburgh. The one against the Cubs was achingly beautiful: first-pitch strikes to twenty-three of thirty batters, fourteen groundball outs, a fastball combination of straight four-seamer and sinker, a wicked 12-to-6 curve he had such confidence in he threw it on 2-0 counts, eighty-two strikes out of 117 pitches.

If there was *anything* that marred the performance against the Cubs, it was that last number, the ball and chain of pitch count, not because of anything Morris had done wrong but because of a disturbing trend. La Russa kept track of pitching performances as he kept track of everything, with pencil and ruler and lined legal-size paper that went wherever he went. In the case of Morris, the series of numbers looked like this:

7/8/5/106   8/3/0/103   8.2/6/3/122   6/5/0/104   7/5/2/73   6/5/2/115
9/6/2/124   8/10/3/111   6/5/4/77   9/4/0/117   9/9/0/123   7.1/6/3/107

La Russa wasn't adverse to computers, although he has never used one for baseball. He knew that he could rely on Duncan—

who in another life would have made a fine hacker, given his ability to tunnel inside without leaving a trace — and was up-to-date on all the latest technology trying to predict player trend lines. La Russa appreciated the information generated by computers. He studied the rows and columns. But he also knew they could take you only so far in baseball, maybe even confuse you with a fog of overanalysis. As far as he knew, there was no way to quantify desire. And those numbers told him exactly what he needed to know when added to twenty-four years of managing experience. Each line was a concise history of Morris's twelve outings through the end of May, and the numbers within each line reflected the following: innings pitched, hits allowed, runs given up, and pitches thrown. They told La Russa a story just like his matchups did, and this particular one contained dark foreshadowing.

They showed that, out of Morris's twelve starts through the end of May, he'd exceeded the 100-pitch threshold ten times, including three games in which he had thrown more than 120. It was a lot of pitches early in the season. Woody Williams's numbers were similar, but there was little La Russa could do about it, given the bullpen's nightmarish performance without Jason Isringhausen. Pushing them was the only way to stay alive, just as figuring out a solution to Pujols's elbow had been the only way to stay alive. He worried that if they both kept it up at this pace, it was only a matter of time before they would get physically drained. But the alternative to not taking his two primary starters deep was no alternative if the Cards wanted to stay up with the Astros and the Cubs. The team had to win games somewhere.

In June, Morris developed some crankiness in his arm because of a knot behind his right shoulder. It wasn't enough to put him on the disabled list, but it forced him to alter his mechanics, which can be beneficial as well as risky, as so much of pitching, like love, is about feel and therefore as elusive as it is beautiful. It was also enough for La Russa to start juggling the rotation to give Morris more rest in between starts. Because the rotation is scheduled out roughly six weeks ahead, with a key pitcher, such as Morris, placed into as many key games as possible, La Russa's pencil and eraser took a beating as he swapped starts and reslotted. In July against the Dodgers, Morris wobbled through five innings. He did some things well, but he threw nothing fastballs to several hitters and the result was a five-run inning. His fastball velocity was down into the high eighties, and he was suffering the worst slump of his five-year career, with thirty-four earned runs given up in thirty-three and two-thirds innings. An MRI on his shoulder failed to reveal any structural problems.

But *something* was wrong, a loss of concentration that could be fatal to the team if it kept up and something that, as a manager, La Russa had to figure out how to pinpoint and handle. Of course, the early rigors of the season had taken a physical and mental toll on Morris, but La Russa suspected that more fundamental aspects of human nature had greater influence. Morris's record stood at 8-6 heading into the All-Star break: not terrible but not great. His ERA had ballooned from 2.37 at the end of May to 4.19, a numerical indicator of mental health for a pitcher as good as Morris. In his multiple roles of Doctor Phil, Doctor Ruth, and Doctor Seuss, La Russa wondered whether what Morris felt was pretty simple.

The season had just gotten messed up, 8 and 6 exactly what it sounded like — barely above mediocre — when with any help from the bullpen, it could have been 11 and 3 and on the way to the twenty-win grail. He privately acknowledged to Morris the tragedy of the bullpen early in the season and how it had screwed the starter. He emphasized his crucial place in the rotation, that he still had an easy shot at fifteen wins. He pointed out that if the team made it into the playoffs, Morris would have another opportunity, as in the previous two seasons when the team had gotten there, to show millions that he was in the highest echelon of pitchers. It all sounded good, but La Russa backed up his pep talk with pragmatism, giving Morris a full ten days off, including the All-Star break, before his next start, against San Diego.

But maybe something else altogether was wrong, an absence as literal as it was emotional — a permanent vacancy at the locker two down from Morris's. It was empty except for the uniform shirt of the player who had once worn it, a shirt of deep Cardinals red hung on a white plastic hanger, the name across the back in proud capital-letter symmetry like a highway sign announcing the next town.

It was unaffected by its surroundings and would forever be unaffected, and there was terrible cruelty in that. And Morris still felt it, not as much, maybe, as at the beginning. But something like that didn't simply tick away. The player who had once worn that shirt had been a mentor to him, helped teach him not only the rigors of pitching but also the rigors of the baseball life: the road trips, how much to tip the clubhouse attendant, the pacing, the mental art that must go in lockstep with the mechanics.

D.K. It's what his teammates called him.

II

SOMETHING had been bothering Darryl Kile in June 2002. He was off his stride, and La Russa knew that he was off his stride, the psychological challenges of pitching impacting the mechanics and the mechanics impacting the psychological challenges. He was working his ass off. He always worked his ass off. But he was languishing at the .500 mark, the last two seasons when he had gone a combined 36 and 20 feeling more and more like a lost horizon. Something was up, and La Russa felt that he had to take it on, fathom the inside of Darryl's head a little bit.

Darryl wanted to win as much as ever, hated it when he had taken back-to-back no-decisions against the Astros, even though he had pitched well and deep — a *no-decision,* as if you hadn't even been there. But Darryl was distracted, preoccupied in a way La Russa hadn't seen before, and it worried him. A pitcher's head is far more precious than his arm and far more inscrutable. An arm could show you it was tired. It could exhibit shoulder crankiness or elbow crankiness. It could be balmed, rubbed, bandaged, iced. It could demand rest or even surgery: *Stop treating me like this.* But a pitcher's head wasn't always so clear. And during the two and a half years that Kile had been with the Cardinals, his head had been so focused, so absent the clouds that can cause temporary insanity in any pitcher at any time. His performance reflected it — the ace of the staff — so what was happening now was more than simply a blip.

He had been something of an enigma when he came over to the

Cardinals in 2000 in an off-season trade with the Rockies. He had put together one spectacular year with the Astros in 1997, going 19 and 7. But then the Astros didn't want to pay him. So he signed with the Rockies, willing to endure the Bataan Death March of Coors Field, so littered with the skeletal psyches of pitchers who started the first and got to the fourth with the score 8–7 and men on second and third and no outs and the ball frolicking in its freedom. Because the ball carried like a space capsule in the thin air, outfielders tended to play deep, meaning that bloopers blooped. The thin air also took some of the snap out of your curve ball, a killer 12 to 6 morphing into a very mortal 12 to 3. Sinker ballers did okay there. So did guys who weren't afraid to live with their changeups. But Kile had a good fastball and a curve that did go 12 to 6 when it was snapping right, and this wasn't the right place for him.

He went 8 and 13 with an ERA of 6.61, four runs more than the 2.57 he had put up during that sensational year with the Astros. The Cards ended up getting him after the season, La Russa and Duncan wondering whether that 19-and-7 season in Houston had merely been some first act with no second one but believing that there were grounds for replication.

Spring training is valuable for La Russa in assessing new pitchers; he closely observes how they respond to the absolute pull-your-hair-out tedium of it. Before the start of exhibition games, they throw only every other day, so there isn't much to do other than the same drills over and over, pick-off drills, fielding-bunt drills, hitting drills in the cage. How a new guy reacts to it—gets after it or sloughs through it—tells La Russa a great deal. He keenly watched Kile, trying to gauge that elusive quality called professionalism. He watched one day. He watched another. He got reports from the other coaches handling the drills, including Duncan, of course. And what he said to Duncan about Kile was crisp and pointed because he almost couldn't believe how serious Kile was about everything:

"I hope this is not a façade. I hope he's not fooling us."

Kile went 20 and 9 for the Cardinals in 2000. Along the way, working with Duncan, he developed a forkball. The more he used it, the more he seemed to like it, with its wicked downward tumble. On many days, it became an equally effective out pitch for him as his fastball and curve. In 2001, he went 16 and 11, polishing his reputation as a bulldog worker, maybe the toughest in the National League. It marked the fourth season out of five in which he had been in the top ten in the league in innings pitched, games started, and batters faced. In fact, Kile took great pride in never having been on the disabled list, *never,* a truly Herculean feat for a starting pitcher.

Kile had other qualities that marked him as far more than a power pitcher who had thrown 232$\frac{1}{3}$ innings in 2000 and 227$\frac{1}{3}$ innings in 2001 and seemed destined to do the same in 2002. He was a wonderful husband to his wife, Flynn, and she was a wonderful wife to him. They had three children together: the twins, Kannon and Sierra, who had turned five in January, and the little son, Ryker, who was less than a year old. They were a gorgeous American family, blond and floppy-haired. You looked at them and wished that everybody in the entire world, including your own family, looked that way. They stood together during picture day at Busch in a tight little rainbow, everybody holding on to one another.

There was also Kile the teammate. *Teammate* is a hackneyed term like so many terms, overused and overwrought. But it still can be beautiful, two powerful words that under the right conditions can take on even more powerful significance when merged together. A ballclub is a family, the most forced and unnatural family imaginable — players passing through like container cargo in the continual money juggle of baseball. How it comes together or splits up, takes in its newest members or spits them out, struggles through hard times or splinters apart, is a crucial element of its success. To be successful, it must have steadying influences, particularly in the emotional trough of late June and early July, when you look around the clubhouse and see faces that maybe you already wish you didn't ever have to see again. Nerves get frayed. Egos become hypersensitive: a pitcher pissed off because he got an early hook, a batter plotting insurrection because he got pinch-hit for. Even the question of what video to slip in the clubhouse VCR in the slow hours before a game can produce a shouting match, comedy versus drama. Cliques form. An ever-widening language gap separates the Latino players, who speak mostly Spanish, and American-born players, who speak English, and the lone Japanese player, who doesn't speak either.

Kile was a great teammate, the ultimate bonding agent. He was a mentor to Rick Ankiel and Morris as they rose and struggled and struggled and rose. He gave Matheny, who caught him, a Rolex watch after he won his twentieth. He put his arm around Jason Simontacchi when he was a rookie pitcher, still dazzled by the intimidating wonder of it all, and took him out for dinner. He was always digging into his pocket and paying for meals, although just about everybody at the table made at least a million or two or three or four. Then there were the little things he did in the clubhouse, the rituals that made everyone laugh: announcing like a lighthouse foghorn three hours before game time that there were three hours to game time, singing in the summer heat that ridiculous little song about "let it snow, let it snow, let it snow."

Kile was about more than comic relief, though. La Russa knew that the best clubhouses don't have a single team leader; they have a small cadre of guys you can count on to cosign what you say and convince their teammates to accept what you say, assuming, of course, that what you have said makes sense. You could not function without their support; they could empower a manager, or they could sink him by letting the inevitable disgruntlements elevate into mutinies.

Kile belonged to that cadre, a key component. It was essential for Kile to buy into what La Russa said. It was essential because of the impact that Kile had in the clubhouse, not just the presence of personality that players felt comfortable with but a competitiveness that they admired and rubbed off on them. He considered nothing in life more insulting than the intentional walk, went toe-to-toe with La Russa on several occasions because of his recalcitrance to throw one. La Russa worried that other pitchers, wanting to emulate their leader, would kick up their heels as well when the order came from the foxhole to put pride aside and simply put the damn guy on first. But La Russa had trouble getting too terribly upset with Kile, because as much as he loved talent in a player, it was the add-on of competitiveness that created the possibility of the spectacular.

Kile's influence stretched past the players to the entire extended family that also make a clubhouse different from any place on earth: the equipment managers, the attendants, the guys running the video, those who ensure order but toil in obscurity underneath the surface glamour of working for a big-league ball club. It was easy to condescend—the upstairs-downstairs mentality, those who play and those who never will. But Kile made sure that the guys coming up never took them for granted, never acted with entitlement when their own presence here was just a matter of genes and the blessings of fortune that came and went. Because who knew what could happen? Who really knew...?

III

LA RUSSA SIMPLY liked talking to Kile as he made his floating rounds during spring training. He liked probing him about the Astros, because, ever since coming over to the National League in 1996, La Russa had admired how the Astros had played. He wanted to know what made their clubhouse tick, and Kile told him about the influence of Craig Biggio and Jeff Bagwell, the steady tone they set and how their steadiness spilled over onto the field. Then one day, Kile asked La Russa to name the ten people in his life who had truly put it all together: the blend of talent and heart and work ethic. The question came up in the context of an article in which La Russa had been quoted in *Time* on the greatness of Michael Jordan. It was a deep question, almost philosophical, a player probing beyond mechanics and the downward tumble of a forkball into something perhaps unfathomable. La Russa appreciated the depth of it. He told Kile that a question as serious as that deserved an equally serious answer, which meant that La Russa would take it and play with it in the quiet hours when men who should be sleeping are sleepless. As he mused on the question, he was struck by what it suggested about Kile, a player who knew he was on the cusp of greatness and wanted to map out the final steps.

Which is what made June 2002 so troubling. Kile had had arthroscopic surgery on his shoulder during the off-season. It had thrown a whack into his spring-training regimen, curtailing the amount of work he could put in. A lot of pitchers simply would have stayed down in Florida once the team moved north, get in four or five starts to put the wheels back in motion and then rejoin the club on May 1. But Kile didn't like the idea of putting his team in the hole like that.

"Who are you gonna pitch in my place?" he asked La Russa.

"That's not the way we look at it, Darryl. It's a six-month season. You come back May first ready to go, we'll still be in contention."

Kile refused the opening offered to him. He had never spent a day on the disabled list, and he wasn't about to start now. He was a starting pitcher. He was paid to start. And that's what he did right from the beginning of the season. He pitched well, incredibly well given how much of the spring he had missed. But as much as he hated to admit it, because it implied some excuse, and he was from the old-time school where any excuse was just that, he was still recovering. By the beginning of June, his record was 2 and 3, including those two no-decisions against Houston. He pitched well against Pittsburgh—six hits in seven innings and one run—to get to .500. Although he struggled in his next start against Kansas City, he still got the win to push up to 4 and 3. La Russa and Duncan liked the way he was coming back physically from the surgery. They were pleased with his progress. They admired his progress. He was beginning to look right. But something wasn't right inside. He was quiet. He really wasn't saying anything, no foghorn blast to the assembled three hours before game time, not even that stupid little song about snow.

"You okay?" they separately asked him.

"I'm okay. Just trying to get my stuff right."

And that's all he said. La Russa talked to Duncan about it, and Duncan thought that Kile's moody silence was simply an expression of frustration, that it was June and he wanted to be pitching great all the time and was barely over .500. La Russa let it go, but then came the Seattle game. His stuff was pretty good, but "within the ears," as La Russa described it, he simply didn't seem to be there. In the pregame meeting, Duncan had stressed several crucial points to Kile, including not to throw anything soft and breaking to John Olerud. But during the game, Kile was doing the exact opposite of what Duncan had told him. It happened a couple of times. From the dugout, La Russa, who had sat in on the meeting, watched and thought, *What the hell was that? Why did he do that?*

Then Olerud came up, and Kile threw exactly what Duncan had told him not to throw, a soft breaking ball, and Olerud hit it out for a two-run homer. It was abundantly clear to La Russa that Kile's head simply wasn't into it. So in the fifth, he came out to the mound and took Kile out. Kile was surprised. He made a bid to stay, but it was too late.

"I've already signaled from the bench. I've already got a guy coming in. Give me the ball."

Kile gave him the ball, an act of surrender even more humiliating than an intentional walk. After the game, on the plane back to St. Louis, La Russa went back to talk to some of the players. He tried to make eye contact with Kile, but the pitcher turned away. La Russa let it go, because he knew that Kile was hard-wired with pride. A hook in the fifth was more than some glancing blow.

Over the next several days, La Russa and Kile continued their dance of avoidance. When the pitcher saw the manager, he went the other way. Then Duncan called La Russa and said that something was wrong with Kile.

"I tried to talk to him about a couple of things. He's not being rude. But he's not listening. He's not into it."

He simply wanted to get his pitching in, which was entirely uncharacteristic of him. "He's bothered about something," said Duncan.

There was a game against Kansas City that Sunday. La Russa waited until all the reporters had gotten their quotes and left the clubhouse. Then he tapped Kile on the shoulder and asked him to come into his office.

"Look, you get the ball Tuesday and there's an off day tomorrow," said La Russa. "For you and for us, I want to have this conversation."

Most times, La Russa would start off a conversation with a player by asking a question and listening to the player's response. But now he began differently.

"I got three things I want to say to you, and I'd like to get all three things out. Then you can say anything you want to. Or say nothing if you want to. But I'd like to say those three things." Kile nodded.

First, La Russa reaffirmed the fact that nobody believed in him more as a pitcher than La Russa and Duncan did and that nothing had happened this season, *nothing,* to change that. His second point had to do with why he'd hooked Kile in the fifth inning in Seattle. It wasn't to humiliate the pitcher but because of the mental mistakes Kile had made.

"As a manager, there is only one way a player and a team improves—if something gets done wrong, you address it, unless it's a hiccup. It's common sense but it's hard to accept if you're the individual involved.

"Do you think that's a bad philosophy?" he asked rhetorically. "If it was you, would you just let mistakes happen?"

La Russa's third point, and perhaps the most important one, was to let Kile know just how important he was to the team—a core player, a core leader—and the responsibility that implied. "That means if you're in Seattle and something happens and you get taken out of the game, you can react however you want. This is America. You can get mad at me. You can dispute my decision. What I would challenge you to dispute is my intention to do the right thing for the team and for you. I think it's real important that you walk out of here today knowing that you're a key guy and that any decision I'm trying to make is for us and for you."

Finished with what he felt he had to say, he asked Kile for his response. "This is totally about me," said Kile. "It's not about you guys. You address things. You work on stuff. You don't ignore things."

"That means I can't ignore it when it involves you."

"I understand that."

"Well, you understand that you're a key guy?"

"Tony, this is totally about me," he repeated. "It's been really hard for me to struggle like I've been struggling."

At that moment, La Russa understood what was eating at Kile, and he respected him more than ever for it. "Darryl, do you understand how few pitchers could have gone through what you did with the arthroscopic surgery and would be determined not to miss a start?"

"I just go out there," Kile lamented. "I pitch four innings. I pitch three innings. I pitch five innings."

La Russa pulled out the legal sheet showing that Kile had also pitched six innings, seven innings, including those two no-decisions against Houston where he had worked his ass off.

"Darryl, we still have four months to play. It's all in front of us."

"It's hard for me. It's just hard."

"Your arm strength is good. Your stamina is good. Cut yourself some slack. You've already gone through the hardest part."

"I'm bouncing back good. I feel strong. Then I get these no-decisions."

La Russa looked at him and said the only thing that was left to say, because no matter how much money you made and how much adulation you received for doing what you did, you could never hear it enough.

"We can't make it without you."

IV

KILE PITCHED two days later against the Angels on a star-crossed night marked by the passing of Cardinals broadcaster Jack Buck. He went seven and two-thirds innings, his longest outing of the season. He gave up six hits and one earned run. He was lights out, his best performance of the season, and the 7–2 win put the team into undisputed possession of first place. On a sad and painful evening—because losing Buck was to St. Louis like losing the Mississippi—Kile had been magnificent.

Five days later, in mid-June, he was set to go against the Cubs at

Wrigley. Flynn Kile felt that something was amiss as she talked to her husband in those days leading up to the start in Chicago. He suddenly asked her to remarry him. He seemed overly emotional and affectionate, as if he were preparing for something, getting ready for something, even if he had no idea what it was. That Friday night, from his hotel room at the Westin off Michigan Avenue, he talked with her for an hour. He didn't want to get off the phone. She remembered him saying that. *I don't want to get off.* But he did because there was a game the next day, and Kile, just as he prided himself on never missing a start, also prided himself on never being late to the ballpark.

There were so many things that happened the next morning, images that could not be erased no matter how much you wanted to erase them. You could see Mike Matheny urging someone, anyone, to check on Kile's whereabouts when he still hadn't shown up in the cubbyhole of the visitor's clubhouse of Wrigley after the team bus had arrived. You could see the head of security for the Westin breaking into room 1102 after repeated phone calls had gone unanswered and finding him there, still in his bed, wearing the black eyeshades that helped him sleep, with one arm across the pillow and the other across his upper torso. You could see Barry Weinberg rushing off the field with Walt Jocketty after a phone call. You could see Buddy Bates, then the equipment manager, fall into a chair in the clubhouse and cup his head in his hands. You could see reliever Dave Veres whispering, "They found D.K. They can't wake him up," then retreat into the tiny equipment room to sob in private. You could see Matheny pleading with Bates to tell him what was wrong, asking him, *Is Darryl still alive?* and lifting Bates by the collar when Bates didn't know what to say because how do you say something like that until he just nodded no and Matheny pulled off his jersey because baseball simply didn't matter anymore. You could see Tony La Russa standing in the middle of a circle of players and saying softly, *"They found Darryl. He's dead."* You could see Joe Girardi, then playing for the Cubs, come out onto the field of Wrigley and announce to the sold-out crowd with tears in his eyes, almost unable to speak, that the game would be postponed because of "a tragedy in the Cardinals family." You could see all those things and so many more things and still not believe it: a player, a teammate, there with you the night before doing the things players do on the road—grabbing dinner with friends at Harry Caray's, getting back to the hotel at 10:30 to call his wife, rejecting Morris's invitation shortly after midnight to have a drink in the hotel bar—because *you know what, Matty Mo, I feel a little tired. I just feel a little tired.*

You could think of Darryl, the way he competed and the impatience with which he treated himself, not cutting himself any slack, because that's what quitters did and baseball had enough quitters in it already, and when you thought of Darryl, it was impossible not to think of his wife and those three beautiful children. You could grope for things to say, ways of realizing it, or somehow making it less real.

You could listen to Tony La Russa in a closed-door meeting that night on the sixteenth floor of the Westin, recounting that last conversation he'd had with Darryl, how he had told him how important he was to the team, how he had said, *"We can't make it without you."* And then you could listen to Dave Duncan, Duncan the Quiet Assassin, Duncan the Deacon, Duncan whose words were so sparse they were called biblical. You could see the tears well up in his eyes as he spoke about his fallen pitcher who had died of a heart attack in his sleep at the age of thirty-three. You could see him stop to steady himself. And then you could listen to him in the sterile antiseptic wash of that hotel conference room when he talked about what a privilege it had been to work with Darryl Kile. You could listen to him describing how wonderful it had been to talk the bittersweet beauty of pitching with him, the timeless and impossible science of trying to figure out what precisely made it work, which was why it was always worth talking about. And you could listen to him when he said that for now and forever, he would use Darryl Kile as a model in his own life, to attain the same professional heights and more than just that because there was so much more than just that: the humanity of Darryl Kile, the exquisite humanity.

· · ·

The Cardinals foundered in the immediate aftermath. There was the incomprehensible loss of Darryl Kile and beyond that, the soul-searching every player went through as they privately wondered, maybe for the first time ever, just how important baseball really was anymore. They knew that Darryl had left behind a wife and three children, and they also thought of their own families: the vulnerability of them, how everything in life could change so very much from one day to the next, there and then not there. The team was still in the thick of a race for the division, and as the manager, La Russa's mandate was to get them to compete. But he also did not want to trample on those who asked themselves, because it was worth asking themselves, why the race for the division mattered. In the week following Kile's death, the team won only two of seven games, and the atmosphere in the clubhouse was ghostly even in the rare victories, players walking in quietly and then showering and then leaving as fast as they could.

La Russa continued to search for the right thing to do. He mourned as they mourned, but he was still a manager. In the past, he had always relied on the advice of his mentors, but they were of no help now because nothing they had been through was parallel to what he and his team were going through. Then he read a column by Bernie Miklasz in the *St. Louis Post-Dispatch.* And it hit him: a way maybe, just maybe, to recapture the hearts and minds of his players back to where he felt they should be.

Several hours before the game to be played that night, he gathered the team into the eating room in the clubhouse. "We're all examining what's right in our lives and what's right for our families," he said. "We mourn Darryl and we worry about his wife and kids and it's not like you can go to the office and hide since we all compete in front of each other." He acknowledged that he wasn't sure what to do, how the coaches weren't sure what to do, how appropriate was it now to get after a player who didn't hustle, to seize on the very things that had once been so automatic before Kile's death. Then La Russa pulled out a piece of paper in which he had copied down a small portion of Miklasz's column, actually something that Kile himself had once written about the death of his own father. "This is what helps me," La Russa told his players. And while he wasn't sure it would help them, he also felt it was worth reading aloud:

> I don't think I'll ever get over it, but my father was my best friend. But in order to be a man, you got to separate your personal life from your work life. It may sound cold, but I've got work to do. I'll never forget my father, but I'm sure he'd want me to keep on working and try to do the best I can do.

The pall began to lift after La Russa read those words. A team that had stopped competing discovered that it was okay to compete again because of what their teammate was telling them: letting them know, just as he had once learned, that there *was* still work to do, that the very definition of a professional *was* to separate out the personal. Which is why, when the Cardinals went on to win ninety-seven games and the division title that year—when they beat Randy Johnson and Curt Schilling of the Diamondbacks in back-to-back games to win the division series, when they came within a breath of going to the World Series—it was a performance in every way remarkable for the sorrow that had been overcome, except maybe to Darryl Kile.

It would have to be enough. For every teammate who had known him, heard that silly and comforting foghorn reminding them that it was three hours before game time, watched him pitch his ass off and argue with Matheny like a stubborn old woman to the point that Matheny would just as soon strangle him and stuff him in a box except that he loved him in the way that only a catcher can love a pitcher.

Whatever they felt and remembered would have to endure. For La Russa and Duncan. For Matheny and Williams and Bates and Veres. For Pujols and Simontacchi and Renteria. For Morris, whose locker, so stoked with the stuffing of the game it looked like Santa's sack, was just down the row from the one that was bare except for the uniform shirt hanging on the white plastic hanger, there long after the last light had been turned off and Morris and everyone else had gone home knowing, as much as they ever knew anything in life, that they would be back at it the next day three hours before game time.

13

THING OF BEAUTY

I

● ● ● SAN DIEGO WAS the perfect place for Matt Morris to get back into the groove after the All-Star break. The very name of its stadium—Qualcomm—sounded like an over-the-counter herbal remedy guaranteeing sweet dreams, the fans equally relaxed so there would be no extra burden on his performance beyond the burden of performance itself.

He came back strong, the ten days' rest clearly of benefit. His delivery and mechanics were smooth. His composure was in place, essential for Morris because he tended to fall out of his delivery and rush his throws when he got excited. In his brief absence from the game, he had rediscovered love.

As La Russa watched him in that first inning against the lead-off hitter, Ramon Vazquez, he couldn't help but feel that a huge obstacle had been overcome. The Cardinals could not win without Morris. His prolonged absence would affect the club like an oil spill, an ecological catastrophe whose black ooze would eventually touch everybody, not only the pitchers who would have to fill in for him but also hitters who would feel the extra burden to attain crooked numbers without his regular presence on the mound.

Morris struck out Vazquez on a 92-mph fastball, and there was *baseball* to La Russa, just *beautiful baseball.* It had that pop, that sweetest sound, the same sound that had moved Cal Eldred to defy the laws of nature with his patched-up pothole of an elbow and return to the game. Morris threw a curve to start the cat-and-mouse against the second-place hitter, Mark Kotsay. He swung through it, not simply a curve but one of those curves that almost genuflects by the time it's through, and there was *baseball* to La Russa, more *beautiful baseball.* Kotsay was able to turn on the next pitch, lining it up the middle. It was the ninth pitch of the game for Morris. And then came a different sound altogether, the sound of ball against bone.

The ball hit Morris's right hand. La Russa and Duncan and the assistant trainer, Mark O'Neal, ran to the mound to try to assess the seriousness. Morris threw a warm-up toss that hit the backstop, and that was it. He was lifted, and even the home plate umpire told La Russa that it was a shame, because Morris had been *on,* his fastball clocking at 92 and 93 and 94 mph. A resulting CT scan showed a nondisplaced fracture of his pitching hand, above his right index finger, that would sideline him anywhere between three and six weeks.

In desperate times, men of course do strange and desperate things. In La Russa's case, the urgency was exacerbated by another bedrock theory of his: When in doubt, *try something.* Jeff Fassero was thrust into the starting rotation in the hope that this jumper cable would give him some spark. He had been a starter for most of his career with Montreal and Seattle, and he responded. He liked the challenge of starting, which is why La Russa threw him up there. Garrett Stephenson needed a different path. La Russa gave him a carefully designed whacking—*We're sending you to the bullpen*—the only words a starter fears more than *Can I talk to you a minute?* And, later, when he was promoted again to the starting rotation, he too responded. Brett Tomko, the number three starter, was so laid back on the mound that he confessed to actually feeling sleepy on his pitching day, despite stuff of such quality that Duncan in spring training pegged him for eighteen wins. He also got whacked with the threat of long-term banishment, and he started winning. Danny Haren was promoted out of Double-A, even though he probably wasn't ready yet, and he started winning. Pujols embarked on a thirty-game hitting streak. Bo Hart, who during the previous off-season had worked in a department store to make ends meet, was still hitting the flying crap out of the ball after his send-up from the minors.

When they came into Philly from Pittsburgh in early August, they were tied for first after dropping three and a half back in the immediate aftermath of Morris's injury. They had gone 14 and 8 in his absence. They had played four three-game series, and they had taken the rubber game of each, and now Morris was coming back. It had the same uplift of a midsummer trade in which the Cards had landed a great number one starter without giving up anything.

Anticipating his return, La Russa and Duncan went to work in the plane to Philadelphia on the Thing of Beauty. The most pressing question was where to fit Morris within it. The last game of the three-game series against the Phillies was also the Sunday night Game of the Week on ESPN, and both men wondered how fair it would be to throw Morris into the fire like that when he hadn't pitched for three weeks. The alternative was Tomko, and they worried about Tomko in a situation like this. In high-pressure moments on the mound, you could see the confidence drain from Tomko's body. He lost faith in the curve in these moments. He pretty much lost faith in everything. So Duncan walked to the back of the plane to tell Morris that he would start the Sunday night game and also to tell Tomko that he wouldn't start the Sunday night game.

Then they went back to work on the Thing of Beauty. La Russa penciled in and erased and then penciled in some more and erased some more, the tricky goal to maximize starts for Morris and Woody Williams while ensuring that they also pitched in the pivotal series left on the schedule, in particular the three games against the Cubs at the end of August. By the time the plane landed in Philly, they had the Thing of Beauty worked out. They had mapped out the rotation for the team's remaining forty games, and it *was* a Thing of Beauty, the defining document for the rest of the season, their Magna Carta. Morris would be getting eight starts and Williams nine. Their presence would be guaranteed in the Cubs series, as well as series against the Astros in August and September. It was the first time all season that La Russa and Duncan had felt excited about their chances to compete and win from here until the end. They looked at each other on finishing the Thing of Beauty—without saying a word, of course—but thinking the same lofty thought: *Man, maybe we can pull this thing off.*

Until the phone call from Weinberg.

II

ON THURSDAY NIGHT after dinner with several teammates in Philadelphia, Morris had slipped on a small set of marble stairs in the lobby of the Four Seasons hotel. He didn't think much of it at the time and headed for the elevators. His ankle felt a little tender, but he wrapped it and went to sleep; when he woke up the next morning, it was sizably swollen. Which is when Weinberg was called. Which is when Weinberg called La Russa on the way to the hospital for an x-ray. Which is when La Russa's mood, tentative on game day to begin with, crashed.

The word was that Morris would be out a minimum of *two weeks,* maybe *three.* The ankle was significantly sprained, and the injury had occurred on his landing foot, meaning that every pitch he threw might exacerbate it. The Thing of Beauty was worthless now. It would have to be completely reworked; the immediate repercussion was that Tomko, after being told he wouldn't start Sunday night, would now be told that he would be starting Sunday night, akin to parents saying that they want to adopt you and then deciding against it and then taking you anyway because nobody else was left at the orphanage.

Morris came into the clubhouse, limping noticeably. Steve Kline looked at him.

"How'd you do that?" he asked. It was a question requiring an answer that Morris clearly didn't want to go into.

"The lobby," he curtly replied. And then he limped into the asylum of the trainer's room, which was off-limits to reporters.

For La Russa, it was a pivotal moment, one of those moments in which managing the team *mentally* was more important than managing *strategically.* He was adamant that none of what was happening would defeat them. The team had regrouped and rebounded when Morris had gotten hurt against San Diego, and they would do the same now. He was trying to be positive, but it wasn't easy. He couldn't help but agonize over the upcoming series against the Cubs, knowing that Morris, slotted for Game 3, could not pitch it. He also knew that the Cubs were about to embark on a hellacious road trip, nine games in ten days, culminating in the series against the Cards. He hoped they would go 0 and 6 before they arrived in St. Louis, because wouldn't that be lovely, send the punky boys packing. But what if they broke even, or they went 4 and 2? What if they came into Busch thinking they could win because they could win? What if they threw Prior and Wood and Zambrano at them versus Stephenson and Williams and Tomko? What if what if what if what if?

And *what now . . .*

The Phillies three-game series was a disaster, an accumulation of miseries. Williams couldn't keep the ball down in Game 1. Matheny failed on a *hit-and-run.* Haren was great until the sixth of Game 2, when he challenged and lost and gave up two home runs. Edmonds turned an inside-the-park homer into a double when he ambled to first, thinking he'd hit it out of the park; if he'd hustled like he should have, he could have made it home when the ball landed in an unpopulated portion of the outfield. Martinez left eight men on base. Tomko was as shaky as La Russa had feared in Game 3 with six runs and two homers in three innings. Even Pujols wasn't immune. He got the flu and missed one game entirely. The series ended on a fitting note when La Russa got ejected in the ninth for exhorting the umpire to eject Phillie pitcher Turk Wendell for hitting a Cardinal after several Cardinals had already been hit. In doing so, he pulled his little cheat sheets out of his back pocket and ripped them up, and while the fluttering of those little torn pieces to the artificial turf might have made him feel momentarily calmer, it also meant that he would now have to do them all over again because the Phillies were coming to St. Louis the following weekend.

But the three-game series is the perfect drug; by definition, it leaves the system quickly. It is over, finished, and then on to the next one. Pittsburgh was in next for three games, and something stunning happened during that series: the setback that had occurred five days ago now offset by such amazing news that it sent La Russa dancing out of his office in what looked remarkably like an imitation of Jackie Gleason on his old variety show. Which was almost as amazing as the news itself.

III

"MORRIS LOOKED pretty darn good. I was really surprised."

La Russa, still in his uniform after an ugly first-game win against the Pirates, smiled for the first time all season when he heard those words from team doctor George Paletta.

"Hallelujah."

Paletta thought it was possible for Morris to go against the Cubs in Game 3, as it was still nine days off. The biggest risk was making sure that his mechanics were proper, in particular that he took a normal stride and landed correctly on his follow-through. A bullpen session with Morris had been scheduled for the next day. Paletta cautioned Duncan and La Russa to scrutinize him closely. He also advised that the only way to tell for sure how his ankle was healing would be to have him pitch at game-level intensity.

Paletta left, and La Russa pounced. Because Morris had to pitch at game-level intensity anyway to make sure he was okay, La Russa sounded out Walt Jocketty on the prospect of letting Morris pitch Saturday against the Phillies on a limited pitch count, instead of heading down to the minors for a rehab game or, worse yet, waiting until the Cubs' series. Pitching against the Phillies would give Morris all the intensity he needed, La Russa reasoned, and, more important, would give him a start before jumping into the fire against the Cubs.

Jocketty was dubious. But before he finished his sentence, La Russa was doing his *away-we-go* Jackie Gleason move to the trainer's room to talk to Weinberg. Jocketty could have canceled the idea, but what La Russa was suggesting made sense, as Morris would have to pitch somewhere before the Cubs' series.

When La Russa came back a few minutes later, he was smiling as broadly as the kid who got the train set for Christmas and the lifetime subscription to *Penthouse*. He pulled out the Thing of Beauty that had become so ugly in the immediate aftermath of Morris's ankle.

"Let's go to work now," he said.

He continued to toil in his uniform, the clubhouse emptied out until the only person left was the assistant equipment manager, Buddy Bates, rattling through with a set of white plastic hangers. He slotted in Morris for Saturday against the Phillies. He slotted him in for Game 3 on Thursday against the Cubs. He restored the initials MM in six other places so that he and Williams had fourteen starts of the games still remaining. "That looks better," he said when he was done. Then he said what he always said when something worked, or at least looked like it *might* work: "*Son of a bitch.*"

Morris went five innings that Saturday, his pitch count recorded in the dugout like the heartbeat monitor of a hospital patient:

Eighteen in the first. Up to twenty-nine by the second. Up to forty by the third. Up to fifty-seven by the fourth. Up to seventy-five by the fifth. If you push it any more, he's going to need a defibrillator.

He threw fifty-two strikes out of those seventy-five pitches. He gave up six hits and left on the short end of a 1–0 Phillies lead. He kept his team in it, and an inning later, the Cardinals turned the tables into a 5–1 lead that held up. If his ankle hurt—and it must have, given what it had looked like a few days earlier, a sight so gnarly that Morris himself regretted looking at it right after eating lunch—he didn't give in to it. He threw mostly fastballs and sinkers, but he didn't try to overthrow. His mechanics were smooth. His curve ball was still pissed at him for that month of rust, doing what curve balls so often do when they've been slighted, refusing any immediate offers of conciliation. His competitiveness was his kill shot, and you couldn't help but wonder if something private and indescribable had passed through to him from someone else who had pitched the exact same way.

He had done what he had been asked to do, just as five days later he would be asked again, this time against the Cubs in the rubber game.

14

KISS MY ASS

I

● ● ● LA RUSSA REMEMBERED the first time he had ever heard the mention of Morris's name. It was late in 1995, and after a ten-year run with Oakland, La Russa was thinking about his future. He was trying to figure out where to go next—maybe Baltimore—when he found himself sitting at a dinner banquet next to Walt Jocketty.

Jocketty had become the general manager of the Cardinals in 1994 after spending almost all of his major-league, front-office career with Oakland, so he knew La Russa well. He was from Minneapolis originally, and the combination of that Minnesota accent, where every answer still seems in the form of a curious question, along with the white hair as finely woven as pasta, exuded Rotarian solidity. He didn't seem like someone who tried to BS his way through as a general manager—make up complete lies about the talents of players who needed to be traded—when some would argue that the whole point of being a general manager was to lie, make your BS better than the other guy's BS. Almost uniquely, he had survived, and survived well, by telling the truth.

Jocketty's style also reflected something else—an increasing anachronism in baseball today. He believed that direct communication with a manager and coaches on personnel decisions could only *enhance* the quality of a ballclub. He showed none of the tendency to treat the manager as *middle* manager, there to be seen in the dugout but never heard, a few steps up from batboy. He listened carefully to the evaluations of La Russa and Duncan on possible players coming in and possible players to be shipped out. He respected their expertise and intuitions, which isn't to say that he always agreed with them or only listened to them exclusively. The decisions were Jocketty's, but La Russa—similar to his experiences with Rollie Hemond on the White Sox and Sandy Alderson on the A's—never felt deserted. But Jocketty was still a general manager.

He was by nature a hyperbolist, an enthusiast who could put a good spin on anything, find truth and justice in a three-card monte. At the table that night, he told La Russa and Duncan, who was there as well, about all the great young pitchers the Cardinals had coming up in the system. Alan Benes was mentioned, and so was someone named Matt Morris. He argued convincingly that the Cardinals had a strong pitching core, and he got La Russa and Duncan fired up, as they had been through enough to know that no matter how prodigious a team's hitting, it is pitching that always carries a team into the October light.

It was pretty much on the basis of that dinner that La Russa and Duncan, traveling in loyal tandem as usual, decided to make St. Louis their next stop. When they got down to spring training in 1996, they liked what they saw not only in Alan Benes but also brother Andy, who had signed as a free agent. But there was this other kid, Morris, even younger, whom the Cardinals had taken in the first round out of Seton Hall. The pitchers were throwing off the mound, and La Russa and Duncan were watching them. They looked up and down the row, and their eyes kept coming back to this 6'5" kid with the delivery, the way he arched his back, the way he got over on his front leg, the way the ball left his hand so *beautifully.* "Everything was so gorgeous," La Russa remembered. And although La Russa knew enough to heed his own admonition— *Never fall in and out of love too early in the spring*—forget it.

He was smitten, and by and large the love has been rewarded. But tonight in Game 3 is different. Different because of Morris's still uncertain ankle. Different because the Cardinals are going against a pitcher who has won six of his last seven starts and last time out, six days ago, carried a no-hitter into the eighth. Besides his competitive heart, Morris is also going to need the return of his stuff. He has to keep the ball down, and his curve—unhittable when it's on, because of its vengeful drop at the plate—must drop the picket signs and get back to work. It's also the rubber game of the three-game series, and in the 162-game season of baseball, trying to make it manageable, winning the rubber game of every three-game series is the way La Russa stays in contention. It's why he tells his players to think of it as if it's the seventh game of the World Series.

Morris is long and spindly on the mound, almost bow-legged. He likes to work quickly, sometimes too quickly when he's excited, which he obviously is tonight in Game 3, given the stakes. The Cardinals' win last night, coupled with Houston's victory over Los Angeles, have only perpetuated the seesaw torture of the standings: three teams separated by 11 one-hundredths of a percentage point:

HOUSTON	70-62	.530	—
ST. LOUIS	69-63	.523	1
CHICAGO	68-63	.519	1½

It only adds to the pressure on Morris tonight, and there's something else to watch for besides his ankle. It's a concern for Duncan and La Russa every time Morris pitches, as baseball may be the only organized profession in the world where theft is perfectly legal. There are virtually no rules about it. Instead, like suspected cattle rustling, it's taken care of with an impromptu code of justice much like a batter getting hit by a pitch. It is not tolerated if discovered, and there are some who will resort to the threat of death. But everyone is up for grabs—the pitcher, the catcher, the third-base coach, the first-base coach, the manager, the bench coach—because of a tendency to inadvertently spill secrets.

In recent years, since so many major-league pitchers are moved up before they've learned the subtler aspects of the game, La Russa has noticed a new twist on baseball theft. Preying on that virginity, players sit on the bench watching for whether a pitcher is tipping off his pitches in the process of his wind-up by the way he reaches in for a forkball or fans the glove on a curve; the wider the glove, the easier the detection. It's a burgeoning phenomenon because so many pitchers, with so little experience in the minors, haven't learned how to conceal what they're throwing. Some players, like Shawn Green of the Dodgers, can figure out a pitcher's pitches with uncanny accuracy. And this is only one of an assortment of attempted thefts that La Russa has seen in his managing career.

There are also the "peekers"—runners on first who try to peek into the catcher's glove to see what he is throwing as a basis for whether or not to try to steal second. There are runners on second who, with their bird's-eye view of the catcher, will try to tip location or the type of pitch to the batter with how they lead off second. There are relief pitchers in the bullpen who will communicate location to the batter by how they drape their arms over the bullpen wall. There are first-base coaches who will tip location with a series of sudden movements. There are coaches who will spend hours staring into dugouts to see if they can figure out the pitchout sign, like Cardinals bench coach Pettini did when he broke the Pirates earlier in the season.

There are ways to combat all of this. A manager, knowing he is surrounded by all these cat burglars, will act like he's putting on a sign when it's simply a series of dekes. La Russa does that sometimes when he goes to his leg or touches his hat, much ado about nothing. Aware that an opponent may be watching on television with its intimate camera angles, a catcher such as Matheny may have as many as six different sets of signs for a starter that he will change with a tap on his mask or a thump on his chest. Outright threats are effective as well—like the one Roger Clemens once gave to a runner on second whom he suspected of tipping. He called time, walked up to the runner, and stated succinctly that "somebody was going to get killed" if he kept it up. But attempted thefts still go on throughout a game, an underworld of deceit and deception. Early in his career, when he was with the White Sox, La Russa learned the value of sign stealing from a third-base coach named Joe Nossek. Nossek was the Willie Sutton of his day—he stole signs because they were there—and rare was the sign he couldn't crack. He got La Russa to pay attention to the science, and La Russa was a good student.

In 1983, as the White Sox were making their run to a division championship, they played the Yankees in a three-game series at the Stadium in August. Suddenly La Russa realized that he had figured out the steal sign from the Yankees' third-base coach Don Zimmer after it had been conveyed to Zimmer by manager Billy Martin from the dugout. The White Sox bench was fond of Zimmer. Everybody in baseball was fond of Zimmer. To not be fond of Zimmer was un-American. But the White Sox coaches also knew that Yankee manager Billy Martin had a reputation for being tough on his coaches, calling them out after games if he thought they had done something wrong.

So La Russa set up a decoy to use against Martin so he would not figure out that the White Sox theft had come from Zimmer. La Russa parked coach Eddie Brinkman in the front of the dugout with strict instructions to do nothing but stare at Martin. During the game, the Yankees tried a steal of second and it failed because the White Sox knew it was on. As ordered, Brinkman just stared at Martin and Martin glared back. Late in the game it happened again, another Yankee thrown out attempting to steal, this time Omar Moreno. Brinkman just kept on staring. Martin threw up his hands in disgust, now thoroughly convinced that he was the one whose steal sign had been filched. And Zimmer was saved from getting scalded.

During Game 3 tonight La Russa will pay close attention to a runner on second to see if his movements off the bag are coordinated to where Matheny is setting up behind the plate. If the runner takes a little jab step to third, does that mean he's signaling to the batter at the plate that the ball is coming in on the third-base side? If he takes a little jab step back toward second, does that mean the ball's coming into the first-base side? La Russa wants Matheny to give a good target to the pitcher. It's an essential component of a pitcher making his pitches. The best way for the catcher to set up the target is to frame the pitch nice and early. But because of a concern that the runner on second is telegraphing pitches to the batter, the catcher will move around, or he may purposely not set up early. Which combats the telegraphing but also deprives him of giving the most effective target. So for every plus there's a minus, and for every minus a plus, those pulleys and levers working overtime yet again.

Maybe it's simply paranoia on La Russa's part, one more thing to look for and worry about. But this is not a new issue between the Cubs and the Cardinals. There is some history to it. The prior season, the two teams almost engaged in hand-to-hand combat over suspicions of theft. It happened in May when the Cards were facing the Cubs at Wrigley. Sosa hit a home run in the first inning off Morris; as far as the Cardinals bench was concerned, something wasn't right about it, the way Sosa just seemed to know what was coming. And come to think of it, what exactly was the Cubs' first-base coach Sandy Alomar doing over at first? Why was he *falling* to his knees like that? Why was he *coughing?* The Cards became convinced that Alomar was tipping location to Sosa. When the inning was over, the third-base coach Oquendo ran over to Alomar as he was coming off the field and asked him *what the hell* was going on. Alomar said nothing, but the belief only grew deeper that there was something rotten. Angry words were traded after the game. The Cubs issued denials and the Cards made continued affirmations. There was no resolution beyond the war of words, but the suspicion still lingers, which is why La Russa will have his eyes peeled tonight.

Kenny Lofton comes up to begin Game 3 in his customary role as the Cubs' lead-off hitter and incessant rabble-rouser. He's 4 for 9 in the series, and he's been at the center of just about all the offense the Cubs have been able to muster. He hits Morris for better average than any other hitter in the Cubs' lineup tonight, the matchups in La Russa's back pocket revealing a subplot of 6 for 15. But there's an even more tangled subplot between the two, dating back to the fifth and final game of last year's National League Championship series against San Francisco, when Morris hit Lofton with a pitch in the bottom of the fourth. Given the circumstances of what was at stake, this wasn't some payback plunk, but in Game 1 of the series, Lofton hit a homer off Morris. He paused at first base to admire his prowess, and Morris silently stared at Lofton as he continued around the bases with the subtlety of a rifle scope.

All this adds considerable intrigue to the first at-bat, in addition to the already considerable intrigue imposed by Morris. There's the ankle factor. There's also the excitement factor, which can cause him to fall all over the place on the mound in his hurried delivery, which sends balls that should be located down into the sweet hitting zone of up. There is the tipping factor.

Morris begins the game by throwing a nasty sinker to Lofton on the outside corner for a called strike. If there is still bad blood between the two, Morris is not going to draw it. Tonight is about pitching, not the settling of Hatfield-and-McCoy baseball feuds. He comes back with a sinker to the other side of the plate, and Lofton hits it harmlessly to Scott Rolen at third for an easy popout. He uses another one to get the second-place hitter, Martinez, on a ground out to Edgar Renteria at short. He's notched two outs in five pitches. From the foxhole, La Russa looks into Morris's eyes and feels confident that he has the right look tonight: focused, suitably anxious to get it on, but not rushing his pitches to his own detriment.

Sammy Sosa comes up in the third spot. Morris goes after him with a sinker. Sosa looks it in without lifting the bat. It's just outside for 1 and 0. Morris comes in with another sinker, clearly the pitch that he is favoring tonight. Sosa cocks the bat, ready to swing, but he lays off. Strike on the outside corner for 1 and 1. Morris throws another sinker the other way, working the inside of the plate. Sosa takes a whiplash swing, visions of the 402-foot sign in center field swirling in his head. He misses for 1 and 2.

Morris has him where he wants him. It's a perfect waste-pitch opportunity: Try to get him to chase, prey on Sosa's ego to go downtown. He throws another sinker, up and away, to even the count at 2 and 2. But it's still a pitcher's count. There's no reason to risk anything here, still a situation in which you can get Sosa to go for something he doesn't really like, still ample room to prey on his feelings of omnipotence. Morris throws his fifth straight sinker. It's up and out over the plate.

From the dugout, La Russa cringes as he sees it, a slight bracing as if he is readying for some terrible explosion. His arms are still folded, his eyes still locked, but his lips have clamped down more tightly than usual, as if this is it, the final heartbreak out of the thousands of them that he has experienced in all those years of managing. He's never going to open his mouth again, say another word.

Morris has made a mistake. All pitchers make them, and they often get away with them. But Morris has made a mistake with Sosa, and Sosa is a mistake hitter. On the scorecard La Russa keeps, he will make a one-word notation to describe what has just happened: *stupid.* No tipping of location here.

Sosa gives a little cha-cha dance step as he hits it, as if maybe the move will propel the ball a few extra feet. In center field, Edmonds turns on his heels and runs back. He keeps running, ever closer to the western front of the warning track. He has his head on the ball as he runs back. He has a bead on it. He knows where it is. Nobody in baseball right now, maybe nobody in the history of baseball, goes back better on a ball than Edmonds does. He makes spectacular over-the-fence grabs look so routine that he's expected to make them. But now he slows to a trot and lifts his head back to watch the ball sail over him, over the 402-foot sign in deep center, landing on a little patch of berm with the silence of a tee shot plump on the fairway.

Morris steps off the mound and walks a few feet as Sosa rounds the bases, not dawdling, but not setting any speed records, adding his own tenderizer to the slab of beef that Morris just served up. Morris removes his glove and wipes his hand, as if to preoccupy himself with anything besides the fact that Sosa just tagged the living crap out of him; the last thing he's going to do is watch Sammy's eternal victory lap. Sosa rounds third and gives a little fist to the third-base coach. Then he touches home and gives a little kiss to the heavens. 1–0 Cubs.

II

KERRY ROBINSON leads off the bottom of the first for the Cardinals, fresh from building another addition on his doghouse, this time for his positioning in right field in Game 2. First-base coach Dave McKay, who handles the positioning of the outfielders, had trouble getting Robinson's attention: Before the start of Game 3, La Russa called Robinson into his office and flat-out told him he'd bench him if there were any more communication problems. In La Russa's mind, it's just another example of Robinson's wobbly fundamentals. His failure to be aggressive in an RBI situation against the Phillies still burns, and it's difficult to think that the relationship between the two can go any lower. The only way for Robinson to redeem himself would be with a spectacular at-bat, and the odds of that plummet as he strikes out on three pitches, all sinkers, groping with late, punchless swings.

Carlos Zambrano is the least known of the Cubs' formidable starting trio, barely a glimmer behind the punky aura of Prior and Wood. Zambrano has neither the redwood thighs nor the sneer. Nor does he have the lineage, signed as a nondrafted free agent out of Venezuela when he was sixteen. But he is hardly some add-on. Prior is Prior, and nobody on the Cardinals disputes that Prior is Prior, a limitless future *if* he stays injury free. Wood is also Wood, tough because he's nasty and nasty because he's tough, and nobody disputes that, either. But at the age of twenty-two, Zambrano has already developed an instinct on what to throw and when to throw it. At certain times during the season, he has been the Cubs' most effective pitcher, and August has been one of those times.

"I'm surprised at how quickly he's become a pitcher," says the Secret Weapon, who from his blurry-eyed sessions in front of the monitor knows the difference between those who have stuff and those who have Zen and those who have both. Blair means it as the ultimate compliment. He's seen countless clips of Zambrano's splitter, his hard slider, his straight powerball four-seamer, and his lights-out two-seamer sinker that clocks in the low nineties with late movement, resulting in a plethora of weakly hit groundballs.

He comes in with a record of 12 and 9 and an ERA of 2.94. His ERA since the All-Star break has been 1.51, and his last three performances give La Russa particular agita:

DATE	OPP.	IP	H	R	ER	HR	BB	SO	GB	FB	PIT
Aug. 12	Houston	9	5	0	0	0	2	10	12	4	121
Aug. 17	Los Angeles	7	5	2	2	0	3	5	14	2	105
Aug. 22	Arizona	9	3	1	1	0	2	4	18	7	93

Nobody in baseball has put together recent numbers like that, the ratio of groundballs to fly balls a remarkable 3 to 1. It makes him the best unknown pitcher in the game right now, an anonymity defined by the little putt-putt green of a partial goatee, centered on his chin, that has become standard equipment among pitchers.

He gets Hart to fly to right; after five pitches, he has two outs. Pujols works a single—the eighth consecutive plate appearance in which he's gotten on base: reason 10,456 why he is the best hitter in the game. But then Edmonds strikes out to end the inning. Zambrano has thrown twelve pitches, nine of them strikes, including first-pitch strikes to three of the four batters he faced.

Morris settles down in the top of the second. He dispatches Simon, Ramirez, and Gonzalez in only six pitches.

Zambrano handles his half of the second by working Rolen and Martinez for easy grounders to third and second. Zambrano shows his precocity with his first pitch to Renteria, a get-me-over slider that most hitters, including Renteria, wouldn't look for. He doesn't lift the bat, and Zambrano has the 0-and-1 advantage. He continues to work Renteria with a combination of sliders and sinkers. The count goes to 1 and 2. Renteria is almost up on his tiptoes as he adjusts to the batter's box, delicate and storklike. Zambrano comes with a nasty sinker inside and low. Renteria simply stays with it, doesn't try to do too much with it, and singles a liner to right.

Matheny, who hasn't had a hit in the entire series so far, lines a single into left. It puts runners on first and second with two outs, a scoring opportunity, but baseball, just a mean bitch sometimes, places Morris into the batter's box.

Morris carries a pretty good bat. But he is clearly overmatched by Zambrano, who is throwing free and easy in the midnineties, his strength rising from thick thighs and chunky buttocks. Even if Morris does manage to make contact, running on that bad ankle subjects him to far more pain and jeopardy than pitching does. On a 3-and-2 count, he hits a slow chopper to the left side, not slow enough for a guaranteed infield hit, not hard enough for an easy out, but exactly in between. Meaning that there will be a play. Meaning that the outcome will hinge on Morris's ability to get down the line to first.

The ball bounces once, twice, past the mound as Zambrano lunges for it and fails. It's heading into that patch of no man's land on the infield grass between third and short, where the lines of personal responsibility between third baseman and pitcher blur. Morris is hustling his buttocks off to get to first because the Cardinals rally will stay alive if he makes it in time, and he will perhaps atone for his mistake with Sosa. The ankle is hurting him like hell. He isn't openly limping, but his stride, with no natural serenity, is halting and choppy, as if he's running against the tide.

Ramirez at third moves toward short to get it on the third bounce. He makes the throw, but the angle is awkward. Simon at first has to dive to get it. He falls off the bag like a skyscraper toppling, and here comes Morris, and it's going to be close, real close. Simon finishes toppling. Because he's big and hardly a garden of coordination, you can almost hear the thud. Morris is on top of the bag. The umpire sees what he sees in the chaos.

He's out. The Cards are still down 1–0 after two.

Morris makes another mistake in the top of the third, rushing a curve ball to Zambrano as if it's a chore, the pitching equivalent of your mother's telling you to take out the garbage and you leave half of it in a paper-towel trail through the house. Zambrano, looking almost surprised to get a cookie like this, slaps it into left to put runners on first and third. If you seek omens, and baseball is all about omens, you can find one in the fact that Zambrano produced a hit, whereas Morris couldn't in his first at-bat. Another omen is Morris's tendency to get the ball up this inning. It's never a good thing, and La Russa is worrying more than ever that Morris's ankle, still throbbing from the close play at first, is definitely starting to affect his concentration and mechanics.

With runners on the corners, Lofton lines a scorcher up the middle, but Hart at second doesn't have to move an inch to get it. It's a blessed break—maybe even an omen that favors the Cardinals—because if the ball goes a foot one way or a foot another, it would carry the Cubs into the land of the crooked number. Morris jams the next hitter, Martinez, with a sinker. It's a nasty pitch, but he gets enough of it to send it into center for a sacrifice fly that ushers home the man on third.

Sosa follows, but Morris handles him far more surgically than he did last time. He bears in on him with a sinker to go 0 and 1 and open up the outside of the plate for himself because Sosa, now inside conscious, is looking for something in the same location. He hits a weak grounder to short for a force-out, ending the top of the third. La Russa is buoyed by the Cubs' failure to reap the crooked number. But the score is still 2–0.

III

IN THE ENTIRE three-game series, the Cardinals have managed exactly one run against the Cubs' starters. It's a horrible trend, and it shows no signs of improvement when Robinson grounds out to short with another overmatched swing and Hart follows by striking out. It brings up Pujols in the three-hole, who finally squeezes out a walk on the seventh pitch of the at-bat when Zambrano's fastball wanders a little high. It's the ninth straight appearance in which he has gotten on base: reason 14,988 why he is the best hitter in baseball.

La Russa, still looking sour, paces forward and back and sideways in the parameters of his foxhole. His habits have become superstitions and his superstitions have become habits. He glances every now and then at the lineup sheet. He takes the little cheat sheets out of his back pocket and puts them back, takes them out and puts them back. He's searching for a spark now, however tiny, to get a fire going, Paul Richards's advice resting on his shoulder: *Make something happen.*

So he tries to sneak a steal, an unlikely moment to try it with the cleanup hitter at bat and Pujols, no speedster, on first. But the unlikelihood of the situation makes him try it. Zambrano can be quick to the plate when he's in the mood, but he gets slow—about 1.5 seconds—when he's not concerned about the runner on first. He doesn't seem particularly worried about Pujols's going anywhere; he's loosing a high, mighty leg kick that speeds up his throw but slows down his overall delivery. He's focused on the batter, so La Russa makes his move. With a dozen pairs of eyes always on him, deconstructing his every gesture, the sign to steal does not come directly from him. Instead, he communicates it to someone else in the dugout, who in turn communicates it to Pujols. Edmonds himself does not know that the steal is on, because the batter can sometimes inadvertently tip something. He swings away as Pujols goes. He fouls the pitch off, and La Russa takes the steal off after that because the element of surprise, the best thing going for his ploy, has evaporated. After Edmonds hits an easy tapper back to the pitcher to end the third inning, La Russa's conviction only strengthens that a run will be a rarity tonight. Zambrano is pitching well with nice rhythm. He's thrown fifty pitches, hardly a taxing amount, and he's gotten first-pitch strikes on nine of the thirteen batters he's faced. The Cardinals have responded with three singles, and nobody has made it past second.

Morris moves easily through the fourth. Five pitches dispense with Alou, Simon, and Ramirez.

Zambrano handles his half of the fourth in thirteen pitches.

Morris takes ten pitches to put away Gonzalez and Bako and Zambrano in the top of the fifth. He's retired nine in a row. With the game now more than half complete, he's thrown a remarkably economical forty-eight pitches. But he's still behind 2–0, and La Russa thinks about pinch-hitting for him here in the bottom of the fifth because there's no way of knowing how much he has left or when that ankle might give way. But how he retired the side in order in the top of the fifth tells La Russa something, so Morris leads off the bottom of the inning. He fouls the first pitch toward the third-base side. He steps out of the box, takes a breath, steps back in. Zambrano comes with a nasty sinker low and away.

Morris reaches for it and clips it down the right-field line into the corner. Again he'll have to run like hell on his bad ankle, and it's agonizing to watch. He makes it around first with a noticeable limp, and his pace slackens as he nears second, catching a slight break when the ball caroms into the corner and Sosa has to root around for it. That saves him from having to slide, which might just wreck his ankle altogether.

Robinson, up next, has a simple task. With no outs, he needs to advance the runner to third. La Russa has his players work on this maneuver religiously during batting practice. Robinson's options have been clearly delineated. He can either try to pull the ball into right, as that placement, far from third base, gives Morris the best chance to advance. Or he can bunt down the first-base line for the same reason.

A smart pitcher like Zambrano might know what Robinson's up to and sink the ball away, making it more difficult for him to pull it to right field. But this simplifies the hitter's task, as now he need only choose between:

1. Taking the pitch.
2. Bunting toward first base.

But Robinson settles on a third choice when Zambrano wisely throws a sinker away. Robinson tries to pull it to right, even though doing so flouts the laws of physics.

He hits it to left field, *short left field,* the very worst place to put the ball if you want to advance the runner from second. Alou comes in from left to make the easy catch. Morris remains at second. La Russa seethes in the dugout. Robinson has failed to apply the lessons of Baseball 101, and his relationship with his manager, which really couldn't go lower, has now gone lower. Few things infuriate La Russa more than the modern player's steadfast refusal to play the game right. It irks him all the more as a reflection on his own managerial abilities; he can imagine a baseball man in the stands turning his head in disgust as he watches a play like that and saying to himself, *This is simply bad baseball,* a basic move-the-runner-over play that doesn't come out close to right.

Hart is up with one out and goes down swinging on four straight sinkers from Zambrano. Where once there was a runner on second with no outs, there is now a runner on second with two outs.

Pujols is up and, with first base open, Zambrano pitches around him for the walk. Edmonds walks as well and the bases are loaded for Rolen. It's the best scoring opportunity the team has had all day, and the fans' chorus rises to its feet in a pleading swell, making it clear that this is it. The game's karma will be determined right here.

In the dugout, the knotted cliques draw tighter, except for the hermit J.D. Drew, who sits alone on the stairs at one end of the dugout, staring blankly from the familiar detachment of the disabled list. The dugout is quiet, perhaps because the players feel the same queasy expectation that the fans do.

Zambrano grips the ball behind his back, then shifts it to his glove for one final readjustment of fingers on seams. Rolen comes to the plate and performs the same ritual he performs before every pitch, gently touching his bat to the border of dirt just outside of the plate and then the center of the plate itself and then the inside border, an expectant magician warming up his wand. In an obvious RBI situation like this, La Russa preaches aggressiveness—take a swing at the first good pitch—and Rolen embraces the dogma zealously.

Zambrano throws a sinker inside and low. Rolen swings. He launches a foul toward the seats past the dugout on the first-base side. He watches as it hangs. Players pop out of the Cards' dugout like a collective jack-in-the-box—Perez and Palmeiro and Williams and Tomko and Haren—all saying the same thing with their outstretched necks: *How far will it carry?*

Simon runs from first to make a play. The ball is definitely headed into the seats past first base, a row back, maybe a row and a half. He's already earned his keep today when he fell to earth to get Morris by a step. Now he has to bend and gyrate and stick his glove into a morass of goopy hands and see whether he can pull something out. He dips his clam-digger-sized glove into the goop. For a moment, it's buried, submerged. Then he scoops it out of the muck to see what it contains.

He has the ball. The inning's over, and the karma has declared itself:

	1	2	3	4	5	R	H	E
CUBS	1	0	1	0	0	2	3	0
CARDS	0	0	0	0	0	0	5	0

Eight men left on base through five. Robinson so deep in the doghouse for not advancing the runner that La Russa turns to the third-base coach Oquendo and snaps without charity: *"If that son of a bitch starts another game this year, I'll kiss your ass."*

15

THREE NIGHTS IN AUGUST

I

● ● ● MORRIS RETIRES the side in order in the sixth, the final pitch a sweet 12-to-6 curve that Sosa misses by so much, even the Arch smiles. He has now retired twelve in a row, no Cubs batter reaching base since Zambrano got that cookie in the third. He has thrown only sixty-one pitches.

But the game continues to play wicked mischief, the primary motivation to make Morris run on that gimpy ankle as much as possible. He comes to the plate in the bottom half of the sixth, with Edgar Renteria on first and two outs. This seems like the place for La Russa to bring in the lefty Palmeiro to pinch-hit, as Morris has done more on the mound than anybody had a right to expect. La Russa further forecasts that possibility by having Cal Eldred already warming up to take the seventh.

But La Russa is juggling the variables here and looking ahead to the ninth. Palmeiro is the only left-handed bat on the bench, and La Russa needs to save him for the ninth, on the assumption that Dusty Baker will inevitably give the ball to his right-handed closer, Borowski. So Palmeiro stays put for now. The other option would be pinch-hitting for Morris with a righty to go against the righty Zambrano. But the bottom line in La Russa's mind is that Morris has the best chance of anyone on the staff of getting three outs in the seventh because of the way he is pitching.

So he lets Morris hit with the two outs, even though there is a man on. Given what he has already been through on the basepaths tonight, simple human compassion begs that Morris quietly pop up on the first pitch or simply strike out. Please, don't run any more.

Zambrano throws a sinker on the inside corner for 0 and 1 as Morris doesn't swing. He comes in with a sinker on the next pitch. It's a fat pitch, almost dead center on the plate. Morris pops it foul to the first base, and now he's in the 0-and-2 trough.

Baker calls for a pitchout on the next pitch. It's an effective move even if nothing is on, as it has a tendency to shut down an opponent's running game. Baker has also seen La Russa in action for more than twenty years. He even played for him briefly in Oakland. He knows that La Russa has a thieving heart behind that Mount Rushmore façade. He's already tried it once before in a less likely situation than this. Renteria at first is a good base stealer. He is capable of going at any time. If he makes it, he's in scoring position. If he doesn't, it's really no bad thing. It ends the inning, thereby preventing Morris from having to finish the at-bat and risk any more agony to his ankle. He can go out and pitch the seventh, which will definitely be his last inning. Assuming that he gets through it, La Russa can then pinch-hit for him in the bottom of the inning, with the world fresh and uncomplicated and three outs available.

Renteria stays put: 1 and 2. Zambrano throws a slider that viciously slides outside. Morris gets the tiniest sliver of it to foul it off: still 1 and 2.

Zambrano comes with a sinker to the other side of the plate. Morris taps a slow roller to the left side of the infield, slow enough that *here we go again*. Baseball has produced yet another seemingly impossible moment, nothing quite like it in all the vast statistical annals that could fill the Atlantic and the Pacific: a pitcher with a bad ankle, barely able to run, comes to bat *three times* and puts the ball in play *three times* with the game's potential outcome on the line *three times*.

Morris's ankle basically gives out on him, causing him to slip as he leaves the batter's box. He's going as fast as he can, but the ankle is killing him, and everybody in Busch can virtually feel his pain every time he lands on it as he makes his choppy run down the line. Zambrano fields the ball on one hop. He has plenty of time to make the throw. But he takes a little bit off it. As Morris chugs closer and closer to the bag, the ball bounces in front of Simon at first. Can he handle it?

He can't. Morris is safe at first.

Robinson comes up, with Renteria now on third and Morris on first and with two outs. Robinson takes the first pitch for a strike. It's a sinker that doesn't come close to sinking, so it's down the pipe. La Russa mouths obscenities from the dugout, because *Haven't we been through this before, Kerry, haven't we? HAVEN'T WE!!!! IN AN RBI SITUATION, YOU MUST SWING AT THE FIRST GOOD PITCH!!*

The ball is right on the plate. It's right down the middle. It's an urban garden in the wasteland of garbage that a good pitcher like Zambrano relies on. So it's a fait accompli — another wasted scoring chance, ten men now left on base with only nine chances left — because Robinson won't get a better pitch than that.

He doesn't. The next pitch is a sinker away. Its location is devilish, but Robinson swings and slaps it down the left field line for a double.

Renteria scores to close the gap to 2–1. Morris winces his way around second and heads for third. The dugout, so tongue-tied all night, finally expresses itself. The separate cliques of coaches and pitchers and position players momentarily dissolve. A line forms to greet Renteria, as if he's been away on an epic journey, with the usual assortment of fist kisses and helmet smacks and butt pats.

But the joy is short-lived; there's trouble at third. Morris managed to make it to the bag without sliding, but he arrived in a noticeable limp. La Russa runs out to see whether he's seriously injured. So does Barry Weinberg. La Russa takes his glasses off.

"You don't look too good. You're hobbling. How sore is it?"

"Pitching is the part that hurts me the least. The running hurts much more."

Morris gives La Russa enough reassurance to leave him in

there. But as La Russa runs back to the dugout, he's fretting, the system of pulleys and levers pumping away. He let Morris bat because he wanted him to pitch the seventh, but now he has to face the consequences of Morris as a base runner. If there's a wild pitch, Morris will not only have to break for home on that ankle but also slide. He could put in a pinch runner, but if he doesn't give Morris the seventh, the game could slip away, because he's pitching so well. But, realistically, how much does Morris have left?

Hart grounds out to end the inning, which alleviates the wild-pitch worry. Morris trots gingerly back to the dugout, gets his glove, and heads back to the field. Now La Russa can focus on worrying about how much his starter has left. With one out in the top of the seventh, he gives up a single to Simon and walks Ramirez.

Duncan runs out to the mound to review the MapQuest against the next batter, Gonzalez: how he has a tendency to sit on breaking balls late in the game. La Russa reaches into his back pocket, pulls out his cheat sheets, and finds a little relief: Gonzalez is 0 for 11 against Morris coming into the game. With a ground out and fly out in his two previous at-bats, he's now 0 for 13. It's a perfect matchup. He works Gonzalez into a 0-2 deficit on two pitches, the second the best curve ball he has thrown all night.

Pitch no. 3: Gonzalez is sitting on a fastball. He gets a fastball and fouls it straight back, an indication that he missed pulverizing it by an inch. Still 0 and 2.

Pitch no. 4: A sinker low and away. Gonzalez lifts it foul to the right side. Still 0 and 2.

Pitch no. 5: A curve inside and high for a ball. It suggests that Morris is tired: It's nowhere near where it was supposed to go. A band of sweat has formed on his cheekbone. It's still sultry hot, the mighty river pushing out cookie tins of humid heat. His ankle has gotten a workout that no one could have cooked up, worse than any reality show. Morris simply wants to get Gonzalez out here, finish him off: The last thing he needs right now is this cat-and-mouse torment. He steps off the mound, then hauls himself back on those spindly legs.

Pitch no. 6: Another curve. Foul behind home plate. Still 1 and 2.

Pitch no. 7: A sinker inside. Another *foul*. Still *1 and 2*.

Morris is exhausted now. He knows it. La Russa knows it. The dugout knows it. Everybody knows it.

Pitch no. 8: A sinker on the inside of the plate. Gonzalez hits it fair on the ground. It's a shot. He got to it. It's also right at Rolen, who doesn't have to move as he makes the throw to Hart at second. Who makes the throw to first. A double play to end the inning.

Morris is done for the night after this. With the score 2–1, he may still end up the losing pitcher, and he won't even have a chance to get the win, unless the Cardinals mount an immediate rally. The agate in the box score the next day will show that he gave up four hits in seven innings, an outstanding quality start. On the batting side, he will be listed as 1 for 3 with a double. No statistic will show what he did on the basepaths, the war he waged with his ankle with every step he took. If the Cardinals lose, the focus won't be on Morris's performance at all but on the Cubs' finally conquering the jinx of Busch by taking two out of three. His heroism tonight will evaporate.

Working the bottom of the seventh, Zambrano jams Pujols on a sinker to induce an easy ground out to third, then strikes out Edmonds in a fricassee of forkball and fastball and curve ball and finishing sinker. The three and four hitters in the Cardinals' lineup have just gone down without defiance, and Zambrano looks as sharp as he has all night. It brings up Rolen, who is hitless not only tonight but also in the entire series. His back hurts. His neck hurts. His whole body hurts. He needs a day off. He's chasing high fastballs. He hasn't hit a home run in more than two weeks.

But he hits one now into the right-field seats: 2–2.

II

STEVE KLINE comes in to relieve in the top of the eighth. The fans go crazy at the sight of him, his hurdy-gurdy style on the mound with all those tics and jerks, one step away from hyperventilating into a heap or body slamming the home plate umpire because he didn't give him the corner. He's a left-handed reliever who went to the University of West Virginia, so he's profoundly crazy, but that's normal for a left-handed reliever. He is never dressed before the start of a game, not even his jock strap, on some occasions. He likes walking around the clubhouse in the buff, then stretching out on a couch behind Chad Blair, offering largely irrelevant commentary as the Secret Weapon watches the game on his little monitor and keeps the pitching chart, doing six things at once and keeping his equilibrium. Kline apparently thinks of the clubhouse as a nude beach; it's his way of staying loose, not letting nerves overcome him, something to preoccupy him for a couple of hours anyway, as his life has no real meaning until the late innings.

The fans love Kline for his lack of pretense. He loves the fans back, in that regard a throwback to a different era in which players soaked up the whole atmosphere of it all like sun worshippers, or at least pinched themselves before and after each game as a reminder that what they did for a living would never be confused with work.

Kids particularly like Kline. They edge the front row of the stands before games like starving refugees, yelling his name as if they have some special relationship, even though they've never met him — *Steve! Steve! Over here! Kliner! Kliner! Over here!* He returns the favor by signing the balls and the pictures and the baseball cards that pour out of their bottomless pockets like rabbits out of a hat. Then he lets them smell the peak of his hat, the smudgy stinky smelly odiferous hat filled with rosin and sweat and horsehide and leather that Kline insists on wearing the entire season. The kids crinkle up their noses when they smell it, but they also close their eyes when they smell it, because they are kids and therefore savvy enough to know that they are taking in the scent of something pure regardless of its reek.

The situation is set up nicely for him here, coming in as a lefty to face the lefty Bako. He gets him on a grounder to Hart for the first out in the top of the eighth.

Baker brings in Doug Glanville to pinch-hit in the ninth spot, It's an expected move, as Glanville is a righty and Kline a lefty. La Russa could bring in another pitcher here, and he's certainly not above doing it. But with Lofton the lefty on deck, Kline is staying right where he is. In addition, the presence of Kline prevents Baker from going to the lefty bats he has lying in wait on the bench.

He throws a good slider that tails away. Glanville swings and makes contact. He hits it hard on the ground. If he had hit it to the right spot, it would have been an easy single through the infield. But it's straight at Hart. He comes up on the ball. And the ball stays down, skittering through Hart's legs into the outfield. Glanville is on first on the error, and bad karma once again soaks the night. Because now Lofton is up. And it isn't simply that Lofton is a pain in the ass, at his age still able to get on base and advance chaos in his shuffling glide.

He is Kline's eternal nemesis, the psychotic ex-girlfriend who sends you creepy notes through the mail to remind you she's still around. Some pitchers truly do have Kung Fu serenity. They react to nothing; that blank stare when they give up a homer is a two-way mirror into the blankness inside them, blessedly free of any and all memory. Kline is not like that. He remembers every pitch he has ever thrown in the major leagues since he first came up with Cleveland in 1997. He catalogues them in his head like an anal-compulsive librarian. And he remembers what Lofton did to him in the ninth inning of the 2002 National League Championship series, when there were two outs and runners on first and second and Kline came in specifically to face Lofton, and Lofton hit a hanging slider on the first pitch to right center to win the game and the pennant.

Now he's facing Lofton again, this time in the top of the eighth of a 2–2 game with a runner on first and one out. Regardless of past history, La Russa has the lefty-versus-lefty matchup he wants. But it's the late innings of a razor-close game, one of those games in which nothing ever turns out to be entirely harmless.

Kline throws a slider on the first pitch, a nice crispy slider tailing to the outside. Lofton takes it. A called strike: 0 and 1.

Kline throws another slider. It goes into the sweet spot of the plate, not only against the wishes of Kline but also Matheny, who has set up outside. La Russa has seen this pitch before; it's the same pitch he threw Lofton in the National League Championship series.

Lofton nails it. He tags it, drills it, creams it, drives it, powers it, powders it, smokes it, kills it, commits every baseball cliché of hitting and then some.

It's headed for the gap in right center between Robinson and Edmonds: The only thing they can do is to vainly chase after it. Glanville is easily around third and on his way to home, and Lofton will have a stand-up triple out of this thing. It's a disaster, a 3–2 Cubs lead with one out and a man on third and the meat of the order coming up.

Until the ball bounces off the dirt of the warning track and into the stands. It's a ground-rule double. Which means that Glanville has to go back to third instead of scoring the go-ahead run. It's a potentially enormous break, and Lofton has only himself to blame; he was so eager to humiliate Kline once again that he simply hit the ball too damn hard.

Kline is out, replaced by the righty DeJean, with Martinez due up. He's a righty, so it only makes sense for Baker to bring in a left-handed pinch hitter. He has several on the bench, but Baker doesn't make the move, and La Russa assumes it's because Baker knows his team better than anyone else.

La Russa signals for the infield to play in. The count goes to 1 and 1 on Martinez. DeJean throws a forkball that doesn't tumble down. Martinez gets a piece of it and lines it to center field.

Edmonds is playing shallow. He likes to play shallow, a reflection of his confidence and penchant for drama. He takes two steps in and catches the ball high in the glove, glancing for a split second in the stitch of the webbing to make sure he caught it. He has his momentum going for him, and he's going to need it because Glanville is tagging up from third and trying to score and here comes the best craziness in all of sports.

He's running full bore and he's quick and Matheny moves two steps up the line, awaiting the throw, and Edmonds makes an over-the-top throw with beautiful carry and La Russa can see it and so can Duncan and so can Morris as he leaps off the back bench because it's gonna be close, it's gonna be really close, and while it's all happening fast, very fast, there's also a slow-motion quality to it as Edmonds throws the ball and Matheny awaits the ball and Glanville comes down the line, hoping he gets there before the ball and who will intersect with what when?

The throw is dead solid perfect. It gives Matheny time to take those two steps up the third-base line and set up in a stoic crouch. It's going to be a wreck at home plate, a serious wreck. Sosa, due up next, leaves the on-deck circle and, like a bystander vainly trying to ward off a car crash, motions to Glanville with his hands to *get down, get down*. But the throw is too far ahead of Glanville, his only choice to go for the high-impact head-on collision. He barrels into Matheny, using his forearm to hit him in the face. He uses the rest of his body to try to flatten him. Matheny does a full 360-degree pirouette. His glove goes flying, and if the ball is still in there, Glanville is safe, and the Cubs will win because there's no way you lose after a play like this.

It takes a second, maybe two, the crowd going berserk and two entire dugouts up on their toes and the home plate umpire bending his neck into this Bill Gallo cartoon swirl of arms and legs and what belongs to whom and who belongs to what, charged with answering everybody's question: *Where is the ball?*

Where is the ball? It's in Matheny's bare hand. He switched it from his glove right before impact. Glanville is out.

HE'S OUT!!!

The crowd goes more berserk, the mix of love and relief and maybe a few I-told-you-sos, although nobody could have ever told you so, a double play like this to end the inning. Edmonds trots in from center field into the dugout into a sea of high-fives led by Rolen and Renteria. He sits in the back of the dugout with his cap off, sweaty and luxuriant, his hair, so carefully slicked back before each game in his Hollywood style, now standing at attention in certain spots. It's a great play, so great that La Russa leaves his foxhole to congratulate him, an almost surreptitious shake of the hand because he believes that this is a player's moment to be shared by other players and that the last place a manager should be is in the middle of it, as if he somehow had something to do with it. Then he goes back to the foxhole because it's still not over, one of those games that just might reach into infinity, the karma meter flopping so wildly, there's no point in trying to glean anything from it, except that whatever happens, it's not going to be emotionally simple.

III

REMLINGER GETS the call from Baker in the bullpen to replace Zambrano. He retires the side in order in the bottom of the eighth.

DeJean answers in the top of the ninth by retiring Sosa and Alou and Simon.

Remlinger is still there in the bottom of the ninth, with Robinson due to lead off. It makes sense for Baker to leave Remlinger in there, as he's getting a lefty-versus-lefty matchup. La Russa knows that, of course, but he doesn't counter off the bench with a pinch hitter. Because of Remlinger's anomaly, better against righties than his own kind, he's leaving Robinson in the game. But the decision should not be confused with a newfound faith in Robinson after his last at-bat, when he doubled and drove in a run. One double does not demolish a doghouse. Robinson himself has no illusions. Between halves of the inning, when La Russa went to Cairo on the bench and told him to get ready to pinch-hit, Robinson assumed that Cairo was going in for him.

"No, no, no," La Russa told him. "You go ahead and hit."

He's hoping that Robinson can use his speed to his advantage here and maybe get on even if it's weakly hit. He's actually thinking less about Robinson than about what moves he will make if Robinson does get to first. It suggests an opportunity to have Cairo bunt him over to second when he pinch-hits for the next batter. But if Robinson advances to second, it will also mean that first base is open, which will take the bat out of Pujols's hands, as Baker will surely walk him. Which in turn will make the matchup between Edmonds and Remlinger the key matchup of the inning. So he isn't quite sure what to do here, and he won't know for sure until Robinson's at-bat is over.

Remlinger is in the Popeye mold of a pitcher, squat and short-looking, even though he's listed at 6'1". His physiognomy suggests power but his best pitch is his changeup, and he will use it anywhere in the count.

The Cubs are thinking that Robinson will want to use his speed here; they're playing him in at the corners and conceding him the right-field line, as he never pulls it that far. He's thinking about using his speed, too, showing bunt on the first pitch but pulling off and taking a strike looking for 0 and 1. He fouls off the next pitch to dig himself an immediate 0-and-2 dungeon. La Russa, one hand on the staircase railing, has a feeling that he can stop musing over whether to have Cairo bunt Robinson to second, because Robinson isn't going to make it out of the batter's box.

Remlinger throws a curve ball a little low to make the count 1 and 2. He throws a fastball up and in to make the count 2 and 2. He throws another fastball high to make the count 3 and 2. Robinson doesn't walk very much, but maybe he can squeeze a walk here, keep the spigot open for the bigger boys. Bako, the catcher, wants a changeup. But Remlinger shakes off the sign; he wants a fastball, so a fastball is what he's going to throw. He comes with it, and Robinson makes contact.

He pulls it into right the exact way he should have pulled it in the fifth when he needed to advance Morris to third. At the very least, La Russa will have to give him credit for getting to the fastball and putting a good swing on it.

But suddenly, everybody in the dugout rises in synch. They're watching and watching and watching because he just hit the living hell out of it, and they're watching some more because it always seems to take forever and every pair of eyes is turned the same way and willing it the same way, with those eyes stretched north because *Can you really believe this, is this really happening?*

And then the catch is made in right field. By Simontacchi, in the bullpen, with his cap.

3–2 Cardinals. It's over.

Players pour onto the field as if there's a fire drill. They run to home plate and form a line like a wedding party. Robinson jumps on the plate and is enclosed, buried beneath Pujols and Rolen and Edmonds and Hart and Matheny and Renteria and Morris and Williams and a dozen others. They form a circle around Robinson and start jumping up and down in lovely unbridled joy, their faces bent and bursting: thirty-year-olds, some of them with the exuberance of fifteen-year-olds. It lasts for a few seconds, this circle bouncing up and down to its own beat, and you really wouldn't mind if it lasted the whole night. You could simply sit back and watch, because it shows you what baseball can still be when it wants to be: a game for little boys that grown men are lucky enough to play.

La Russa hugs Robinson when he finally escapes from beneath the bodies, making it clear that under certain circumstances, managers have even shorter memories than relievers. Robinson runs off to do the postgame TV interview because he is the star this night, maybe the star of the season in some utterly improbable way. Then Oquendo whispers something to La Russa that has nothing to do with his coaching responsibilities at third base. La Russa laughs, actually *laughs,* so you know that whatever Oquendo just said has to be worth something.

"When are you gonna kiss my ass?" Oquendo asks him.

For the first and only time during these three nights in August, La Russa is out of moves.

The spontaneous combustion ends once Robinson escapes. The players disengage and trot down the steps of the dugout into the tunnel that winds under the ratty pipes to the clubhouse. They are still excited, still chatty. They have taken the rubber game of the three-game series. They have taken two out of three against the Cubs. They are tied for first place in the division on a summer night that should always have baseball somewhere within it. They are also tied for first in the traffic jam of the Wild Card. With one victory, they've earned two possible trajectories to the playoffs.

The effects of this experience will linger, stay in the blood of these players: a few of them stars and a few of them recognized outside of the city in which they toil but most of them only anonymous pieces in the vast puzzle of the game that will go on and on after their spaces are taken up by other puzzle pieces. They will think about the three-game series they have just played. Robinson will think about it, the way in which he traveled from the doghouse to heaven at the same velocity as the home run he just creamed to right. Morris will think about it, a performance that no doubt brings a smile to the face of the silent protector who stays near him wherever he goes. Williams will think about it, the way he went head to head against Wood and outpitched him with quiet verve. Martinez will think about it, the momentary relief of standing on first just having done what maybe, just maybe, you weren't sure you could do anymore, although you would never admit that to anyone. Drew will think about it, knowing that by not playing in a single inning these past three nights, his days in a Cardinals uniform are probably numbered, better for him to start over somewhere else, unburdened by burdens. Eldred will think about it, how he shouldn't be here at all. Stephenson will think about it, the unforgiving repercussions of pitching with too much of your heart and not enough of your head, although come to think about it, Stephenson *probably* won't think about it. Rolen will think about it, quietly, very *very* quietly. Pujols will think about it, wondering why he didn't get a hit on *every* at-bat. Kline will think about it, continued nightmares of being told to kiss the bride and lifting up the veil and seeing that it's frigging Lofton, Lofton at the register when he's in the checkout line searching for his bonus card, Lofton in the car next to him when he stops at a red light, Lofton asking him whether he prefers a window seat or an aisle, Lofton, Lofton, Lofton, smiling in such a way that it does resemble a hit into the gap.

La Russa will think about the three-game series. So will Duncan. So will Oquendo, who probably knows, despite unimpeachable witnesses, that La Russa will never dole out what he so emphatically promised in the bottom of the fifth in his impassioned vow *never ever* to start Robinson again.

Player or coach, star or invisible man, hustler or somebody who simply hustles, happy to be there or unhappy to be anywhere, the future in front of you or the future behind you, it doesn't really matter right now. Each and every one of them will let the three-game series just played continue to sit and settle for a little bit. They will allow themselves the pleasure, for at least as long as it takes to strip off the uniform to grab the shower to change into the street clothes to go to the airport to fly on the charter to sleep in the hotel room to arrive at the ballpark to start another one beginning tomorrow, still what it is despite so many efforts to make it feel like something else, still a part of us even when we say never again, what La Russa believes it to be and will always believe it to be because a quarter century in the foxhole of the dugout, if it has taught him anything, has taught him this.

Beautiful. Just beautiful baseball.

EPILOGUE

● ● ● TONY LA RUSSA waited in the dugout after the game was over. Dignity and professionalism required it no matter what he felt inside: an almost surreal deflation. He waited to see whether Red Sox manager Terry Francona would look over from the Busch visitor's dugout to acknowledge him so that La Russa in turn could give his own acknowledgment, the silent language of the victor and the vanquished.

The Red Sox had done it in 2004. They had won the World Series, not in seven games or six or even five, but in a four-game sweep over the Cardinals. La Russa waited for a minute or so—although the dugout was the last place he wanted to be, just a further rub-it-in reminder of the scene of the crime—the bearlike bodies of the Red Sox with their mountain-men beards and grizzly hair in a Rubik's Cube hug less than a hundred feet away. But Francona was understandably busy, caught up in the joy of his players. So La Russa left, walking by himself into the tunnel, passing beneath the exposed pipes on the way to the clubhouse, which right now had to be the saddest single place in the world. He walked toward a terrible coda on what by any measure had been a fantastic season for the Cardinals, maybe the most special team that La Russa had ever managed.

Even after that delicious third night in August, the Cardinals still lost the Central Division to the Cubs in 2003. As for 2004, none of the pundits had any faith in St. Louis. With the Astros making moves for starting pitchers Roger Clemens and Andy Pettitte, with the Cubs still stoked by the triumvirate of Prior and Wood and Zambrano, the Cardinals were universally picked to finish third. Their starting pitching wasn't good enough. Their bullpen wasn't good enough. With J.D. Drew traded to Atlanta, there was a problem in right because J.D. at 75 percent was still better than many right fielders at 100 percent. There was also a problem at second, because Bo Hart, as valiant as he was, could not sustain the rigors of a full season as a starter. In the off-season, the Cardinals looked on like envious children as the superbrats made the multimillion-dollar moves that still define the game—Schilling to the Red Sox and everyone else to the Yankees.

In the middle of May, the Cardinals were mired at 16 and 16 after losing two out of three to the Montreal Expos. They were lurching along, vainly trying to find a way. La Russa's contract was up for renewal after the season. The front office approached him then about re-upping, but he didn't want to negotiate, in part because he thought it would look bad to players who were potential free agents and wanted their own contracts negotiated, but also because he wasn't convinced that the Cards would even want him back if the team continued in its mediocrity. It was his ninth year with the team, and the history of managing suggested that nine years with one team was maybe too long.

But then, at the end of the month, something happened, and the twenty-five pieces of the puzzle became a team. Using the unit of the three-game series as a yardstick, the Cardinals played twenty-one of them from June to the end of August. They swept eight, lost only three, and had a record of 87-44 going into September in running away with the division. Their record at the end of the season—105 wins and only 57 losses—was the best in baseball.

The Cardinals opened the playoffs by beating the Dodgers three games to one to advance to the National League Championship series against the Astros. In the aura of the irresistible "reverse the curse" narrative as the Red Sox improbably prevailed over the Yankees in the ALCS by winning four straight games after falling behind 3–0, the Cardinals-Astros series was barely noticed.

But it too was brilliantly played, filled with the flip-flop of drama, the Cardinals going ahead two games to nothing at Busch, then losing three in a row to Houston in their boisterous house, then returning to St. Louis to win the next two, including the final seventh game against eventual National League Cy Young Award winner Roger Clemens.

Then came the World Series and the Red Sox thrashing. First and foremost, La Russa believes that Boston deserved to win because they were the better team, got the pitching they needed when they needed it, got the timely two-out hits by making pressure their friend. But he also believes that there is no way—at least no rational way—the Cardinals should have gotten swept. The team was too gifted for that to happen. Except that it did happen.

After his typical sleepless search for pragmatic explanations to unintended results, he now wonders if it all moved a little bit too quickly, a film at fast-forward where everything just became blurred. After the epic win in Game 7 against Clemens, La Russa tried to tell his team that there was still work to be done. "We just earned a ring, but it's not *the* ring," he said. But he also honored human nature; for various players who had been on the team for several years, finally winning the NLCS—after two failed tries in 2000 and 2002—was a huge monkey off their backs. The same was true for La Russa himself: an end to the local media's intimations that he clutched in the clutch.

The team celebrated hard that night, lingering in the clubhouse until three or four in the morning, feeling both the joy and the relief that destiny was still theirs. They got to their respective homes late, stole a little sleep, began to make travel arrangements for their families, heard from people they hadn't heard from in a thousand years yearning for World Series tickets, arrived at a hotel parking lot near the airport at 11:30 A.M., and by noon were on a plane to a cold, sodden Boston to face a Red Sox team buoyed by both talent and mythology.

If it wasn't the World Series, La Russa would not have had the team work out that day. But because it was the World Series, they were required to make an appearance. They arrived in Boston at

4:45 P.M., then got a police escort to Fenway Park because they were late. They were supposed to start working out at 5:00, but didn't arrive until 5:15 and had to wait for the equipment. After their workout ended, the last bus left Fenway at 8:15 P.M. and made its way to the hotel the Cardinals had been placed at by the Red Sox—since it was the home team's responsibility—located not downtown near Fenway, but forty minutes away in Quincy. The Cardinals were told that there were several large conventions in Boston that had taken up all premium downtown hotel space.

When a team loses, and loses badly, all explanations sound like excuses. The fact of the matter, as La Russa put it, is "that either you do or you don't and we didn't." But he did feel that in the rush to the World Series, the team lost an edge.

Game 1 the following night, in contrast to the sweet spectacle of both the American League and National League Championship series, was like a sloppy Little League game. The chilly weather made the ball slick, which in turn made it difficult for starter Woody Williams to ever get the right feel and establish effective command. Early in the game, when Matheny set up down and in against Orlando Cabrera and Williams ended up hitting him on the shoulder, La Russa could feel the curse of his own Bambino. Cardinals pitchers gave up eight walks. Red Sox pitchers gave up six of their own, and the Boston defense made four errors.

In the top of the eighth, the Cards scored twice to tie the score at 9–9. They had the bases loaded and only one out with Rolen due up followed by Edmonds. During the season, the two of them had combined for seventy-six home runs and 235 RBIs while each hitting over .300. But in what may have been the most pivotal at-bats of the World Series, Rolen popped out to third. Edmonds then struck out looking to end the inning. A superb chance to steal a win at Fenway had been lost, and what it portended was even worse. Rolen would ultimately go 0 for 15 in the World Series and Edmonds 1 for 15. (Throw in Reggie Sanders, who batted sixth in the first three games, and the Cardinals four-, five-, and six-hitters went a combined 1 for 39.) When Mark Bellhorn hit a two-run homer off reliever Julian Tavarez in the bottom of the eighth to give the Sox an 11–9 lead that would hold up, it really did seem that the Bambino had simply switched sides.

The eerie fate of indignity only continued in Fenway's parking lot, where the Cardinals' last bus sat idle for twenty minutes because it was blocked by a security guard's car. The bus arrived at the Marriott in Quincy at 1:45 A.M. The hotel had agreed to keep its restaurant open an hour after the last bus arrived. The hotel staff was less specific about what kind of food would be served; when La Russa walked into the dining room, he saw players and their families eating hamburgers and pizza: basic junk food. This *wasn't* a World Series *moment.* It was dreary and depressing, and La Russa blamed himself because he should have seen it coming. In the aftermath, arrangements were made for one of Boston's better downtown restaurants to stay open after Game 6 so players and their families could feel as if they were in the World Series, instead of the high school state playoffs. But there would be no Game 6.

In Game 2, Matt Morris retired the first two batters, then walked the next two to face Jason Varitek. Duncan had told Morris and Matheny in the pregame deconstruction of the Red Sox hitters not to throw a changeup to Varitek. But with the count 1 and 2, Morris still threw a changeup because he thought he had Varitek set up for the pitch. Varitek stroked a two-run triple.

In the same game, Reggie Sanders missed second base on his way to third on a successful *hit-and-run* and had to go back to second. It was the kind of fundamental miscue the Cardinals had almost never committed during the season, and the ecosystem of baseball wouldn't tolerate it now. A batter later, La Russa pulled a run-and-hit with Matheny at the plate. The runners went early and Matheny hit the ball sharply. But third baseman Bill Mueller, coming toward the bag to cover Sanders' attempted steal, serendipitously found himself in perfect position to snag the ball and easily put the tag on Sanders for a double play, because Sanders was coming right at him. The irony was that Mueller's positioning would have been different had Sanders made it to third in the first place; Mueller wouldn't have been racing to the bag to cover a steal because there would have been no steal, which would have meant

Matheny's line drive snaking down the line instead of being caught, which would have meant a possible crooked number instead of an inning-ending double play.

Schilling was on the mound for the Red Sox in Game 2. La Russa had seen him enough to know that this wasn't vintage Schilling. His Frankenstein ankle, the tendon held together by stitches blotched with blood, was clearly bothering him. He was hittable, but he also made pitches when he needed them, particularly with his off-speed. When he needed to get his forkball down, he didn't miss by throwing it over the plate—an example of how to compete under pressure that the Cardinals starters could not emulate.

The Cards lost the second game 6–2 to fall behind in the World Series two games to zero. La Russa assembled the team afterward. What he told them was similar to what he had told them after Game 5 of the NLCS, when the Astros had risen from the dead to win three straight at home and take a 3–2 series lead. "Listen, nobody controls what we think and how we are going to act. You are going to get blistered right now and overwhelmed with people in the media trying to tell you how you should feel. How you guys are getting ready to mug a great season. But we control. The big thing is we control how we feel and how we act and how we play." La Russa knew his team had not been itself in the first two games at Fenway. But they were going back to Busch Stadium now, and Busch had been the postseason Promised Land for the team. They hadn't yet lost a playoff game there, and they were too good to fold up now. Which made what happened at Busch—the Cardinals scoring a total of one run in the next two games, while losing both—the part of the World Series that haunts him the most. Because what did happen? Where did the offense—the best in the major leagues—go? Why for the first time all year, with the possible exception of a three-game series sweep by the Pirates at the end of June, did the Cardinals start taking poor at-bats—uppercut fly-ball swings—instead of hitting through the ball hard to take advantage of a Red Sox defense that had made *eight* errors in the first two games?

Beyond the strategy and the psychological head games, managing is the art of survival: learning somehow not to become crippled by the decisions that even when you make them right, still turn out to be wrong, not to mention all the things you cannot control no matter how much you want to control them. Over the past quarter century, La Russa had learned to survive in the foxhole by examining his own actions first: a detached clinical examination to avoid wallowing in the mud of what just occurred. As he stood in the corner of the dugout waiting for Francona, he knew that his team had just played its worst baseball of the entire season: silent bats, poor base running, over-the-plate pitching. He also knew that he had just lost his eighth straight World Series game; the last time he had been to the Series, fourteen years earlier in 1990, had also been a four-game sweep.

In fact, La Russa's whole managerial experience in the Fall Classic had the pallor of Greek tragedy. He had been in the Series four times and the number of games he had managed, seventeen, was only one more than the *minimum* of sixteen. In 1988, he had lost in five games, after the Kirk Gibson home run that had rocked the world. In 1990 and 2004, his teams had been swept. In his one World Series win in 1989, his Oakland A's had swept the Giants, but even this victory had been improbably upstaged: interrupted by an earthquake and the indelible image of players on the field with their families just before Game 3, frozen with the terror of not knowing if Candlestick Park would hold together.

That kind of history could eat away at a man. He could become spooked, jinxed, irreparably tortured. But La Russa hearkened back to Paul Richards and the most enduring piece of advice he has ever received, as much about life as about managing: *It's your ass, it's your team, so take responsibility.* The fault was not his players, because they had been too brilliant all season long to simply collapse like this. He concluded instead that the fault was his, something he didn't do—a breakdown of his obligation to prepare his players, never mind how hard he had tried. But he also knew that simply taking the blame, an act of ultimately meaningless self-flagellation, wasn't enough.

So the day after the Series ended, as players flushed out a season's accumulation of balls and bats and gloves from their lockers, he met with his coaches to constructively delineate what had happened, why the bats had gone silent, why the pitchers couldn't find the black of the plate. They mused over the edge that had been lost in the fast-forward rush to the World Series. They wondered if the euphoria of winning the pennant, beating no less a force than Clemens, had been *too* euphoric. La Russa himself wondered if maybe the team had over-prepared, affected by a comment ESPN announcer and Hall-of-Famer Joe Morgan made to him afterward that in his own World Series experience, he didn't want a lot of information, just the bare bones of how hard a particular pitcher threw and how he used his off-speed. La Russa and his staff also discussed personnel changes, because it was inevitable that some players who had been cornerstones of the Cardinals in 2004 would be gone in 2005, either through free agency or salary realities or trade.

The questions came easier than the answers, but during the off-season, La Russa would be determined to find them. And the one thing he would *not* do is let the World Series overshadow a magnificent season. There were the obvious proofs: winning more games than any team in baseball, taking the division by thirteen games, winning the National League Pennant. There was the team itself, with its stoked lineup and vintage five-man rotation and fine mix of relief with two lights-out lefty specialists: a team that hit hard and ran hard and defended hard and gave pleasure to rival scouts and front-office men and managers who always thirst for baseball played right. But there were also the smaller subtleties, the little edges, not as apparent to the outside world perhaps but just as important and maybe even more memorable.

When the Cardinals clinched the NLCS, Elaine La Russa and the La Russas' daughter Devon were there. As soon as the game ended, their husband and father looked up to the stands and beckoned them to join him. They descended along with the players' families, a flood onto the field. Bianca, their elder daughter, hadn't come because she had nobly agreed to stay behind in California to take care of the house and the large brood of pets. Elaine thought of her in that instant, wished she could be here. But it was still a joyous moment for Elaine—no, a perfect moment—a long way from the stag-night parties and men-only restrictions of the Bard's Room of Comiskey. For the first time in a long time, she fell in love with baseball again, felt the beauty of it. As she looked at her husband, she also felt something else, something that she hadn't always felt during the preoccupation of his career. She felt that he was thrilled she and Devon were there, that as much as he reveled in the joy of winning the National League Pennant, there was something else he reveled in more, and that was his family.

Two days later, when the Cardinals conducted their workout before Game 1 of the World Series in the frigid froth of Boston, La Russa wanted his players to do what they had to do on the field and then get back to the clubhouse as quickly as possible. Like a mother hen, he walked the outfield shooing his players inside. But Cal Eldred lingered despite the cold. Standing before the Green Monster of Fenway, he had a huge smile on his face, soaking in every second of the fact that after fourteen years of ups and downs and too many elbow reconstructions for any elbow to bear, he had arrived. He didn't want to leave no matter how cold it was, so La Russa let Cal Eldred be. He just let him be, in the shadow of the Green Monster.

Six days later, after the World Series ended and La Russa walked through the tunnel to the clubhouse, he saw his players for what would be the last official time. There was nothing to say, all the bullets spent. If they were complicated men, they were also professionals, and no empty words of solace from a manager would do any good anyway.

In a couple of minutes the media would burst into the clubhouse with their predictable stream of hard questions. But for now, the clubhouse was sacred, intimate, a team and only a team. The players stood in front of their lockers in silence, perhaps because they were still expecting their manager to give some little speech. Instead, La Russa did something he had never done before. He had his coaches and all the clubhouse personnel form two lines. Then one of the lines went to the right and the other to the left to shake hands with each player, circling until they were done. La Russa knew what his players had done during the season. He loved them for that—took great pride in them as a manager and as a man—and this was the best way he could think of to tell them he would never forget it.

POSTSCRIPT

THE CARDINALS

Rick Ankiel, following rehabilitation from reconstructive elbow surgery, pitched in the major leagues for the first time since 2001, after being activated by the Cardinals in September 2004. He gave up one walk over ten innings in five relief appearances. In October 2004, he won his first major-league game since April 8, 2001, surrendering one run in four innings to the Milwaukee Brewers.

Chad Blair continued in his role as the Cardinals' video coordinator in 2004.

Miguel Cairo, after hitting .245 for the Cards in 2003 as a utility player—in which he played first base, second, shortstop, third, and the outfield—became a free agent and signed with the Yankees in 2004. He emerged as the team's regular second baseman and hit .292.

J.D. Drew was traded after the 2003 season, along with Eli Marrero, to the Braves for pitchers Jason Marquis, Ray King, and prospect Adam Wainwright. La Russa's feeling about Drew—that he might thrive with a different manager—was proven true. Healthy most of the season in his free-agent year, Drew had over 500 at-bats for the first time in his career, hitting .305 with thirty-one home runs and ninety-five RBIs. But the trade was one of those rare ones in baseball that benefited both sides. Marquis established himself as a bona fide starting pitcher at the age of twenty-five, going 15 and 7. Coming out of the bullpen, the lefty King had an ERA of 2.61 and gave up only forty-three hits in sixty-two innings. Despite Drew's breakout year, the Braves still chose to let him test the free-agent market. He signed a five-year, $55 million contract with the Dodgers.

Dave Duncan, in his twenty-second season as La Russa's pitching coach, had perhaps his most satisfying year ever in 2004, guiding a staff that before the season had been doomed for mediocrity by virtually every baseball pundit. The team's ERA, 3.75, was second in the National League and nearly a run less than in 2003.

Jim Edmonds was the subject of trade rumors after the 2003 season, because of a lackluster second half in which he batted only .214. After shoulder surgery in the off-season, he returned to the Cardinals and hit .301 in 2004 with forty-two home runs and 111 runs batted in.

Cal Eldred, after leading Cardinals relievers in wins in 2003 with seven, appeared in fifty-two games in 2004 with a record of 4 and 2 and an earned run average of 3.76. After the season, Eldred was among ten Cardinals players eligible for free agency. He elected to remain in St. Louis.

Bo Hart started on the Cardinals in 2004 but was sent down to Triple-A after thirteen at-bats.

Jason Isringhausen, healthy all year in 2004 as the closer, tied for the league lead in saves with forty-seven.

Walt Jocketty was named major-league Executive of the Year by the *Sporting News,* based on the myriad moves he made as general manager in shaping the 2004 Cardinals without ballooning the team's payroll.

Steve Kline had his best year in the majors as a lefty specialist out of the bullpen in 2004, recording an ERA of 1.79 in sixty-seven games. In keeping with his personality, he also gave La Russa the finger from the bullpen during a game in June when he became upset at not being used. When La Russa found out about it afterward, he steamed into the shower to confront Kline. "I don't think he'll be mad," Kline later told reporters. "He loves me too much." He became a free agent after the season and was not re-signed by the Cardinals. He inked a two-year deal with the Baltimore Orioles.

Tony La Russa, after an 85-77 finish in 2003, managed the Cardinals to a 105-57 record in 2004 and a franchise-record 112 wins including the playoffs. If he wins eighty-one games in 2005, he'll move into third place on the all-time list of managerial wins, behind Connie Mack and John McGraw. He has 2,114.

Tino Martinez was traded after the 2003 season to the Tampa Bay Devil Rays for a minor-league player. The Cardinals also agreed to pay $7 million of the $8.5 million due on his contract. He hit .262 with twenty-three home runs and seventy-six runs batted in.

Mike Matheny won the Gold Glove as catcher in 2004, just as he had in 2003. He became a free agent at the end of the season, and signed with the San Francisco Giants.

Matt Morris went 15 and 10 in 2004 but was plagued by inconsistency. His velocity was noticeably down and his record in the postseason—0 and 2 with an earned run average of 5.91—was disappointing. A free agent, with an uncertain future after once being heralded as one of the best young pitchers in baseball, Morris had arthroscopic surgery last November on his pitching shoulder. Rather than test the market, Morris re-signed a one-year contract for $2.5 million with incentive clauses. The amount was $10 million less than what he had made in 2004, a rare case in baseball of a player opting for honest reappraisal instead of greed.

Orlando Palmeiro, after hitting .271 with the Cardinals in 2003 as a role player, signed with the Houston Astros. He appeared in 102 games and hit .241.

Eddie Perez, after hitting .285 with eleven home runs in 2003 off the bench, signed with the Tampa Bay Devil Rays. He tore his Achilles tendon early in May 2004 and missed the remainder of the season.

Albert Pujols, after leading the National League in hitting in 2003 with a mark of .359, in 2004 became the first player in major-league history to hit thirty or more home runs his first four seasons. He also joined Joe DiMaggio and Ted Williams as the only players to drive in 500 runs or more their first four seasons. Pujols hit .331 with forty-six home runs and 121 runs batted in.

Edgar Renteria hit .287 at shortstop in 2004 and drove in seventy-two runs. He became a free agent at the end of the season and signed with the Boston Red Sox.

Kerry Robinson was traded by the Cardinals shortly before the 2004 season to the San Diego Padres for outfielder Brian Hunter and shuffled back and forth between Triple-A and the parent club. He appeared in eighty games for the Padres, with four extra-base hits in ninety-two at-bats, all of them doubles. He hasn't hit a home run since the one described in this book.

Scott Rolen had his best year in the majors in 2004, hitting .314 with thirty-four home runs and finishing second in the National League in runs batted in with 124, despite missing much of September because of a strained calf muscle.

Garrett Stephenson did not pitch in major-league baseball in 2004 because of an injury.

So Taguchi continued to improve as a player off the bench for the Cardinals in 2004, hitting .291.

Woody Williams, bothered by shoulder tendinitis in spring training, got off to such a terrible start in 2004 that he contemplated retirement. But he finished strong to go 11 and 8 and was chosen as the Cardinals starter for the first game of the World Series. He filed for free agency after the season and signed with the Padres.

THE CUBS

Mark Prior, after going 18 and 6 in 2003 and finishing third in the National League Cy Young voting, discovered his own mortality in 2004 in his second full season in the major leagues. He missed the first two months with a sore Achilles tendon and elbow, and finished with a record of 6 and 4 and an ERA of 4.02.

Sammy Sosa had his worst year ever for the Cubs in 2004, hitting .253 with thirty-five home runs and only eighty RBIs. He was fined $87,400 for arriving late to the Cubs' season finale at Wrigley and then leaving fifteen minutes after the game had started. Sosa, who makes around $17 million, then accused the Cubs of mistreating him.

Kerry Wood missed several weeks of the 2004 season because of tendinitis in his triceps, only adding to the injury woes Wood has experienced since breaking into the major leagues. He went 8 and 9 with an earned run average of 3.72. He also hit eleven batters in 140 innings, including three Astros in a single game.

Carlos Zambrano emerged in 2004 as the most effective starter of the Cubs triumvirate, going 16 and 8 with an ERA of 2.75 in 209 innings.

The Cubs, based on their finish in 2003 in which they advanced to the National League Championship series, were picked by many pundits to make it to the World Series in 2004. Plagued by injuries, they did not live up to expectations, but were still contending for the NL wild card late in the season. Then at the end of September, a one-and-a-half game lead turned into dust when they lost seven of eight games. As only the Cubs could do and only baseball could do to them, the slide began when they lost to the Mets in extra innings after being ahead 3–0 with two outs in the ninth.

AFTERWORD

● ● ● IN THE YEAR since *Three Nights in August* was first published, both Tony La Russa and I have received hundreds of comments from those who count the most, readers, praising the book for its depiction of the exquisite strategy and humanity of baseball. My ambition was high: not to write a season-in-the-life account of La Russa and the St. Louis Cardinals but instead a timeless book applicable to any season, to be enjoyed by any fan regardless of team affiliation. The fact that so many readers grasped the intent from all over the country is the best news that an author can ever receive.

I have to confess that I also thoroughly enjoy the significant place that the book has taken in what the *New York Times* called in August 2005 "a theological dispute" in baseball over what matters more, statistical analysis or the unquantifiable human factors of intuition and instinct. It's the humanists versus the statisticians, the old guard versus the thirty-something (and sometimes younger) general managers with their MBAs and law degrees. It's the disciples of Michael Lewis's book *Moneyball* versus the disciples of *Three Nights in August,* or what one blogger dubbed the Moneyballistas versus the LaRussaistas. It's a war, a baseball war, so maybe it should not be taken too seriously, but I have also learned that few things in life are approached with more righteous fervor than the game of baseball.

So for all the wonderful comments I have received, I have also taken my share of criticisms from the sabermetricians who study the game with the same grim sense of purpose that Oppenheimer brought to the Manhattan Project. I have challenged their theories with the approach I have taken in *Three Nights in August,* mocked the complex formulas they apply to the game. I also have to confess that I riled them on purpose. In the book's preface, I wrote of baseball's new generation, and by implication its hundreds of thousands of adherents, the following:

> It is wrong to say that the new breed doesn't care about baseball. But it's not wrong to say that there is no way they could possibly love it.

I have thought a great deal about those two sentences over the past year. I certainly don't regret them. But if I had to do it over, I would rephrase them as follows:

> It is wrong to say that the new breed doesn't care about baseball. They love it, although I think that what they really love is the deconstruction of it.

I will always object to the Moneyballistas' cold and clinical deconstruction of baseball to the point where the game itself, the beauty and poetry of it, seems of no use to them. They rely so much on the percentages that they consistently miss the emotional component that can break a game open. Maybe the hit-and-run, for example, is not a great percentage play. But as La Russa points out in *Three Nights in August,* a hit-and-run can become a percentage play if you take the time to teach it. A hit-and-run is also exciting. It's tumultuous, unexpected if it's executed right, and it can crush the morale of an opposing team, turn a snooze of an inning into a roar. It's the same with the bunt. In the summer of 2005, the *Washington Post* ran a lengthy story on whether or not the bunt is a good percentage play. James Click, a writer for Baseballprospectus.com, analyzing data from the 2003 season, called the bunt an "archaic, outdated strategy." The old guard, led by the Washington Nationals manager, Frank Robinson, objected to Click's conclusion as being just the kind of thing you expect to hear from someone who has never set foot in a big league stadium as a player or manager or coach: "I don't live by the numbers, and don't manage by the numbers. I put on the bunt when the situation calls for a bunt."

But beyond the numbers, there is an emotional element to the bunt just as there is in the hit-and-run. Sweetly laid down in that no man's land between the pitcher's mound and the third base bag, it can propel a team in certain situations. It's the same with the suicide squeeze, which the Cardinals executed an astounding thirteen out of sixteen times in the regular season last year. I have no doubt that as they read this, the Moneyballistas are combing through a hundred years of baseball box scores looking for evidence that the Cardinals' success ratio was just luck or statistically meaningless. But whatever the research shows, it will not take into account the way a suicide squeeze, if it's successful, can just break the spirit of an opposing team, and change the whole rhythm of a game.

For all their stated reliance on hard, quantifiable facts, the Moneyballistas go through all sorts of strained machinations in trying to support their theories. Clearly the patron saint of all Moneyballistas is the Oakland A's general manager, Billy Beane. He was canonized in Lewis's book, and it was Beane who started the theological war with his bloodless analysis of the game and rejection of such sacred cows as bunting, stealing, and fielding. Lewis's book was provocative, smart, and literally got millions of people to think about baseball in a whole different way. He is to be admired and applauded for that. So is Billy Beane for daring to be different in a game that too often hides its head in tradition. But Billy Beane's real genius has been in setting the bar low for himself, the-hey-I-don't-have-any-money-so-you-shouldn't-expect-anything-from-me-anyway standard he lives by so that all the Oakland A's have to do every year is hover close enough to the playoffs for Beane to maintain his guru standing. He fields interesting teams. He operates well within a limited payroll (as do other teams, such as the Minnesota Twins, that nobody ever talks about). But as far as I know, the purpose of baseball is not simply to get close but into the thick of the playoffs. None of Beane's teams have ever been in the World Series, much less the league championship series. The last two years, his teams haven't even gotten to the playoffs. But because he comes close, the sabermetricians hail him as proof that building a team by the numbers does work. To me, it's a little bit like saying a hitter should be hailed for belting a lot of 375-foot outs into left center.

Moneyball also touted Beane's ability to find diamonds in the rough, but a little scrutiny degrades this Svengalian ability into the same difficulties that all general managers have in trying to predict future baseball talent. He had seven of the first thirty-nine picks in the 2002 draft and the point, hammered away over and over again by Lewis in his relentless hero worship, was how Beane used the numbers to uncover talent rejected by those horrid tobacco-spitting traditionalists known as scouts. So how has the vaunted *Moneyball* draft performed?

Two of them, Nick Swisher and Joe Blanton, made contributions to the A's in 2005 and are bona-fide big leaguers. Blanton went 12-and-12 and could become a great pitcher. Swisher, given all the *Moneyball* hype of being the next great thing, hit .236 with a less-than-stellar on-base percentage of .322. He did have 74 RBIs, a seemingly impressive number, but since the Moneyballistas and sabermetricians reject the value of RBIs, as they reject virtually all traditional baseball barometers, perhaps they should be ignored. Mark Teahen was traded in 2004 for closer Octavio Dotel (after Beane opined in *Moneyball* that just about anybody could be a closer). The other four were still in the minors last season, including catcher Jeremy Brown. Lewis spent almost as much effort lionizing Brown as he did Billy Beane. The book ended with a beautiful description of Brown, whom the tobacco-spitters thought of as a slow and punchless catcher from the University of Alabama, hitting a home run. But despite Lewis's poetic gifts, Brown is still waiting for his first at-bat in the major leagues.

It was also Billy Beane in *Moneyball* who made a fool of the Chicago White Sox general manager, Ken Williams, the same Ken Williams who helped win the White Sox a World Series in 2005. In creating the White Sox, Williams traded Carlos Lee before the season for Scott Podsednik. The Moneyballistas went crazy over the trade, since Lee had great Holy Grail numbers in on-base percentage and slugging percentage and Podsednik did not. Looking at the numbers, maybe it wasn't a great trade. But the very limits of looking at the numbers were revealed after Podsednik came over to the White Sox and set an entire tone for the team, defining its hustling swagger and chemistry. As for the Oakland A's last season, they made their usual close-but-not-close-enough run. The team was buoyed by reliever Huston Street (a fine Beane draft pick, but hardly a diamond in the rough since everybody in baseball knew he was the real deal). The Athletics got to 88 wins, presumably good enough for the Moneyballistas to keep the Billy Beane bobblehead in the car rear window. But not good enough for anybody who believes in postseason play.

In their frantic attempts to claim some sort of victory, the Moneyballistas also cite the 2004 Red Sox who won the World Series. Moneyballistas liked the Red Sox because they had an under-thirty general manager named Theo Epstein with a law degree. They liked the Red Sox because they'd hired statistical guru Bill James (who is far more sane and sober about the numerical hysteria in baseball he spawned than any of his worshipers). The Moneyballistas went wild with joy when the Red Sox won. It made for some very nice newspaper columns by facile columnists praising the *Moneyball* approach, conveniently ignoring the fact that the Red Sox carried a payroll of well over $100 million and never would have won the World Series had they not signed Curt Schilling to a three-year deal for over $35 million.

Other patron saints frequently cited by the Moneyballistas have had brutal comeuppances, or have figured out that the religion of baseball is still money. Paul DePodesta, the assistant general manager to Beane when *Moneyball* was written and another figure canonized by Lewis, took his Harvard degree and his supposedly legendary skill for number crunching and became the general manager of the Los Angeles Dodgers. It should have been a good situation for DePodesta, but in rejecting such emotional elements as desire and chemistry and the ability of teammates to get along, De-Podesta shoved the team into chaos. He went into the free agent market to sign J. D. Drew to a five-year, $55 million contract. Drew is a player with great Holy Grail numbers, belied only by the fact that he has a history of injuries and has never shown any discernible interest in playing to his maximum. Drew got hurt in 2005 and had only 252 at-bats, an inevitable outcome to anyone who knew him. He has no *heart*—maybe the word Moneyballistas despise most because how can a heart be deconstructed? But Drew's tragic lack of competitive fire was obvious to others, including Tony La Russa. It made the Dodgers ever more reliant on the volatile temperaments of Milton Bradley and Jeff Kent, a time-bomb combination waiting to explode, which ultimately did explode with ugly accusations. The Dodgers were terrible in 2005, under .500 by 20 games, and DePodesta was fired.

Another *Moneyball* icon, J. P. Ricciardi, the Toronto Blue Jays' general manager, has also realized that the romanticism of doing more with less in baseball is far outweighed by the real-world need to do more with more if the goal is to get to the World Series. With $30 million more of payroll money at his disposal, Ricciardi made a big splash in the postseason by signing reliever B. J. Ryan, starting pitcher A. J. Burnett, and first baseman Lyle Overbay. In other words, *Moneyball* theories are fine, and bottom-fishing for talent both noble and sweetly enchanting, but actual money is still a lot better if you want to win it all.

But are the Moneyballistas entirely wrong in their thinking? Of course not. Beane is shrewd, and he has produced American League Rookies of the Year the past two seasons through his draft picks. Bill James's great work is extremely valuable. I read the *Baseball Prospectus* annual guide every year and see some spectacular research. I marvel at the ability of its writers to predict the future performance of certain players with uncanny accuracy, just as I also marvel at sentences that read: "Our Run Differential would be reflective of what we know the team scored in its first inning for the Team, and the first 5 innings for the Opponent. Thus, Win Expectancy does not always directly map to an actual point in the game where this state actually existed. This is important for understanding Win Expectancy's relationship to Support Neutral pitching statistics, which will be described later on."

Notwithstanding Win Expectancy's relationship to Support Neutral pitching statistics (first cousins, I presume), the human components of the game cannot be undervalued, and that was an essential thesis of *Three Nights in August:* successful teams such as the Cardinals combine both the statistical and the emotional. Tony La Russa pays attention to statistics, obsessing over match-ups between hitters and pitchers and the parables they tell. So does pitching coach Dave Duncan, who uses a computer as much as anyone in providing a blueprint for his starting pitchers each and every game. So does general manager Walt Jocketty. But they also don't ignore the factors of chemistry and heart and desire and performance in the clutch, because they can't be ignored.

It's Curt Schilling in the 2004 playoffs pitching on that Frankenstein ankle with blood oozing from his sock. It's Ozzie Guillen managing the White Sox a year later as if he's an Al Pacino character in a Brian De Palma movie, electric and alive and in-your-face and *don't mess with me, bro.* It's Cardinals shortstop David Eckstein with that little-boy physique, playing each and every game at five hundred percent and catalyzing an entire team that won the most games in the major leagues last year. If *Three Nights in August* squarely favors the human, then so be it. After all, I am one, and so are baseball players, whatever the numbers say.

—Buzz Bissinger
December 2005

A NOTE ON SOURCES

Close to 90 percent of what appears in *Three Nights in August* was based on personal observation and interviews. I spent several weeks with the St. Louis Cardinals during spring training in 2003 and attended about fifty regular-season games. In the depictions of various players and personalities in the book, I also used written sources. The archives of the *St. Louis Post-Dispatch* were invaluable. I also utilized articles from *Baseball America,* the *Chicago Tribune,* the *New York Times,* the *Sporting News,* and *USA Today.* In writing of the events leading up to and following the death of pitcher Darryl Kile, an article in the St. Louis Cardinals' publication *Gameday Magazine* was particularly helpful, as was an interview with Flynn Kile on ESPN. This book also could not have done without the historical box scores compiled by the Web site Retrosheet.org, which go back more than a hundred years. The Web sites of Espn.com and Mlb.com were enormously helpful as well. Below is a list of selected bibliography.

Baseball America 2003 Almanac. Durham, North Carolina: Baseball America Inc., 2003.

Baseball America 2004 Almanac. Durham, North Carolina: Baseball America Inc., 2004.

Baseball Register 2003 Edition. St. Louis: Sporting News Books, 2003.

Baseball Register 2004 Edition. St. Louis: Sporting News Books, 2004.

Birnbaum, Phil, Deane, Bill, and John Thorn. *Total Baseball: The Ultimate Baseball Encyclopedia, 8th Edition.* Toronto: Sport Media Publishing, 2004.

Castle, George, and Jim Rygelski. *The I-55 Series: Cubs vs. Cardinals.* Champaign, Illinois: Sports Publishing Inc., 1999.

Gentile, Derek. *The Complete Chicago Cubs.* New York: Black Dog & Leventhal Publishers, 2002.

Golenbock, Peter. *Wrigleyville.* New York: St. Martin's Press, 1999.

———. *The Spirit of St. Louis.* New York: HarperCollins, 2000.

Holtzman, Jerome, and George Vass. *Baseball, Chicago Style.* Chicago: Bonus Books, 2001.

Honig, Donald. *The Man in the Dugout.* Chicago: Follett Publishing, 1977.

James, Bill. *The Bill James Guide to Baseball Managers: From 1870 to Today.* New York: Scribner, 1997.

Koppett, Leonard. *The Man in the Dugout.* New York: Crown Publishers, 1993.

Lau, Charley, with Alfred Glossbrenner. *The Art of Hitting .300.* New York: Penguin Books, 1991.

Lewis, Michael. *Moneyball.* New York: W. W. Norton, 2003.

Libby, Bill. *Charlie O. and the Angry A's.* Garden City, New York: Doubleday, 1975.

Light, Jonathan Fraser. *The Cultural Encyclopedia of Baseball.* Jefferson, North Carolina: McFarland, 1997.

Logan, Bob. *Miracle on 35th Street: Winnin' Ugly with the 1983 White Sox.* South Bend, Indiana: Icarus Press, 1983.

Myers, Doug. *Essential Cubs.* Chicago: Contemporary Books, 1999.

The Scouting Notebook 2004. St. Louis: Sporting News Books, 2004.

Smith, Curt. *Voices of the Game.* New York: Simon & Schuster, 1992.

Will, George. *Men at Work.* New York: HarperCollins, 1991.

ACKNOWLEDGMENTS

There are many people to thank for the creation of *Three Nights in August,* but first and foremost is my editor at Houghton Mifflin, Eamon Dolan. A few lines of praise are inadequate to describe the seminal role that Eamon played from beginning to end with patience, support, love, tough love, a few necessary head slaps to the overly fragile psyche, and everything else that counts in the creative process. He demanded with a quiet relentlessness, dedicated to making this book as good as it could possibly be. In a profession in which the invaluable art of editing is becoming a lost art, he proved himself to be a Picasso.

Among the St. Louis Cardinals, the list is long because of the graciousness that was consistently shown. Pitching Coach Dave Duncan must be highlighted not only because he unfailingly answered all my questions despite continual interruptions to his concentration but also because he helped me fix my laptop when it became besieged by a virus one terrible morning in Houston. Bench Coach Joe Pettini provided valuable help on the Zen of just about everything that was baseball related. Bullpen Coach Marty Mason provided valuable help on the Zen of pitching, and of course there is the Secret Weapon, Video Coordinator Chad Blair. Traveling Secretary C.J. Cherre made my life infinitely easier in trying to keep up with the blistering seasonal schedule of the Cardinals during 2003. Equipment Manager Rip Rowan and assistant Buddy

Bates made me feel like a welcome presence in the clubhouse despite working twenty-five hours a day. So did Head Athletic Trainer Barry Weinberg and Bullpen Catcher Jeff Murphy.

Other members of the Cardinals organization who must be thanked include Chairman of the Board and General Partner Bill DeWitt, Jr., Vice Chairman Fred Hanser, Limited Partner Dave Pratt, General Manager Walt Jocketty, Assistant General Manager John Mozeliak, and team media gurus Brian Bartow, Brad Hainje, and Melody Yount. Among the Cardinals players, all of them were giving of their time despite continual demands by the media. Several in particular went above and beyond the call of duty during the 2003 season: Steve Kline, Cal Eldred, Mike Matheny, Orlando Palmeiro, and Eddie Perez.

Outside the Cardinals family, a tip of the hat to Joe Strauss, who covered the team in 2003 for the *St. Louis Post-Dispatch.* The same to Rick Hummel of the *Post-Dispatch,* who may well know more about baseball than any other person in the history of the game. On the broadcast side, television announcers Al Hrabosky and Dan McLaughlin always made for interesting bus trips from the hotel to the ballpark, and it's difficult to think of anybody in life who has more character and more stories than the radio voice of the Cardinals, Mike Shannon. There is also Ed Lewis and Jim Leyland and Rollie Hemond and Jerry Reinsdorf, baseball men to the core.

Last but not least, thanks to agent David Gernert for putting Tony La Russa and me in the same room together at the outset. And, of course, there is La Russa himself, a manager of unique distinction, but more important, a man with qualities of loyalty and honor and decency as rare as they are gratifying.

INDEX

BUZZ BISSINGER (left, with **TONY LA RUSSA**) is the author of *Friday Night Lights* and *A Prayer for the City*, as well as *Three Nights in August*, which spent a total of twenty-six weeks on the *New York Times* hardcover bestseller list and was selected as a Best Book of the Year by the *Chicago Tribune*, the *Rocky Mountain News*, and the *Christian Science Monitor*. A contributing editor at *Vanity Fair*, Bissinger has won the Pulitzer Prize and the Livingston Award, among other honors.